DOGMA➤ *Volume 5: The Church as Sacrament*

A PROJECT OF JOHN XXIII INSTITUTE
Saint Xavier College, Chicago

Edited by T. Patrick Burke

DOGMA

by Michael Schmaus

5 *The Church as Sacrament*

Translated by Mary Lederer

SHEED AND WARD: KANSAS CITY AND LONDON

6700 Squibb Road
Mission, Ks. 66202

Nihil Obstat: Thomas J. Beary, Ph.D.
    Censor Librorum

Imprimatur: +John A. Marshall, *Bishop of Burlington*
January 14, 1975

Library of Congress Catalog Card Number 74-276 44
ISBN: 0-8 362-0616-9

Manufactured in the United States of America

Contents

I

The General
Sacramentality
of
the Church

◄ 1

The Meaning of Sacramentality

Sacramentality can be understood only within the perspective of general salvation history: it is the goal of salvation history which lights up its meaning. This goal is for mankind to reach God in order to carry on a blessed dialogue with him in eternity. God himself calls men to this future through the word and the sign. For God cannot be seen or heard directly: in order that his summoning word and inviting sign may be heard and seen within history, he must convey them in a concrete, audible, and visible form. Thus he must make use of a visible means. This is what the Church is, and it is qualified for that role in proportion to its commitment to Christ.

If we are to have an adequate understanding of this, we must first have some clear idea of God's relationship to Christ and to the Church. Let us recall what was said in the earlier volumes of this work about the tripersonal life of God. In an act of self-communication God eternally brings forth a Son, his Word, the Logos. God intended from eternity that this self-communication should take a human form. His design reached its fulfillment in the incarnation of the Logos; the man Jesus has in the Logos the ground of his existance and subsistence. God reveals himself to Jesus as the eternal Father: Jesus becomes his representative in history.

Jesus is the historical representative of the eternal divine ontology, but at the same time he is the first born of many brothers.

If God's plan aimed at the incarnation of the Son he generates eternally, i.e. at the acceptance of the man Jesus into the eternal sonship of the Logos and into his dialogue with the Father, this is a process which has taken place not for one man alone but for the whole human community, and indeed, in its own fashion, for the whole creation. For if other men are not indeed to be taken up, as Jesus was, into the subsistence of the eternal Logos, they are to come into the closest union with the Logos through the sending of the Holy Spirit, who is the Spirit of Jesus, and who seeks to become the spirit of those who open themselves to Christ in faith, recognizing in him their brother and their representative before God. Just as God called to himself the man Jesus, who subsisted in the divine Logos, through his whole human life but above all through his death and resurrection, so that he reached God and lives with him as the "glorified One," so he calls to himself the whole of humanity, whose representative Jesus is. God has called mankind into community with his incarnate Son. In Jesus he has communicated himself definitively and once and for all to men, so that we can reach him in Christ.

Conversely, Jesus opened himself totally to God and let himself be wholly governed by God's call. This means that, since the resurrection he is present in a hidden way in human history as God's representative and that therefore his brothers and sisters know towards whom they must move in response to God's call into the absolute future—Jesus himself; faith in him is the way. He is man's representative standing in the presence of God; and hence man receives God's call if Jesus, his representative, receives it. But this also means that God's call to the future is a call to faith in Jesus Christ. Only through him and with him can man pass into the future.

But where is Jesus to be found? In the Church. Thus the call to Christ takes place through the call to the Church, the people of God, the body of Christ. Whoever responds to the divine invitation to the Church gains a share in the life of Christ, the head of the Church community. For in the Church Jesus' life and above all his death on the cross and his resurrection are made dynamically present. Thus these saving events are made available to all men. This is the basis of the Church's sacramentality: it is a sign and an instrument for the saving call of God to future glory. In this saving call God, who communicated himself to Jesus Christ, communicates himself to his brothers and sisters as the Lord of the future and at the same time gives them constant encouragement to persevere.

Thus we see that the sacraments are primarily orientated towards the future. It is in terms of the future, in terms of God the Father, that they must be understood. For through Christ they come ultimately from God the Father; and in Christ, the Father himself is at work in them. God is the author of the whole of the past universal salvation history. Through his self-communication he gives man the power to move into the future; it is from the future that he calls to men. The important point to grasp here is this: the sacramentality of the Church, inasmuch as it is the body of Christ, is a prime factor in the evolution of the creation, which proceeds from God and returns to God. Let us now consider its sacramentality in detail.

The statement of the Second Vatican Council with regard to the total sacramentality of the Church is probably the most important pronouncement it made concerning the Church, if not the one whose full meaning is the most difficult to grasp. All the council's other statements about the Church are affected by this insight. The key to the new understanding of the Church reached by the council is the teaching on the christocentric character of the Church; and here the council is taking up a concept of the Church which dominated scriptural and patristic ecclesiology, although the statement that the Church is a sacrament does not occur in so many words anywhere in Scripture and is found only very rarely in the Fathers. In the last century Johann Adam Moehler and I. H. Oswald emphasized the sacramentality of the whole Church. The latter said, for example:

The Church as the universal means of sanctification, as the institution for sanctification—that is, the Church in its visible form but based on the invisible work of the Holy Spirit—is not so much *a* sacrament as, rather, *the* Christian sacrament. The Church itself is the sacrament, the means of salvation in the most comprehensive sense of the word.[1]

[1]*Die dogmatische Lehre von den Heiligen Sakramenten der katholischen Kirche,* I, 2d ed. (Münster, 1894), pp. 12-13.

In the years before Vatican II this view was developed by theologians in various ways. Pius XII's encyclical *Mystici Corporis* was particularly influential, although it did not state explicitly that the Church was a sacrament.

The council is cautious in its formulation in that it states in the Constitution on the Church (No. 1) that the Church in Christ is "as it were" the sacrament—that is, the sign and the means—for the most intimate union with God and for the unity of the whole human race as well. But the words "as it were" are omitted in the text which states, in Ch. 2 (No. 9): "God has gathered together as one all those who in faith look upon Jesus as the author of salvation and the source of unity and peace, and has established them as the Church, that for each and all she may be the visible sacrament *(sacramentum visibile)* of this saving unity."[2] The note quotes Cyprian (*Epist.*, 69, 6), who says that the Church is the indissoluble sacrament of unity.

However, the idea itself is more important than its formulation. In the first two chapters of the constitution, the Church is described as the community of salvation which lives from Christ and the Holy Spirit. For as long as the world lasts it is the presence of God mightily working and inviting mankind to dialogue with him, within a society which is hierarchically structured. This expresses the basic character of the Church's sacramentality: all the sacramental events in the Church are an expression and fulfillment of this basic character. In describing the Church as a sacramental reality, we are not adding a new, eighth sacrament to the seven sacred rites we already possess; on the contrary, we are revealing the source from which the seven particular sacraments, according to the will of Jesus Christ, emerge. In them the sacramentality of the Church as such is given concrete expression. Thus the Church's sacramentality has to be understood analogically: just as Christ

---

[2]*The Documents of Vatican II*, ed. Walter M. Abbott, S.J. (New York: America Press, 1966), p. 26. Excerpts from the Constitutions and Decrees of the Ecumenical Council are taken from *The Documents of Vatican II*, reprinted with permission from *America*. All rights reserved. © 1966. America Press, Inc., 106 West 56th St., New York, N.Y. 10019.

is the way to God, the Church, in which he is present performing his saving work, is moving towards God and is the way to God. This is the aspect from which we are to understand the Church's sacramentality: it is orientated towards its goal, and its full significance can be grasped only in relation to this goal. So, too, all the individual sacraments must be interpreted. The fact that they are effective for the attainment of this goal they owe, of course, to their origin in Christ. And here we are speaking not only of the horizontal line from Christ in history but of the vertical line deriving from the fact that Christ is at work in the sacraments. It is important not to forget that it is God the Father, the first person of the Trinity, who is himself working through and with and in Jesus Christ.

CHRIST THE BASIC SACRAMENT

The sacramentality of the Church can be understood only in terms of Christ, in terms of the christocentric, pneumatic nature of the Church. Jesus Christ is the ultimate sign of God's salvation in the world. God has communicated himself in a final and irrevocable way to the man Jesus and through him (in a different way) to all men. God's self-communication acquires its significance, however, only when it is accepted by men. The man Jesus Christ is the locus and the means of God's encounter with man. Thus we can call him the original sacrament.

In order to understand this expression, we must be aware that in Catholic tradition we mean by "sacrament" an effective, visible sign of invisible grace; and by "grace" we mean primarily the self-communication of God as a personal element; and, secondarily, by "sanctifying grace," God's self-communication as a created quality. According to this traditional idea, the sacraments are certain physical things, i.e. water, wine, or oil, which acquire a saving efficacy through the words that are spoken over them. In Jesus Christ, however, what we have is a human nature subsisting in the Logos, i.e. not a thing, but an "I," as an effective sign of grace. St. Augustine helps us to understand the statement that a human being has sacramental quality when he says that a man gives himself to another through his words, i.e. that in his words he gives more than mere information, he gives his own self. In hearing his words the man addressed receives not only a particular spoken content but the speaker himself.

Jesus Christ was, in his whole life, the original sacrament. He is the man who has entered wholly and without reservation into community with God and his fellow men, the man who has become the foundation for peace and community. In him there is the total self-communication of God and the total human response to it. His whole existence—his life, his death, his resurrection—is one immense gesture of reconciliation. But this gesture which on the one hand is a human gesture is on the other the achievement of God. Jesus Christ is the saving presence of God in the world, in his existence and in everything he said and did. There are times during his earthly life when sacramentality breaks through with particular clarity—in the healings of the sick, the raising of the dead, and the other demonstrations of his power.

It is full of significance that from time to time Jesus took the things of this earth, bread or wine for example, and conferred on them the sign quality of his own human nature. This was possible without doing violence to creation because Christ represents the original plan of the divine creative will, and hence everything else in the created universe around him has been created for his sake, ultimately so that the glorified life he won in the resurrection may be achieved, i.e. the attainment of God.[3] In their innermost meaning—which cannot, of course, be demonstrated in any way by science—the things of creation have symbolic character: they are symbols of Jesus Christ himself. If, then, they acquire the sign character of his own human nature, there is fulfilled in them the creative purpose with which they have been informed. By acquiring the sacramental sign character of Jesus Christ's human nature, these things of earth also receive a share in the sacramental significance of the man Jesus. The highest realization of his sacramentality is his crucifixion. It was because, in becoming the representative of the whole of mankind, Jesus

---

[3]For a fuller treatment of this thesis see Volume 1 of this work, *Dogma: God in Revelation* (New York: Sheed and Ward, 1968), pp. 47-51.

assumed manhood as a descendant of Adam, the forefather in whom mankind fell from God's grace, that God's self-communication and the acceptance of Jesus took the form of the cross. The grace won by Jesus' crucifixion includes the reconciliation of men with God, peace among men, liberation from the fear of death, joy, the opening up of a new, imperishable life.

THE CHURCH AS EFFECTIVE COMMUNITY OF SALVATION

Christ gave the Church his own mission. His saving work on earth having been accomplished, he authorized the Church, charged it with the responsibility to make what he had achieved available to all men. That is the meaning of the Church's being and its life.

The Church can be interpreted in two ways: as the community of salvation and as its instrument. The scriptural expressions which describe the Church as the people of God, the temple and the house of God, indicate that the Church is committed as such—and not only through its individual members—to give praise and love to the Father through Christ in the Holy Spirit.

Beyond this, however, the Church, which has already received salvation, has the capacity and the task of communicating salvation, not of its own accord, but as the instrument of Jesus Christ. This gives it the character of a secondary universal sacrament. Because of its function as the transmitter of Christ's saving life to all men, the Church may be called the mother of all men. This was a popular formulation in patristic times, and it has preserved its ancient meaning in the liturgy.

The Church is enabled to be the instrument of Jesus Christ in his work of transmitting salvation—that is, to make present the salvation he has already achieved in the past through his death and resurrection—because it shares in his priesthood. Because of the character of Christ which has been conferred on all its members in baptism it has a likeness to Christ and a participation in his priestly office. The Church would not be fulfilling the reason for its existence if it failed to continue this mediating work. Whatever it does as the Church has the effect of transmitting salvation: in its life there is no area of neutral action. Where the Church is not transmitting salvation, sin breaks in.

The Church is the community of those who believe in Christ, that is, those who have been given the saving merits of Christ and may regard themselves as saved insofar as they persevere in their faith in Christ and do not fall again into the dominion of the powers of destruction. In them the saving activity of Jesus Christ is constantly at work.

The Church is the constant, tangible presence in history of the glorified Lord, from his resurrection until his return at the end of time, because, as the Constitution on the Church says (No. 7), the members of the Church live with Christ's life. They are led by him as their head and united by his Spirit with him and with one another.

The Church is the realm in the world which is reconciled with God, says St. Augustine (Sermon 96; 7, 8), and hence it is an earnest of salvation. It is the germ and the beginning of the kingdom of God, the first realization of the total divine rule to come. It is the preliminary earthly form of salvation. In it the new creation of mankind after the image of the Creator is already realized in a germinal way. Its existence already reflects in advance the unity of the whole human race—not in a mere empty image but in effective power (Constitution on the Church, No. 18). Just as Jesus is the new man, so the Church is the new humanity, and not only in a passive way but in one that is constantly active. As the community of salvation summoned by God from among humanity, it is already a fully real sign of the constant saving work of God through Christ, who is present in the Church in the Holy Spirit. As the human community of freedom, love and joy, it is, for the period between Jesus' ascension and his return, the sacrament of man.

In Jesus Christ the saving sign given by God exists in an individual form, but one which represents the whole of mankind before God. In the Church, which has been gathered together through the saving act of Jesus Christ, united in the Holy Spirit and preserved in the saving love of the heavenly Father, the ever present saving sign has the form of a community. It is clear why: because the one Jesus Christ is present in the community through the Holy Spirit sent by him. This community lives from his flesh and his blood. It is so much a union of brothers that Paul can even say it is "one person in Christ" (Gal. 3, 28). Through this "one person," through the new humanity gathered around Christ, God achieves salvation for all men. To the end of time the Church is to be the effective heavenly sign of salvation for every generation, every people, every individual. It is ordered towards all men, and all men are ordered towards it. In this sense one can say that every man is a potential Christian. Through baptism and through faith, which is the response to the preaching of the gospel and the Church's testimony to Christ, the potential Christian becomes a real one.

It is in accordance also with the physical-spiritual and the social-historical nature of man that God should communicate himself to him *via* the sacramental way of the Church. The Church appears as the full sign of salvation when it does not accept simply one or the other element of the Christian gospel, no matter how important, but the gospel in its fullness. Salvation is also communicated through saving signs that are partial, i.e. those churches in which the fullness of faith or the hierarchic order established by Christ is not completely realized. Here it is of the greatest importance that the full sign not only appears externally as such, but is also filled from within with love, hope, and faith. This means, in other words, that the Church performs its task the more perfectly, the stronger and more intensively it becomes what it already is, namely the community ruled by Christ in the Holy Spirit, so that the presence of Jesus Christ appears ever more clearly on its countenance. The Church stretches out eschatologically, in a constant process of self-reform, towards the whole of mankind. Vatican II stated (Constitution on the Church, No. 9):

Its goal is the kingdom of God, which has been begun by God Himself on earth, and which is to be further extended until it is brought to perfection by Him at the end of time. Then Christ our life (cf. Col. 3, 4), will appear, and "creation itself also will be delivered from its slavery to corruption into the freedom of the glory of the sons of God" (Rom. 8, 21). So it is that this messianic people, although it does not actually include all men, and may more than once look like a small flock, is nonetheless a lasting and sure seed of unity, hope, and salvation for the whole human race. Established by Christ as a fellowship of life, charity, and truth, it is also used by Him as an instrument for the redemption of all, and is sent forth into the whole world as the light of the world and the salt of the earth (*cf.* Mt. 5, 13-16).

The Church's mission to be a sign of God ever present in human history and ever performing his saving work is obscured not only by sin, human selfishness, rapacity, and lust for power, but also by a onesided cultural commitment, such as that to European civilization, a connection with a particular social or economic class, or even a commitment to antiquated forms and formulations.

THE EFFICACY OF THE CHURCH IN FAITH, HOPE, AND LOVE

Although the Church appears as a hierarchically structured society, it can be active only through its individual members. Insofar as these act as members of the Church, particularly insofar as they fulfill the call to faith, hope, and love that is the essential characteristic mark of the Church community, they are acting sacramentally.

The sacramental effect of the individual members is realized in two ways, quite different from each other: in the performance of the tasks of daily life and in carrying out the signs of salvation provided by Christ. The latter way is an official one, the former a non-official one.

So far as the non-official activity is concerned, it is not limited to the work of the laity; but it is primarily through the laity that it is realized. We do not need to repeat in detail what the laity's fields of activity are; but we must emphasize that the work of the laity also is important in the mediation of salvation. The basis of this is their assimilation to Christ. St. Thomas has interpreted the mark of Christ that is conferred on a man through baptism, through the sign of his being received into the Church, in the following way: the believer is committed to two things:

First and primarily to looking forward to eternal glory, for which reason he is marked with the seal of grace. . . . But secondly, every believer is committed to receive that which belongs to the worship of God and pass it on to others, and to this the sacramental mark is ordered in a special way. The whole sacred service of the Christian religion derives from Christ, though it is apparent that the sacramental mark is in a particular way the mark of Christ, into whose priesthood the faithful are incorporated, according to the sacramental marks, which are nothing but particular signs of sharing in the priesthood of Jesus Christ that he himself has instituted. (*Summa theologica*, III, 63, 3)

It cannot be stated clearly how far the mediation of salvation by individuals reaches and what degree of intensity it attains; but it is impossible to doubt the strength of its reality. For everything a member of the Church performs in his faith in Christ is performed by Christ himself. Everything a Christian does as a believer is an act of grace. But grace always has a social orientation. Whatever a person produces of faith and love is an expression of the self-communication of God. The divine self-communication reaches out beyond the one who receives it to others, to those who are united to him in love, but even beyond this group to distant places that are beyond our calculation. Let us remember the words of Christ: "Where two or three have met together in my name, I am there among them" (Mt. 18,20). Vatican II (Constitution on the Church, No. 11) points out that those who are united to each other in sacramental marriage help each other towards sanctification through their life together and the rearing and education of children. The community of the family is, in the council's words, "so to speak, the domestic Church," in which the parents should be, through word and example, the first witnesses to Christ for their children.

The ways in which salvation is mediated through individuals are very numerous indeed. We may say that the whole of life— all one's actions and words—is a proclamation of Christ which mediates salvation. We are not thinking, necessarily, of words which are explicitly Christian in content. All the words of comfort, support, and encouragement—or even of criticism, when it is constructive—are saving words through which God turns towards the person who receives them and gives himself to him. But it is especially in suffering, in the cross, that the Christian mediates salvation to his brothers within the messianic people of God itself, and beyond them to all men, inasmuch as Christ is present in every crucifixion, performing in it his saving work. The cross on Golgotha is the very form of grace, for in it God gave himself to man in an unconditional way. As man's representative Jesus Christ gave a response of unconditional obedience. In his attitude of loving obedience he was so totally open to God that God was able to work perfectly through him, both as judge and as the giver of grace. The latter appeared in the life of the risen Lord.

The crucifixion and the resurrection both extend their effects to all men: or rather, Jesus Christ, marked forever by these events, stretches out towards all men in order to draw them into a share in his own life. But this means a share in his crucifixion and his resurrection. The crucifixion of every baptized Christian is a share in the crucifixion of Christ. Consequently, in the Christian who is carrying his cross, who is suffering, ill, dying, Christ himself is performing his saving work (cf. Mt. 25,31-45). That is why every cross that is carried in love of the Lord is a fountain of salvation whose waters flow one knows not where, or how far. Despite its structure as a hierarchically ordered society, which appears to the world, the Church is like a fountain of salvation ceaselessly flowing in a hidden manner. It is not only in movement towards the fulfillment of the future, it is itself the movement towards the fulfillment of the future; that is, the perfect reconciliation of the creation with God and the fullness of reconciliation of men with one another from which will come a new flowering of man's joy in God and in his fellow men. Then community will cease to be a burden; every man will be a cause of rejoicing for every other.

EFFICACIOUSNESS *EX OPERE OPERATO* AND *EX OPERE OPERANTIS*

In order to avoid possible misunderstandings, it is appropriate here to make a point which is important for the general sacramental nature of the Church and for the seven sacraments. It may help to clarify the problem of the general mediation of grace in the Church. The Council of Trent declared (DS 1608)[4] that the seven sacraments work in the customary way *ex opere operato,* i.e. on the basis of the given sign. The converse of this is a function *ex opere operantis,* i.e. being effective as a result of the attitude of mind in the person performing it.

By this distinction the Church has ensured the saving efficacy of the sacraments: it does not depend upon the attitude of mind, the sanctity or lack of it, of the person dispensing them. For if that were the case, the recipient would be hopelessly at the mercy of the spiritual condition of the man administering the sacraments. It is, of course, necessary that the dispenser of the seven sacraments shall have the intention of performing, at least in an implicit way, a saving sign of Jesus Christ, i.e. a saving sign of the Church: otherwise there would be no action performed according to the meaning of the sign.

That the seven sacraments work *ex opere operato* does not mean that the faith and love of the dispenser are irrelevant to their saving efficacy. The teaching of the Council of Trent does run the danger of this kind of objectification; but it is an unavoidable danger. It must and can be overcome by a constant self-reflection and self-reformation on the part of the dispenser. He who is charged with the office of dispensing the sacraments will carry out his work in the right way only if he tries to live more and more in community with Christ and with the Holy Spirit, which means living out of faith and out of love for God. Thus, to keep to the language of the Council of Trent, the *opus operantis* is combined with the *opus operatum.*

The ideas which entered into the definition of the Council of Trent had a long history before it. They originated in early scholasticism and were given clear development by St. Thomas. The subject and its problems, however, goes back to St. Augustine. Augustine had to deal with the situation in which the Donatists demanded that, in an exaggerated way, there should be what was

---

[4]Denzinger-Schönmetzer, *Enchiridion Symbolorum, Definitionum et Declarationum de Rebus Fidei et Morum* (Freiburg: Herder, 1965[33]).

later called the *opus operans,* i.e. the holiness of the Church, for these sacraments to be valid. In his dealings with Donatism, Augustine created the beginnings of the doctrine of the sacramental character. His view was that, on the one hand, the sinfulness of a priest dispensing the sacraments was not an obstacle to the saving effectiveness of baptism, because the whole Church community gave the baptism and because, ultimately, the Holy Spirit guaranteed salvation; on the other hand, those baptized persons who were separated from the Church dispensed the sacrament, but achieved no saving effect, since peace with the Church, the *pax ecclesiae,* was the condition and the basis of the love that effected salvation.

The imparting of salvation by every single baptized person to any other baptized person, and, beyond this, to others as well, a fact which is based on the sacramentality of the total Church, is guaranteed by the promise of Jesus Christ. But since it is not tied to particular signs that come down to us from the apostolic period, it does not have a concrete form like the seven sacraments we know. It is a communication out of love alone, a communication out of the Holy Spirit. We should not underestimate the significance of the encounter between one man and another which takes place in the communication of salvation. Owing to the character of personal relationships, a large part is played in the purely natural dimension. An encounter between persons has a hidden, limitless quality about it, for when one person approaches another in genuine love, it is God himself who approaches this other. And as the other accepts the movement of love which comes to him, he accepts God himself—or rather, God accepts the movement of love which has issued from the first person in the form of the loved other person. Thus God is both the origin and the goal of every human movement of saving love.

THE WORD AS SALVIFIC ACTIVITY OF THE CHURCH

We have seen earlier that the establishing of divine revelation is one element of the Church's pastoral office. The proclamation of salvation, however, for the sake of which the divine word is established, and which is the whole reason for doing it at all, is not to be ascribed to the pastoral office, but to the consecrating authority of the Church, for the reason that salvation is imparted in it. The establishing of revelation is important because the proclamation is not only a call to faith in Christ and love of Christ, because it not only seeks to arouse *fides qua,* but because it transmits the truth left to us by Christ as the truth of salvation, i.e. because it seeks to arouse *fides quae.* The *fides quae,* in its earliest form, is: Jesus is Lord and the Messiah promised by God.

For the importance of the content (we might say, the intellectual element in the proclamation) we may compare Acts 20,18-35, 1 Cor. 11,18-33, and all the other discourses recounted in Acts. Whenever Paul gives ethical injunctions ("paraneses") in his epistles in general, he always supports them with dogmatic statements, statements of content (cf., e.g., the eucharistic texts of 1 Cor. 10 and 1 Cor. 11).

As we saw earlier, the word of God in the Old Testament has such a powerful dynamism that it may be rightly called a divine action (cf. Jeremiah or Ezechiel or Isaiah). The word of the Church's proclamation shares in this dynamic character of God's word in Scripture. Insofar as the Church is the Church of Jesus Christ, the eternal incarnate Logos, it has itself the quality of a word. The Catholic Church regards itself not only as a Church of the sign, the sacrament, but also, and indeed primarily, as a Church of the word. Its primary task is that of proclamation. The use of signs is part of the Church's task of preaching the word, not *vice versa.*

One cannot, strictly speaking, say that the saving activity of the Church includes the proclamation of the word and the use of signs. Rather, the proclamation of the word is the activity of the Church that includes everything else. Even the use of the signs is, fundamentally, a saving preaching of the word, for two reasons: first, because it is only the word together with the thing that constitutes the sacramental sign, with the word having the chief importance; secondly, however, because the significance of the sign itself is proclamation. Augustine called the sign a visible word, and such that through this visible word God communicates himself to man. Thus this proclaiming sign is an effective and not merely an indicative one. The Church can also use its word to teach, enlighten, and inform. It is involved in these forms of the word as the Church that believes in Christ. Hence they too share in this saving quality.

Proclamation in the strict sense, however, the proclamation of the risen Christ, is more than this kind of reporting and informative utterance. It is testimony that makes Christ present. In the word of the Church's proclamation it is Jesus himself who speaks. Consequently, to hear the word of the proclamation is to encounter Christ. As little as the word spoken by Jesus can be separated from him during his earthly life, so little can the word of the kerygma in the Church be separated from Jesus. The proclamation of the word becomes a saving event. In it, there takes place a double movement: the movement of praise and worship from below to above and the movement of God's self-communication from above to below. God's self-communication takes the form of a word in the proclamation of the word. The presence of Christ in the Church is realized in the word. The saving presence of Jesus Christ has the form of a word in accordance with his own word character.

Even in the natural sphere the word can have an emotional power if it is more than mere information. The word can comfort and depress, it can create joy and despair, love and hope, courage and discouragement, virtue and vice. In the word there is a far-reaching, profound dynamic. There is no need for the word of the Church's proclamation to lack this natural dynamic; but it is the sign and the vessel for another dynamic, namely for the saving activity of God himself. The natural becomes the vessel of the divine.

It is difficult to draw a line exactly between the saving activity of the Church's proclamation and the saving activity of the sacraments, in a narrower sense. In any case we must grant that the word of the Church's proclamation shares in the sacramentality of the whole Church. God's self-communication always takes place here and now in the word of proclamation.

Just as the saving presence of God assumes the form of a sign in the sacrament, it assumes the form of a word in the Church's kerygma. The word of proclamation is always the self-representation—or, rather, the self-realization—of the Church. The Church is always realized in its kerygmatic word, just as it is always realized in the sacrament.

Thus we can see why Paul lays the greatest emphasis on the service of the word (1 Cor. 1,17). We might even say that the saving reality of the word is affected more than that of the sacramental sign by the intensity of faith and love in the preacher. The more open he is to God in his faith and love, the more chance, as it were, he gives God to reach his listener through the word of his proclamation. It must be added, however, that the word of the Church's proclamation also possesses some element of what we call the *opus operatum*; for here it is ultimately Christ, working in the Holy Spirit, who comes to men. Nevertheless, while we can say of the word of proclamation only in general that God gives himself in it to men for their salvation, with the sacramental signs we can see, in each case, a particular concrete mode of the divine self-communication. It must, though, be emphasized that what is true of the total sacramentality of the Church is also true of the Church's proclamation of the word, namely that in it the crucified and risen Christ is active. But this means that in every proclamation of the word by the Church the cross of Christ is itself present, creating salvation. The realization of the cross in the present takes the shape of words in the Church's proclamation. It is also the cross of Golgotha which is present in the sacramental signs, effecting salvation. In them it assumes the form of a sign. Unlike the proclamation of the word, however, it is always possible with the individual sign to state the particular aspect under which the cross of Golgotha is present. Thus we can say of the celebration of the eucharist that the cross and the resurrection are present under the aspect of the self-surrender of the sacrifice of Jesus to God the Father, in the sign of that meal which creates and strengthens community with Christ and through him with the heavenly Father, and thus creates and strengthens brotherly union among those who are taking part. We can say that the cross and the resurrection are present in baptism, inasmuch as they open up the way for us to the kingdom of God. We can say that the cross of Christ is present in confirmation, inasmuch as on the cross he victoriously resisted evil publicly before the world. We shall be developing these particular aspects when we come to discuss each of the sacraments.

◂ 2

The Seven Sacraments and the Sacramentals

As we saw in the preceding chapter, the seven sacraments are part of the total sacramentality of the Church. Remaining within the Church's basic sacramental structure, they constitute concrete forms of it. We shall now turn to the consideration of the historical development of the sacramental system, beginning with the scriptural data.

THE TERM "SACRAMENT"

Sacramentum is the word commonly used in the early North African Bible translations for the Greek word *mysterion,* which had come into the New Testament and Christian theology from the Old, where it had the most varied meanings. In the religious sphere the word refers to God's plan of creation and the purpose he has assigned to the history of the world, insofar as God communicates his plans to those he has chosen, those who believe in him (e.g. Wis. 2,22; Dan. 2,18f.; 27,47). Revelation in this sense means that those to whom it is given are taken up into a relation of trust with God (cf. Mt. 13,11; Mk. 4,11; Lk. 8,10). The communication of the mystery is not a piece of information from God but a realization or actualization of it in those to whom God reveals himself, those whom he has chosen.

In the New Testament the word is used in both the singular and the plural. It is most fully developed by Paul. The influence of Hellenistic religious language is not of great importance here. God is a mystery: this mystery can be known only by a divine decree (Rom. 16,25-26; 11,25; 1 Cor. 2,6). Although the word fluctuates in meaning, it appears from Colossians and Ephesians that for Paul the "mystery" is the gospel itself. The long-hidden but now revealed divine mystery is Jesus Christ himself (Col. 1,26-27; 2,2; cf. also Gal. 4,4). It is the universal, the cosmic, the total Christ, who has opened up to both the Gentiles and the Jews the way to the hope of glory (Col. 1,26-27; Eph. 1,9f.; 3,5.9-12).

In the New Testament, then, the word "mystery" means three different things: God the mysterious, the hidden, the holy, the inaccessible; then God's revelation in Jesus Christ; and finally the act of worship. Through the incarnate, crucified, and risen Christ the divine mystery that was hidden from all eternity has been made manifest in the Church (Eph. 1,4-10; 3,3-12; 5,32; 1 Cor. 2,7;3,1).

Christ is the mystery in person. His actions and his words are manifestations of the mystery that he himself is. In his death and glorification the divine glory appears in a way that is manifest only to believers. The mystery of Jesus is proclaimed by the apostles, and the Church throughout the ages continues to make it constantly present again in the Church's worship. "What was visible in the Lord has passed into the mystery," says Leo the Great (Sermon 74,2). "I find you in your mysteries," says Ambrose (*Apologia prophetae David*, 58). Hence the word "mystery" has comprehensive meaning. Neither in the New Testament nor in the early Church is it limited to those actions which we call sacraments.

In the post-apostolic period the whole of the Old Testament was described as a mystery and regarded as a preforming of the New. Around the year 200 the word meant for Christians the eternal decree of God, who had been at work in the person and the life of Jesus, revealing himself in Jesus as a mighty salvific power. Thus the sense included the person of Jesus himself, who, as the saving event, bears within himself and represents the revelation and realization of the eternal saving grace of God. It also included the preliminary images and prophecies in the Old Testament, in which the mystery of Christ was already at work in a provisional, foreshadowing revelation. Later on, as in Origen, the eschatological perspective of the mystery was emphasized. Jesus, especially in his death and resurrection, came to be seen as the final realization of salvation but not as its full realization. To bring this about is the mission of the Church. Thus the mystery as already revealed and realized in the Church is still orientated towards the future (cf. 1 Jn. 3,2).

Around the end of the second century the word "mystery" or the synonymous *sacramentum* begins to be used, initially by Justin Martyr, to describe the great rites of salvation within the total sacramentality of the Church, i.e. baptism and the eucharist.[1]

LIFE SETTING

Although those seven sacred signs which, after various divergences, came to be known from the middle of the twelfth century as "sacraments" in the strict sense are concretizations and concentrations of the Church's total sacramentality and are only to be understood within this perspective, they are nevertheless not arbitrary manifestations of the Church's sacramentality but ones which correspond to the living situation of the individual and of the Church community. It is clear that the community needs a rite in which it constantly realizes itself (the eucharist); it needs a rite of acceptance for new members (baptism); it needs constant self-reflection and self-renewal (penance); it must deal with the problem of illness and death (the last anointing); it needs an inner structure (the ordination of bishops and priests); it must deal with the question of how the individual Christian lives his Christian faith in his daily life in the face of temptation (confirmation); and the union of the believing

---

[1]P. Smulders, "Die Kirche als Gottes Sakrament des Heiles," in G. Barauna, *De ecclesia*, I, trans. O. Semmelroth, F. G. Gerhartz, and H. Vorgrimler (Freiburg, 1966), pp. 289-327.

man and woman in marriage in the community formed by Christ is a natural expression of the Church's sacramentality (matrimony). Thus the manifestations of the life of the Church as a total sacrament lead to seven particular sacraments, each with a special place in the life of the Church.

CHRIST THE SOURCE

That there really are only these seven concretizations of the total sacramentality of the Church quite apart from sociological deductions becomes fully certain only if we can show that Jesus himself in some way established these saving signs. According to the faith of the Church, the seven sacraments were instituted by Jesus Christ directly or indirectly on the basis of the operation of the Holy Spirit, whom Jesus sent upon his disciples. They originate, in any case, in the apostolic age.

The history of religions school of thought points out, in contradiction to the Church's tradition, that the New Testament says nothing about sacraments. According to this view, the sacramental idea has its roots in Hellenism; and, in particular, was introduced by Paul into Christianity as a foreign element. The fact that baptism and the eucharist were practiced in apostolic times—which these writers cannot deny—is explained by claiming that these were nonsacramental actions.

Let us say first that nowhere in Paul can we discover any connection with the mystery cults. These "mysteries," which flourished from the seventh century B.C. to the fourth century A.D., were rites in which the life, death, and resurrection of a mythical god were celebrated so that those participating would receive deliverance from sin and death and also divine life. As we have already pointed out, Paul understands by "mystery" the hidden saving plan that God has revealed to his chosen ones.

With regard to the Church's tradition, however, if it is said that the individual "sacraments" were instituted by Jesus Christ, this statement needs careful interpretation. Both exegetical analysis and the evidence of doctrinal history show that a number of sacraments were not mentioned by Christ. We would not be giving its due weight to the Tridentine statement (DS 1601) that Jesus Christ instituted the sacraments if we were to hold merely that the foundation of the Church or the preparation for it by Jesus Christ implied the institution of the seven sacraments. If this statement were correct, the question would arise why, on the basis of its total sacramental nature, the Church created seven and no more than seven sacraments. The situations that arise in the life of a community and the individual do not necessarily require precisely seven.

First, we can agree with R. Schnackenburg that the sacraments depend on the specifically Pauline view that combines salvation history (Adam-Christ) and the pneumatic, supratemporal element. This bridging of time and space (between Christ and the following generations) is made possible for Paul by the figure of Christ himself. For on the one hand Christ, for Paul, is the historical Jesus and remains as such the Messiah, but on the other hand he is the glorified Lord who lives through all ages, whose second coming is awaited with longing. Although this is the basis, it is still not an adequate explanation for the seven sacraments. Two other things have to be considered: the sacramental will of Christ and his representational function.

We can speak of the will of Jesus Christ to establish seven sacraments only if we can find texts in Scripture that testify, at least in an incipient way, to this will of the Lord. We do, in fact, find such texts concerning baptism and the eucharist. In the case of the other sacraments, we can say that there are indications for all of them in Scripture. Inasmuch as they originate with the apostles, we can and must consider them as part of the deposit of revelation. There are two points to be made here: not all the saving signs of Jesus related in the New Testament have been developed in the evolution of the Church's faith to the full significance of sacraments (see the washing of the feet); also the evidence in Scripture for what were later to be called the seven sacraments is of greatly varying fullness. Thus, for example, it is nowhere theoretically stated that the consecration of priests or bishops is to be performed by the laying-on of hands. All we have is the statement of the fact that holy powers are imparted through the gesture of the laying-on of hands and prayer, without Scripture reflecting anywhere about it. Also, a long development has been necessary for the rite of reception into the Church to be recognized as a dual sacramental sign (baptism and confirmation). Thus the investigation of the mind of Christ on the sacraments does not, by itself, lead to full certainty.

In accordance with the different degrees of clarity and fullness of evidence for the saving signs in the New Testament, the Council of Trent sees a hierarchy among the sacraments and sets baptism and the eucharist at their head (DS 1603).

SACRAMENTS IN THE OLD TESTAMENT

As far as the second point is concerned, namely Christ's representative function, we must point out first of all that the sacraments in the New Testament have, as Paul in particular testifies, a prelude in the Old Testament. In Paul, we find the linking of type and anti-type. Thus the passage to the Red Sea becomes the model for baptism, and the eating of the manna that of the eucharist (1 Cor. 10,2-4). But Paul is less concerned with the things than with the event, an event that is, in each case, based on a person. Behind the Old Testament event stands Moses; behind the New Testament, Christ. In particular, it is the Adam-Christ parallel which provides the key to Paul's view of the sacraments. Just as Adam was the ancestor of that mankind which had to live under the destructive power of illness, death, and sin, Jesus became the ancestor of that liberated mankind which is able to live in peace and joy. In baptism and the eucharist the salvation Jesus Christ created once and for all is imparted to man (1 Pet. 3,18; Heb. 9,11; 10,14).

Behind these ideas there stands the Semitic conception of the representative or corporate person. Adam and Christ were each the real representatives of the race of men they founded, the one race living under the powers of destruction, and the other freed from those powers. (It is probably the case—though it will very likely never be established with certainty—that the gnostic idea of the "primal man" has had an influence on this thinking.)

PREPARATION IN THE LIFE OF JESUS

The fact that Jesus wanted to leave his own saving work to his disciples in the form of particular symbolic actions was no surprise to those who had been with him during his life and seen him perform, from time to time, symbolic actions such as the healing of the man born blind or the feeding of the five thousand. Some development was necessary, however, from these first beginnings to the conception of the apostle Paul. But the interpretations that Paul gives of baptism and eucharist were themselves able to be the starting point for a fuller sacramental understanding. The scriptural idea that salvation and eternal life were transmitted through matter and word (cf. Eph. 5,26), through earthly gifts given by the Lord (Jn. 6,53ff.), and that in these rites there is effected the mystery of rebirth (cf. Tit. 3,5; 1 Pet. 1,23; 2,2; Jn. 3,3ff.), sanctification (cf. Heb. 12,9ff.), and a lasting union with the Lord (cf. Jn. 6,56f.) shows the development in sacramental thinking. Thus gradually other actions that effected salvation, such as the words "your sins are forgiven you," could be interpreted as sacraments. If Paul considered that these signs (baptism, eucharist) brought about a certain identification with Jesus Christ, the bringer of salvation, it must also be pointed out that communion with Christ not only did not diminish the personal autonomy of the recipient, it brought it to its full realization. For full personal autonomy consists in the freedom from sin and death (Rom. 6, 4.7.11.14). Thus we see that everything Paul says on this subject is an exhortation to live the kind of life that follows from community with Christ.

Again, the symbolic actions on the part of Jesus could not have been a complete surprise for those who witnessed them, for they were acquainted with the symbolic actions of the prophets from the Old Testament. They were in particular familiar with saving signs in religious worship. The most important rite was circumcision. Then there was the paschal memorial meal in which thanks were offered for the liberation from Egypt and the covenant of Sinai, a lasting sign of the loving-kindness of the divine will. In the memorial rite a sense of identity was created between those celebrating it and those who had experienced the exodus from

Egypt and the receiving of the covenant on Sinai: the past became the present.

In the context of Paul's whole theology we may regard the saving sign of which he speaks as the anticipation, guarantee, and seal of ultimate salvation as well as a stage on the way towards it. With the reception of baptism and the eucharist salvation begins, but it is not yet fully accomplished. Just as the whole Church is the great sign in the world that God wants to lead men to final communion with himself in the future, so the individual sacraments are to be understood as the ways in which God calls men through Christ into the perfect future of salvation: they are the signs of the absolute future to come.

HISTORICAL DEVELOPMENT OF THE CONCEPT

The Latin word *sacramentum* as a description of the particular saving event that takes place in the people of God also had a long history before it acquired its present significance at the Council of Trent. The word, which was first used by Tertullian, is connected with *sacrare* or *consecrare*, and the term means a legally valid and permanent removal of a person or thing from the sphere of human law to that of divine law. Thus the oath taken by a soldier in the army is a *sacramentum*. The term can also refer to a sum of money a plaintiff had to deposit at a consecrated place before the beginning of a lawsuit (it reverted to the temple of the particular deity if he lost the case). Tertullian was the first to use the word "sacrament" in a theological sense, although he did not limit its meaning to the sacraments as we understand them today. He understood baptism, in particular, in terms of a military oath.

The concept of sacrament underwent an important development with St. Augustine, who made use, in his treatment, of Neoplatonic ideas. For Augustine a sacrament is a sacred sign, but he differentiates between the sign and the content (*res*) of the sign. With regard to signs the important thing to consider is not what they are but what they mean. But in order that a sign should communicate something other than its own being, it must have some resemblance to what it refers to. The bearers of this resemblance are the natural object used and the word which defines it. The object and the word constitute the visible manifestation of the sacrament. St. Augustine says: "Take away the word and what is water then but water? But when the word is combined with the element, we have a sacrament" (*Sermon on St. John's Gospel*).

In his struggle against the Donatists, St. Augustine distinguished to an almost excessive degree the content of the sacrament and the sign of the sacrament. This was possible because of the Neoplatonic distinction between spiritual and material being, the visible and the invisible. Augustine said that the Donatists had the true sacrament of Christ insofar as they had the sacramental sign but that they did not have any grace, for it depended on the faith of the recipient whether the sacrament could produce the saving reality it symbolized. Only those, he said, who accepted in faith the reality the sacrament represented and made manifest partook of this reality. But true faith existed only in peace with the Church.

In his opposition to the Donatists, St. Augustine sometimes emphasized faith so much that the sign seemed to be superfluous. Thus his idea of the sacrament fluctuates between a realist conception and one that is symbolical and spiritualist. This is why, in later times, both Catholic and Reformed theologians were able to appeal to him in support of their views.

Another step in the development of the idea of sacrament was taken by Isidore of Seville (d. 636). He distinguishes even more sharply than Augustine between the sign and the reality it points to. He does not exactly separate the two things, but he opens the way for this to happen.

We find a powerful conception of sacrament in Hugo of St. Victor (d. 1141). For him a sacrament is an object present to the senses which, because of its similarity with the saving reality established by Christ and the sanctification that it has received, both represents and contains a spiritual grace. Grace is contained in the sacrament as in a vessel.

Peter Lombard goes beyond this when he regards the sacrament not only as the sign, but also as the cause of grace. He speaks so generally of signs, however, that this word applies to actions also, not only to things. To explain the sign, Thomas Aquinas used the Aristotelian terms "matter" and "form," regarding the word as the form and the thing as the matter. This idea does bring some clarification, but it also involves difficulties that are hard to overcome where there is no actual object or physical thing involved, as, for example, in the sacrament of penance or of matrimony.

The twelfth century made an important advance when it began to distinguish between the *opus operatum* and the *opus operans*. Moreover, in the same century the word sacrament was limited to those seven sacred rites that we call sacraments. In the time of Tertullian the word had had a much more extended application. At that time, in addition to those actions and events for which the word "sacrament" was later reserved, it could also be applied to for example, the Christian faith in general, the individual truths of faith, confessions of faith, and individual facts of salvation. Thus the notion that there are precisely seven sacraments could scarcely arise in the first millennium of Christianity because of terminological usage.

NUMBER OF THE SACRAMENTS

Parallel to the development of the concept of "sacrament" there is the development of the question as to how many sacraments there are. The Council of Trent defined that there are seven sacraments, no more and no less (DS 1601). This statement could only be made at a particular point in the development of the notion of what exactly a sacrament is. Trent's action was a terminological regulation: the word "sacrament" is, after all, by no means part of divine revelation. By reason of the ecumenical importance of the question a brief sketch of the history of the number may be helpful.

The first step was taken by Tertullian about the end of the second century, applying the word "sacrament" to baptism and the eucharist. Since confirmation was for long directly connected with baptism and the two together constituted the ceremony of entrance into the Church, it took a long time before it was thought of as a distinct sacrament. Isidore of Seville counted four sacraments: baptism, confirmation, the body of Christ, and the blood of Christ —thus counting the eucharist as two sacraments. Cyprian and Augustine refer to holy orders as a sacrament, but this has little significance because their notion of "sacrament" is so wide. Penance is scarcely ever called a sacrament in the ancient Church: the process was too long and troublesome to fit the prevalent notion of a sacrament. Also, it lacked the "thing," or physical substance like water or bread, which Augustine considered necessary for a sacrament. At most, the act of reconciliation with the Church, performed by imposition of hands and anointing with oil, could be viewed as a sacrament. But for Augustine the real sacrament of forgiveness of sins is baptism. The penitential procedure was seen as a revitalization of the grace of baptism. Likewise the anointing of the sick was not termed a sacrament. That would have been difficult, since penance was often postponed to the end of life, and an anointing was part of it anyway. Marriage was called a sacrament because of the reference to it in Ephesians 5,32 as a *mysterion,* but there is no reference to it in patristic times as a sacrament in the later sense of the word. In Milan the washing of feet was termed a sacrament because of a reference to it in those terms by Ambrose.

During the time from the end of the patristic period to the twelfth century, the view sometimes occurs that as many sacraments as possible should be recognized. Peter Damian (d. 1072) mentions twelve. On the other hand, he lists baptism, eucharist, and ordination among the "chief sacraments."

It was not until the concept of sacrament developed by Hugo of St. Victor that the path was opened that led eventually to the number seven. He gives three types of sacrament: *sacramenta salutaria,* namely, baptism, eucharist, the consecration of a church, and confirmation; *sacramenta exercitationis,* which are not necessary to salvation but are useful, namely, holy water, ashes, the blessing of palms and candles, etc.; and *sacramenta praeparatoria,* namely, ordination, consecration of sacred vessels and vestments.

The canonists of the twelfth century, especially the authors of the glosses on the Decretals of Gratian, such as Rufinus, distinguished between sacraments of salvation, of service, of worship, and of preparation. To the first group belong baptism, eucharist, confirmation; to the second, sacred vessels and the prayers of clerics; to the third, feast days; and to the fourth, the consecration of clerics, of churches, and of sacred vessels. Another grouping put forward by the same authors distinguishes between sacraments of mere dignity, those necessary for salvation (baptism, catechetical instruction, exorcisms), and those which are both of dignity and necessary for salvation (confirmation, eucharist). Sicard of Cremona counts seven sacraments, in the order which has now become customary. The basis of the number seven in his view is the seven gifts of the Holy Spirit.

Peter Lombard was of decisive importance for the eventual official adoption of the number seven. Although he gives little weight to that precise number, still the enormous influence of his *Sentences* brought about a general recognition of the number in the thirteenth century. The basis for it was found not in Scripture or statements of the Church Fathers, but in the sacred number "seven" itself. Some considered the number necessary, others merely convenient.

The number three signifies the Godhead, and four the whole of creation, so that the sum of them, seven, represents the union of the divine and the created. Furthermore, according to Scripture there are seven gifts of the Holy Spirit, there is a seven-branched candlestick, seven showbread loaves in the Temple, a book with seven seals which the Lamb opens, and finally seven words of Jesus on the cross. Theology mentions seven works of mercy, seven cardinal virtues, and seven deadly sins.[2]

CHANGE IN THE SACRAMENTS

History shows us that all seven sacred signs underwent many alterations, some major and some minor. It should be noted in particular that Pius XII declared that the outward sign for the sacrament of order was the laying-on of hands and a particular prayer, but he left open the question whether in earlier times it was not also necessary to hand over the priestly symbols—the missal or the chalice—in order that the sacrament should be brought about. This is an expression of the fact that the decree of the Church is not only concerned with the ornamental trappings of the sacra-

[2]J. Finkenzeller, "Die Zählung der Sakramente," in *Wahrheit und Verkündigung, Festschrift M. Schmaus*, II (Paderborn, 1967), p. 1020.

mental sign but can also determine more exactly the nature of the sacramental sign itself, so that the performance of a sacrament depends on the observance of the Church's ordinances.

This seems to contradict the statement of the Council of Trent that the substance of the sacrament was determined by Christ and is therefore withdrawn from the authority of the Church (DS 1061, 1699, 1728f, 3556, 3857). To help resolve this very real problem raised by historical research it should be pointed out that although the sacramental signs were established in the apostolic age, they are, like every divine self-communication, dependent upon their free acceptance by man. They are on the one hand divine ordinances but on the other an expression of the Church's life, and the Church is not a mechanically functioning apparatus but a community of free men. Although God himself is active in them, it is the Church's own life which is expressed in the sacramental signs through its representatives, in free obedience towards God—a life that is one in faith, hope, and love. If the sacraments are real expressions of the Church's life, ordained but not arbitrarily determined by God, then we must acknowledge the right of the whole Church to decide the way in which it wishes to express its faith, obedience, and love to God within the framework of the divine ordinance.

This can be understood in the following way: the sacramental sign in the sense of a "symbolic area" (*Zeichenfeld*) derives from the apostolic age, and outside this symbolic area it would be impossible for the sacrament to be produced. But within that area the Church, in the course of history, can make the sign more exact and concrete, with the effect that only the sign the Church has decided on in the historical process of concretization produces the sacrament. This concretization of the symbolic field and within the symbolic field is determined by the Church's historical life. The sacramental sign cannot realize its symbolic power in the same way in every culture: it is quite possible that a sign that was intelligible in one century may tend to lose its intelligibility in another owing to a cultural change. In that case, the Church is free to alter the sign with a view to rendering it more intelligible. This alteration must not, of course, have the effect that the Church wholly abandons the symbolic field which originated in the apostolic age and creates an entirely new symbol; the Church is always bound within the limits of the symbolic field.

EFFICACY OF THE SACRAMENTS

We can say of the sign, which is constituted by word and thing, resembling the relationship between soul and body, that it effects salvation by denoting it—that is, it effects grace by denoting grace. Grace means the divine self-communication and the new quality created in man's soul (sanctifying grace). This connection is easy to understand: when the sign is performed, God is making known his hidden, saving presence. The sign is the manifestation and the image of the divine communication of salvation. This statement must not be confused with the opinion sometimes expressed in early scholastic theology (e.g. Hugo of St. Victor) that grace itself is contained in the sign—for example, in the water —as in a vessel. Such thoroughgoing sacramentalism runs the risk of acquiring the connotations of magic. It does, however, contain one element that is correct: namely, that the sign indicates the saving presence of God and that when the sign is made here and now, God's self-communication is made historically tangible in the form of the sign. This becomes even clearer when we recall that the form of the sign is essentially constituted by the word. In the speaking of the word, i.e. the proclamation and promise to a man of God's saving intention, there is realized God's saving will, his self-communication to man. Thus the sacrament can be understood as the real symbolic manifestation, the historical and social-physical expression, of grace. In this interpretation also the sacrament remains within the causal category defined by the Council of Trent. Its causality, however, is not that which we encounter in the processes of nature, but that which is appropriate to the absolute freedom of divine mercy. We can describe it, with Karl Rahner, as the *causa sine qua non.* This view is wholly distinct from the doctrine (condemned by the Council of Trent [DS 1606]) that the sacraments are only the outward signs of grace, for in the present definition the sacrament is seen as the self-communication of God that comes in a historical and social-physical expression to the person receiving it. The recipient is made aware not only that God is communicating himself to him in the sacrament but also that the sacrament is the mode and the means of the divine self-communication to him. Thus the sacrament remains part of the causality of salvation. God's self-communication, i.e. grace, takes place both in the sign and in the fact that it reveals itself in the sign. The sacraments achieve their effect through the act of signifying: *Significando efficiunt quod significant.* They have not only an interpretive function but a creative one.

This interpretation removes the sacraments from the remotest connotations of magic: for here man acquires no power over God, but God has power over the sign man performs. That God communicates himself to the recipient in and through the sign is guaranteed to us by his promise. Man, as the means employed by God but still himself acting freely, has only to perform the sign in dispensing the sacrament and open himself to God in faith in receiving it. Both what the person dispensing it and the person receiving it do are actions made effective by God himself, and the acceptance of the divine self-communication is also grace.

In order to have a full understanding of the whole sacramental complex, it is necessary to consider the different elements in the saving effectiveness of the sacraments. Scholastic theology distinguishes three levels of action in each of the sacraments, which are described as follows: (1) *sacramentum tantum*, the "bare sign"; (2) *res et sacramentum*, the supernatural reality which is at the same time a sign; and (3) *res tantum,* the "sheer reality," which is the union with God by grace that is the ultimate effect of the sacrament.

In other words, first we have the outward visible sign itself, the *sacramentum tantum.* If, as we have seen, matter is the expression of God's concern for man, then this is particularly true of the sacramental sign, for in it God is calling man directly to be with him for eternity. The term *res et sacramentum* refers to the immediate saving effect that the outward sign infallibly produces and regards this first, hidden effect as a sign of faith for the ultimate and actual saving effect, the *res tantum*, i.e. the divine self-communication.

We can begin by making the general point that the direct effect

of the sacrament, the *res et sacramentum*, always signifies a particular relation to the Church. The sacraments are all the Church's
signs: they are all a self-realization, a self-representation, of the
Church. Thus, for example, baptism imparts membership in the
Church. Through the sacrament of ordination a man receives a
special position in the Church. Through sharing in the eucharist he
is again, in a special way, drawn into the brotherly community
of the Church. With this ecclesiological effect of the individual
sacraments there is always combined an encounter with Christ,
issuing in an increase of likeness to him, which may be termed
the christological element. There are three sacraments—baptism,
confirmation, and holy orders—which, according to the indications of Scripture as developed in tradition and defined in the
doctrinal pronouncements of the Church's teaching office, each
impart an indelible mark of Christ, so that a man is marked as
belonging to Christ, in each case, in a particular aspect. It is a
mark which also fits him to undertake particular tasks in the Church.
This christocentric-ecclesiological effect of the sacraments involves
the ultimate real saving effect of each of them, namely, sharing in
the Holy Spirit, the "theological element." Here we recall the words
of Augustine in his controversy with the Donatists: He who is in
the Church has a share in the Holy Spirit; he who is separated
from it cannot share in the Holy Spirit, which is the principle of
the Church's life. The mark of Christ is to be understood as an
irrevocable bestowal of participation in the mission of Christ.

For the sake of clarity we should point out that in theological
language the *res* is divided into grace "in itself" and "sacramental"
grace. The latter refers to the particular color and direction a particular sacrament gives to the communion with God which it imparts. It refers to the particular nature of God's call to the future
in that particular situation.

THE MINISTER

Who is empowered to perform the sacramental signs? Who is empowered to speak the saving word of the proclamation? As we saw
in Volume IV of this work, it is the primary responsibility of the

bishop to proclaim God's message of salvation. Of course, we must distinguish here between mere statement and the saving proclamation which itself involves the self-communication of God. Any man can speak the words of the proclamation for the purposes of information, and the word has a saving effect within the Church whenever it is proclaimed by a baptized Christian to others, whether he has been consecrated as a bishop or priest or not. Thus, for example, parents are the first witnesses and proclaimers of Christ to their children. Let us remember Christ's words: "Where two or three are gathered in my name, there am I in the midst of them" (Mt. 18,20).[3] The laity share in the prophetic office of Christ.

The authentic public proclamation of the word to the people of God, however, is the task of the bishops and of the priests commissioned by him. It is, of course, possible that the bishop can give this task to baptized laymen and women also (cf. the section on ordination to the priesthood). The bishops and the priests, however, are precisely by definition those who are in a special way to proclaim the word of God, through a special mark of Christ given to them in their consecration. This mark of Christ enables them to play the role of Jesus Christ. Hence their authority and their obligation to proclaim Christ is founded in the sacramental sphere— not just in the general sacramentality of the whole Church, but in that compressed and intensified form of it represented by the sacrament of ordination. The special resemblance to Christ that is imparted in the sacrament of ordination means that Christ uses those who receive the sacrament in a special way as his organs.

What is true of the proclamation of the word is true in an even stronger way of the performing of the sacramental signs, especially the celebration of the eucharist. Since the eucharist is the self-representation of the Church, it follows naturally that the person celebrating it is the representative of the Church. Since a particular celebration of the eucharist is always the self-representation of the local Church, the particular representative of the local Church is the celebrant of the eucharist. He is called to this not by a com-

[3]Unless it is otherwise indicated, the excerpts quoted from the New Testament are taken from *The New English Bible, New Testament.* © The Delegates of the Oxford University Press and the Syndics of Cambridge University Press 1961, 1970. Reprinted by permission.

mission from below, but from above. The call from above takes place in a special sacramental act and through the commission, founded in this act, to represent the Church of Jesus Christ among a particular group of men or in a particular place.

With baptism and marriage, however, the representation of Christ and the official utterance of the word of God take place differently. Baptism can be performed, in an emergency, by any other baptized person, or even by anyone at all whose intention it is to perform a Christian rite. Similarly, it is the couple getting married who celebrate the sacrament of matrimony. In the case of baptism, however, it must be said that the usual minister is the bishop or the priest commissioned by him, and that in the sacrament of matrimony the bishop or the priest commissioned by him also plays a role.

In the case of baptism it is understandable that it should be performed in an ecclesial context, for through baptism a person becomes a member of the Church—primarily, a member of the local Church and, through this, at the same time of the whole Church, which has its local form in the local Church. It is natural, then, that the leader of the local Church should be the one who receives the new member into the Church. If in particular cases of emergency other people also are able to administer baptism, this shows the universal saving will of God. If there is no other possibility, anyone can open for another the door to the messianic community of salvation. Behind this idea there stands the christocentric nature of the whole of human history, i.e. the brotherhood of men because of their relationship to their Father in heaven. As far as the recipient is concerned, all men are called to baptism. Baptism is the necessary prerequisite for receiving the other sacraments. In the case of matrimony, some further distinctions need to be made, which we shall do when we come to deal with that sacrament.

THE TEACHING OF THE CHURCH

As theological understanding has developed, the Church itself has given an account of its faith in the sacraments—or, rather, in the merciful God who works through them. We may mention here the Council of Lyons (1274, DS 860) and the Council of Florence (1439-1445, DS 1310), the latter with its pastoral direction for the Armenians; but above all and primarily the Council of Trent. At the Council of Trent in particular, the institution of the sacraments by Jesus Christ was defined, while it was left open in what way Christ did this. Further, the teaching was given of the sacramentality of the seven sacred signs which were in customary use in the Church and of their difference from the Old Testament signs of salvation. At the same time, the saving causality of the sacraments was defined, again without its being interpreted in more detail. Moreover, a special point was made of the fact that the sacraments had not been instituted solely to nourish faith. This statement does not, of course, exclude the assumption that one of the purposes of their institution was to nourish faith: what is rejected is simply the onesided attitude in regard to faith which had emerged in the Reformation. The council takes a realist view of the sacraments when it says:

If anyone says that the sacraments of the New Law do not contain the grace that they signify or that they do not confer that grace upon those who do not place obstacles in the way—as if they were merely external signs of the grace of justice received through faith and insignia, so to speak, of a Christian profession by which men distinguish the faithful from infidels: let him be anathema (DS 1606 in *The Church Teaches*).[4]

This statement is a rejection of the view that justification takes place through faith alone. But of course it does not maintain that the person receiving a sacrament should do no more than remove any obstacle to its reception. As in all the conciliar decisions of earlier times, its aim is simply to reject a onesided view, and this does not mean that the truth that might lie in that view is also rejected.

The council goes on to point out that three sacraments—baptism, confirmation, and ordination—imprint an indelible mark on a man. At the same time it states that not all baptized persons are able to administer all the sacraments. Against the view that the

---

[4]St. Louis: B. Herder Book Co., 1955.

administering of the sacrament depends on the religious and moral state of the minister, it declares that the sacrament is always truly administered if the person entrusted with the authority to administer it at least has the intention to do what the Church does when it administers and imparts the sacraments. As we have already said, this statement by the council ensures certainty in the administration of the sacraments. It is of special importance that the council rejects the view that every minister of the sacraments can alter the sacramental sign as he thinks fit. This does not, however, as we noted above, exclude the possibility that the Church as a whole—i.e., the pope or the college of bishops with the pope at its head—might make alterations within a particular symbolic field for the purpose of making the sign more concrete. The Church has made further doctrinal utterances with regard to the individual sacraments which we shall consider when we treat them individually (DS 1601-1613).

THE PROTESTANT VIEWPOINT

In the view of the Protestant Churches the sacraments can be described as ritual actions instituted by Christ to the performance of which explicit promises of grace are attached. Contemporary Protestantism generally recognizes only baptism and the eucharist as sacraments. The absolution of sins, which was regarded as a sacrament by the early Lutherans, is now regarded as a continuing actualization of baptism. The saving gifts of the sacraments are taken hold of only in faith. Their effect follows not as a result of faith, but simply as a result of the saving word of God working through the sacramental signs. But only faith receives the saving effects: faith itself is at once imparted and strengthened through the sacraments. For Lutherans the proclamation and the sacraments are co-ordinated; they cannot be separated from each other but form a unity. In the other Reformed Churches the sacraments are subordinate to the word and have only a clarifying, cognitive function. There are, however, many differences of view in detail. For Calvin the sacraments have a saving effect only for the predestined.

DIVINE INITIATIVE AND HUMAN ACTION
IN THE SACRAMENTS

The Church is represented in each of the sacramental signs in a particular way: in them it constantly becomes an event, as community in Christ and in the Holy Spirit. This means that the sacraments are symbolic self-representations of Jesus Christ and the Holy Spirit. In them Christ works in the Holy Spirit in a special way in each according to the particular sign. Thus they are encounters with the symbolically present Christ in the here-and-now of history. Since Christ is always present in the Church as the One sent by the heavenly Father, the Father himself is working through the signs. Moreover Christ, as the eternal Logos incarnate, is always an act of God symbolically present, but at the same time always an impulse from him to move forward into the future. The sign is both the event and the guarantee of God's communication of himself.

Since the sign does not function automatically like mechanical natural causality but must be brought about by someone—that is, a person is required for it—the performance of a sacrament always becomes also an encounter between the person dispensing it and the person receiving it. This encounter is something quite different from one which takes place in an official or bureaucratic context. If the dispenser and the recipient understand the sign in true faith, recognizing it, performing it, and receiving it, then this is always an expression of faith, hope, and love: love of Jesus Christ and love of one another—a saving love in which one longs for the salvation of the other and one lays himself open, in this encounter with the other, to receive salvation. Thus this event is wholly determined by persons, even though it is a physical sign—water, wine, oil— that is the occasion and basis of the movement of salvation that descends from God and returns to him by way of man. The degree to which the external sign is part of the movement of salvation is determined differently by the various theological schools (its physical, moral, and intentional efficacy). According to the Thomists, salvation is contained in the object itself. For the Molinists, among whom there are different shades of opinion, the external sign is simply the occasion for the working of God.

But however this relationship is explained, saving causality cannot on any account be ascribed to the object on the basis of its own nature or its own natural structure. Salvation always takes its origin from God. The sacraments do not exercise any compelling influence on God: he retains the initiative. If he gives himself in grace, it is always the consequence of his freely given mercy. Man never, so to speak, has God at his disposal: the sacraments do not work for him like magic. Nevertheless God has assured us of the operation of his saving work when any one of the saving signs is performed.

It is fundamental here that the sign itself—water, wine, or oil —has a certain symbolic relationship to the saving activity, but that the saving significance is really only revealed through the word that is connected with the thing. The water in baptism points to the washing clean from sin; the wine in the eucharist points to the strength and joy, as well as to the communion, that is implicit in the eucharistic meal; the anointing with oil points to the anointing with the Holy Spirit. Thus there is a certain inner fittingness about the signs to symbolize what is worked through them. But it is only the word, the word that is spoken out of faith in Christ, which makes clear their saving significance.

THE SACRAMENTALS

Those saving signs which are called "sacramentals" (little sacraments) are to be understood in terms of the total sacramentality of the Church. They consist in blessings and consecrations in which the Church prays over particular articles or objects with the intention that those who use them shall grow in faith and love. Thus sacramentals are signs of the saving concern of the Church for its members. A person who uses the sacramentals penetrates more deeply into the faith and love of a Church community; he places himself within that movement in which the Church gives itself to Christ. As in everything the Church does, the cross of Christ is at work even in these saving signs of everyday life. Thus they are not like amulets, worn as a charm to protect our earthly life against illness or material losses, but serve Christ's salvation (cf.

the Council of Trent, 7th session, canon 13, DS 1613; cf. also DS 1729, 1746, 1757; cf. the doctrine concerning providence). In sacramentals the Christ-symbolism of earthly things, based on the christocentric nature of the world, is expressed; so too is that brotherly love in which each is concerned for his neighbor and that motherly love in which the Church offers saving aids to all her children in the present world as well as, ultimately, hope for the glory to come. The Christian loves the world, but in this very love he is longing for Christ's return, so that the world may be freed from all its insufficiencies and come to share fully in the glory of Jesus Christ; or rather, through him, in the glory of God the Father.

◄ II

The Individual Sacraments

⬸ 3

The Eucharist: The Scriptural Data

INTRODUCTORY

Through baptism and faith men are incorporated into Christ as the risen Lord who is identical with the crucified Jesus, and they are united among one another to become a community, the people of God and the body of Christ. The community which is founded in Christ as the corporate person who brought about salvation celebrates the memory of its head until he comes. If the resurrection of Jesus had coincided with his return, there would be no celebration of the eucharist; but since the hope of the first Christian community for the imminent return of the Lord was not fulfilled, but a period whose length we do not know was to elapse between his resurrection and his return, the new people of God created by Jesus must celebrate the memory of his incarnation, death, and resurrection and the hope of his return, thus making conscious to itself the meaning of its own life till the end of time. The celebration of the eucharist fulfills that need to celebrate which is part of the Church as of every community of men. The Church's need to celebrate is characterized by its particular quality of being the people of God and the body of Christ. In the celebration the Lord himself is always present in order to give his people a constant share in his saving death. Thus the celebration of his memory becomes a thanksgiving, a "eucharist."

THE WITNESS OF SCRIPTURE

In the New Testament different accounts of the eucharist are found which nevertheless are in broad agreement. We find the relevant passages in the First Epistle to the Corinthians, in the Synoptic gospels, and in another way in St. John's Gospel and in Acts. Contrary to the interpretations of many theologians, it appears that the Epistle to the Hebrews does not contain any reference to the eucharist. Rather, it describes the death of Jesus Christ, against the background of the Old Testament sacrifice, as the final saving sacrifice. In doing this it uses liturgical formulae.

Acts

We shall consider here the passages referring to the eucharist in the order in which they originated. It will be observed that each has a different understanding of the eucharist: thus we shall also be able to see, in this way, the place which each text occupies in the process of the development of eucharistic belief in the apostolic period. That Jesus' command was understood and carried out by his disciples is attested by two accounts in Acts. The three thousand who were converted by Peter's preaching met constantly to listen to the teaching of the apostles, to participate in the community and in the breaking of bread and in prayer (Acts 2,42). When Paul was in Troy, he preached until dawn to those who were gathered at the breaking of bread (Acts 20,7-11). Readers of Acts were so familiar with the expression "the breaking of bread" that it needed no explanation. It describes a ritual celebration, and it has obviously become a technical expression which may refer not only to the act of breaking bread but to the whole ceremony as a ritual meal. We find this comprehensive meaning of the expression nowhere outside the Bible. The word is also used sometimes in Scripture to describe an individual act, namely the breaking and sharing out of the bread (Mt. 14,19; Mk. 6,41; Lk. 9,16; 14,31; Mt. 26,26; Mk. 14,22; Lk. 22,19; 1 Cor. 10,16; 11,24). (Luke 24,30 cannot be considered a reference to the eucharist.) In the writings of the post-apostolic age also the phrase is used to describe the whole celebration of the eucharist (e.g. Ignatius of Antioch, *Ephes.*, 20,2; *Didache,* 14).

Paul

It is Paul who offers us the key to the way the New Testament saw the eucharist and to its whole theology as well. He mentions the eucharist only in chapters 10 and 11 of the First Epistle to the Corinthians, and his remarks are occasioned by the distortions and abuses of the eucharist in Corinth. Paul gives us the original form of the cultic eucharistic celebration. There are not several forms of it in the New Testament but only one, and it is in the First Epistle to the Corinthians that we find it. The text in chapter 11 (1 Cor. 11,17-34) is as follows:

In giving you these injunctions I must mention a practice which I cannot commend: your meetings tend to do more harm than good. To begin with, I am told that when you meet as a congregation you fall into sharply divided groups; and I believe there is some truth in it (for dissensions are necessary if only to show which of your members are sound). The result is that when you meet as a congregation, it is impossible for you to eat the Lord's Supper, because each of you is in such a hurry to eat his own, and while one goes hungry another has too much to drink. Have you no homes of your own to eat and drink in? Or are you so contemptuous of the Church of God that you shame its poorer members? What am I to say? Can I commend you? On this point, certainly not!

For the tradition which I handed on to you came to me from the Lord himself: that the Lord Jesus, on the night of his arrest, took bread and, after giving thanks to God, broke it and said: "This is my body, which is for you; do this as a memorial of me." In the same way, he took the cup after supper, and said: "This cup is the new covenant sealed by my blood. Whenever you drink it, do this as a memorial of me." For every time you eat this bread and drink the cup, you proclaim the death of the Lord, until he comes.

It follows that anyone who eats the bread or drinks the cup of the Lord unworthily will be guilty of desecrating the body and blood of the Lord. A man must test himself before eating his share of the bread and drinking from the cup. For he who eats and drinks eats and drinks judgment on himself if he does not discern the Body. That is why many of you are feeble and sick, and a number have died. But if we examined ourselves, we should not thus fall under judgment. When, however, we do fall under the Lord's judgment, he is disciplining us, to save us from being condemned with the rest of the world.

Therefore, my brothers, when you meet for a meal, wait for one another. If you are hungry, eat at home, so that in meeting together you may not fall under judgment. The other matters I will arrange when I come.

The text of the tenth chapter of 1 Corinthians (10,14-22) is as follows:

So then, dear friends, shun idolatry. I speak to you as men of sense. Form your own judgment on what I say. When we bless "the cup of blessing," is it not a means of sharing in the blood of Christ? When we break the bread, is it not a means of sharing in the body of Christ? Because there is one loaf, we, many as we are, are one body; for it is one loaf of which we all partake.

Look at the Jewish people. Are not those who partake in the sacrificial meal sharers in the altar? What do I imply by this? that an idol is anything but an idol? or food offered to it anything more than food? No: but the sacrifice the heathen offer are offered (in the words of Scripture) "to demons and to that which is not God"; and I will not have you become partners with demons. You cannot drink the cup of the Lord and the cup of demons. You cannot partake of the Lord's table and the table of demons. Can we defy the Lord? Are we stronger than he?

The Synoptics

St. Luke's Gospel (22,7-23) has the following:

Then came the day of Unleavened Bread, on which the Passover victim had to be slaughtered, and Jesus sent Peter and John with these instructions: "Go and prepare for our Passover supper." "Where would you like us to make the preparations?" they asked. He replied, "As soon as you set foot in the city a man will meet you carrying a jar of water. Follow him into the house that he enters and give this message to the householder: 'The Master says, "Where is the room in which I may eat the Passover with my disciples?" ' He will show you a large room upstairs all set out: make the preparations there." They went and found everything as he had said. So they prepared for Passover.

When the time came he took his place at table, and the apostles with him; and he said to them, "How I have longed to eat this Passover with you before my death! For I tell you, never again shall I eat it until the time when it finds its fulfillment in the kingdom of God."

Then he took a cup, and after giving thanks he said, "Take this and share it among yourselves; for I tell you, from this moment I shall drink from the fruit of the vine no more until the time when the kingdom of God comes." And he took bread, gave thanks, and broke it; and he gave it to them, with the words: "This is my body."

"But mark this—my betrayer is here, his hand with mine on the table. For the Son of Man is going his appointed way; but alas for that man by whom he is betrayed!" At this they began to ask among themselves which of them it could possibly be who was to do this thing.

The text of St. Mark's Gospel (14,12-26):

Now on the first day of Unleavened Bread, when the Passover lambs were being slaughtered, his disciples said to him, "Where would you like us to go and prepare for your Passover supper?" So he sent out two of his disciples with these instructions: "Go into the city, and a man will meet you carrying a jar of water. Follow him, and when he enters a house give this message to the householder: 'The Master says, "Where is the room reserved for me to eat the Passover with my disciples?" ' He will show you a large room upstairs, set out in readiness. Make the preparations for us there." Then the disciples went off, and when they came into the city they found everything just as he had told them. So they prepared for Passover.

In the evening he came to the house with the Twelve. As they sat at supper Jesus said, "I tell you this: one of you will betray me—one who is eating with me." At this they were dismayed; and one by one they said to him, "Not I, surely?" "It is one of the Twelve," he said, "who is dipping into the same bowl with me. The Son of Man is going the way appointed for him in the scriptures; but alas for that man by whom the Son of Man is betrayed! It would be better for that man if he had never been born."

During supper he took bread, and having said the blessing he broke it and gave it to them, with the words: "Take this; this is my body." Then he took a cup, and having offered thanks to God he gave it to them; and they all drank from it. And he said, "This is my blood of the covenant, shed for many. I tell you this: never again shall I drink from the fruit of the vine until that day when I drink it new in the kingdom of God."

After singing the Passover Hymn, they went out to the Mount of Olives.

St. Matthew (26,17-30) has the following account:

On the first day of Unleavened Bread the disciples came to ask Jesus, "Where would you like us to prepare for your Passover supper?" He answered, "Go to a certain man in the city, and tell him, 'The Master says, "My appointed time is near; I am to keep Passover with my disciples at your house." ' The disciples did as Jesus directed them and prepared for Passover.

In the evening he sat down with the twelve disciples; and during supper he said, "I tell you this: one of you will betray me." In great distress they exclaimed one after the other, "Can you mean me, Lord?" He answered, "One who has dipped his hand into this bowl with me will betray me. The Son of Man is going the way appointed for him in the scriptures; but alas for that man by whom the Son of Man is betrayed! It would be better for that man if he had never been born." Then Judas spoke, the one who was to betray him. "Rabbi," he said, "can you mean me?" Jesus replied, "The words are yours."

During supper Jesus took bread, and having said the blessing he broke it and gave it to the disciples with the words: "Take this and eat; this is my body." Then he took a cup, and having offered thanks to God he gave it to them with the words: "Drink from it, all of you. For this is my blood, the blood of the covenant, shed for many for the forgiveness of sins. I tell you, never again shall I drink from the fruit of the vine until that day when I drink it new with you in the kingdom of my Father."

After singing the Passover Hymn, they went out to the Mount of Olives.

Comparison of the Texts

The distinctive characteristics of the various texts have led, in the course of theological development, to a differentiation between a Petrine and a Pauline account. According to this view, we find the Petrine account in the gospels of Matthew and Mark, and the Pauline in the gospel of Luke and the First Epistle to the Corinthians. The Pauline account differs from the Petrine chiefly through the addition of the instituting command: "Do this as a memorial of me." Moreover, it is to be noted that Matthew and Mark do not have the addition to the words about the bread, i.e. "for you" or "that is given for you." Paul and Luke have this addition. The fact is especially important that according to the Pauline account, Jesus took the cup after the meal, whereas in Matthew and Mark he took it immediately after the distribution of the bread during the meal. According to Paul and Luke, the eucharist falls into two parts because of the intervening meal. And the words that Jesus speaks over the cup in Mark and Luke are characteristically different from those reported in Matthew and Mark. In Paul and Luke, Jesus says that the cup is the new covenant. It is, of course, closely related to his blood. The covenant is founded and constantly actualized anew through his blood in the cup. The identity of the cup and the blood is not expressed directly, but implicitly and indirectly. Those present are not invited to drink the blood, but they do it without being invited. According to Matthew and Mark, however, the identity of cup and blood is explicitly stated. In Mark the disciples are indirectly invited to drink the blood, and Mark also emphasizes that they really drank out of the cup.

Again, there are notable differences within the two groups. Matthew differs in a number of details from Mark. The formulations peculiar to Matthew obviously serve the desire for clarity and linguistic smoothness. Thus they represent a stage of reflection that goes beyond the Marcan text. The main thing to note is that Mark reports that Jesus explicitly asked the disciples to eat the bread he had blessed. In this he makes clear the meaning of

Christ's invitation to take it. Matthew gives us Jesus' words: "Drink from it, all of you," which correspond with the invitation to eat the bread. Mark says nothing of this invitation to drink the wine. The first thing he mentions is the drinking of the wine, and then he reports the words that Jesus spoke over the cup, without mentioning his invitation. By changing the preposition in the phrase "for you" (*peri* instead of *hyper*) Matthew expresses more strongly than Mark that the shedding of the blood takes place not only for the salvation of the disciples but also in their stead. The most important addition in Matthew is the phrase "for the forgiveness of sins," which is linked to the words over the cup. He expresses even more clearly what Mark says.

The differences between Paul and Luke are still greater than those between Matthew and Mark. Thus in Paul we have nothing about eating and drinking "when the kingdom of God comes." On the other hand, Luke does not have the second command of institution that Paul reports in connection with the words over the cup. He has probably yielded to the desire for brevity. Also Luke adds to the words "for you" spoken over the bread the word "given."

Origin of the Texts

In order to understand the eucharistic texts of the New Testament and their relationship to one another it is important to see how they came to be written. Paul himself in chapter 11 of the First Epistle to the Corinthians refers to the tradition, a tradition from the Lord. It is safe to say that he does not mean here a revelation by Jesus made directly to him personally, but a tradition that goes back to the Lord and has come from him—through other people handing it down—to Paul. After his conversion Paul had many opportunities to get to know the traditions that came from the Lord (cf. Acts 9,6; also Gal. 1,18; 2,1-10). As he says in his epistle, Paul proclaimed what he learned from this tradition on his second missionary journey, in 51, in Corinth. Thus the epistle does not instruct the Corinthians on a truth of faith they did not yet know: it is rather an exhortation to them to celebrate in the right way the rite long familiar to them. Undoubtedly 11,23b-25 are part of the tradition, as are vv. 26-29. Only in v. 30 do the conclusions which Paul draws from the abuses in the Corinthians' celebration of the eucharist begin for certain. The view that the Pauline text is a piece of original tradition is supported by the fact that it is liturgical in character.

The first proclamation after the sending of the Spirit on the day of Pentecost was expressed in the original apostolic *kerygma*. This gave rise to various particular forms which were passed on in the various communities: formulae embodying the faith, professions of faith, liturgical formulae, accounts of the words (*logia*) of Jesus, accounts of his actions. In the gospels, especially in the Synoptics, these various separate pieces are woven into a community tradition and related back to the historical life of Jesus. We have already pointed out (see especially Volume I, *Dogma: God in Revelation,* ch. 10, "The Sacred Scripture") that in evaluating them as narrative and as history it is essential to take into account the problems involved in the history of their form, of their tradition, and of their editing.

It is quite clear that from the beginning the memory of Jesus was celebrated, as he had commanded, in the form of a meal (cf. Acts 2,42; 20,7-11). As time went on and more and more people were incorporated through baptism in the body of Christ, it became more and more necessary for the origin and meaning of the celebration to be explained. In the interpretation and justification of the celebration, it was natural that the major part should be played by the tradition of the words that Jesus had spoken at his farewell meal. It was to be expected that hagiographers would place their accents according to the varying situations in the different Christian communities. In Paul, however, we can exclude this kind of emphasis or variation given to the text. After all, he was arguing against the abuses present among them by reminding the Corinthians of the text with which they were familiar. He would have risked objections being raised against his argument if he had subtracted from, added to, or made any difference of emphasis in words that were familiar to all.

Interpretation of the account of the origin of the celebration performed in the Christian communities involved, of course, much longer texts than what has been handed down to us in the eucharistic passages. These are, as it were, a résumé of what was said at the celebration.

The liturgical character of the texts we have emerges clearly in their tight, precise form, and in the parallelism between the words over the bread and over the cup. These texts are to be seen both as rubrics for the celebration, i.e., as instructions on the way the rite is to be celebrated, and as a statement of faith that testifies to the origin of the celebration and gives information about it. A special weight is to be placed on their historical reliability. This emerges, in particular, from the fact that both the Synoptics and Paul always clearly state the historical framework within which the eucharistic words of Jesus were spoken. (Apart from the eucharistic texts we have, as we have already seen, another important text in the New Testament that can only be explained in terms of liturgy: Matthew 28,20.) The historical value that the texts possess, despite their ritual and liturgical character, is based on the fact that they come from qualified witnesses, namely those who took part in the last meal Jesus ate before his death.

The "narratives" that come from the liturgy are reflections of faith that have matured in different ways. As we have frequently observed, these reflections are under the influence of the Holy Spirit in that they present clarifications or developments of the revelation of Christ. Thus we find that the various texts present various aspects of the one saving mystery. Paul presents the earliest form, and Matthew the most highly developed. The advance in the reflection on belief goes along with development in the understanding of the significance of Christ.

From the point of view of the liturgical character of the eucharistic narratives we can make an important addition to this grouping into two. From the liturgical point of view the Pauline and Marcan institution narratives are closer to each other than both are to the Lucan. In terms of content we find that in the process of reflection, the reality of the eucharistic body and blood of Jesus Christ, as well as the soteriological element, became gradually more and more emphasized.

The Last Supper

It is interesting that both the Synoptics and Paul present the eucharistic words in the context of a meal. We note, however, that Mark and Matthew have kept the memory of the historical framework but are not interested in setting the eucharistic words in a particular place in the meal. In Luke and Paul, or rather the pre-Lucan and pre-Pauline texts, account is apparently taken of the actual course of the meal. This is expressed in the phrase "after supper." Here the words over the cup are set in a particular place in the action. Paul shows as little interest in the Jewish Passover meal as Luke. The words "after supper" seem to be in both, but especially in Paul, a rigid formula like a rubric. They are important, however, for the interpretation, in that they show the closeness in time and in matter of the pre-Lucan and pre-Pauline account, but especially the latter, through the event itself.

It has not been entirely established what type of meal it was that provided the framework for the institution of the eucharist. According to the Synoptics it was a Passover meal, but this is difficult to reconcile with St. John's Gospel. The question is not important for the interpretation of the eucharist. What we know is that Jesus instituted the new rite within the framework of a meal. The normal festive meal did not differ greatly from the Passover meal. Both consisted of three parts: a first course (with the first cup), the main meal, and then a celebration. In the Passover meal, drinking from the first cup (everyone had his own) was followed by a word of blessing connected with the feast day. Then bitter herbs were eaten and the actual Passover liturgy began. This started with the second cup being mixed and passed around. The father of the house explained the meaning of the celebration, and the recitation of the first part of the small *Hallel* (Psalms 113f.) followed. Then the father of the house broke the bread, put bitter herbs on it, and handed it to the others. Then they ate the Passover lamb that had been killed and sacrificed in the Temple during the afternoon. After that, the third cup was passed, which was called the cup of blessing because of the words of thanks spoken for the meal just eaten. After the remains of the meal had been cleared away, the fourth cup was passed. The celebration ended with the second part of the small *Hallel* (Psalms 115-118).

Jesus connected his eucharistic words over the bread with the prayer over the bread at the main meal and the words over the wine and the cup with the thanks spoken at the third cup. Thus the two eucharistic actions of the bread and the cup were separated from each other by the main meal. In any case, Jesus made use of an already existing rite in order to institute his new one. It is not surprising that at a very early stage the two eucharistic actions were brought together, but they still retained their connection with the festive meal.

At his final meal Jesus gave the command of institution of the eucharist. The apostles are to do what he has done: consecrate, as a memory of himself, bread and wine in thanks, so that they may become the mode of the presence of his saving action and of himself. This is reported twice by Paul, both after the words over the bread and after those over the cup, but by Luke only once and by the other two Synoptics not at all.

Following the command of Jesus, the first Christian community celebrated the memory of their Lord in a meal. This consisted of two parts, forming one whole. The first part was a meal to satisfy hunger and the second was the eucharist. We find this form of memorial celebration in the Christian communities of both Corinth and Jerusalem (cf. Acts 2,41; 20,7-11).

INTERPRETATION OF THE PAULINE TEXTS

I Corinthians 11

As we have seen, it was this connection between the eucharist and a meal that led in Corinth to the abuses Paul attacks in his epistle. The Corinthians who were rich and highly placed in society had the responsibility of providing the food for the meal meant to satisfy hunger—the celebration was, then, at the same time an occasion for helping the poor. But instead they were arriving long before the poor, the workers, and the slaves were able to, and beginning to eat and drink. When the members of the community who were low on the social and economic scale arrived after their day's work, the rich, it appears from Paul, were already drunk. The poor received nothing; they even had to sit by helplessly watching the others. This behavior did not burden the consciences of the rich Corinthians, for they could say that the poor did not miss out on the main thing, which was the eucharist. Paul describes their behavior as not only antisocial but an expression of contempt for the community of Jesus Christ. The Lord's meal is meant, as a whole, to be a self-representation of the Church and moreover to impart salvation in that it incorporates its members more deeply in Christ and strengthens brotherly love in the community. The behavior of the rich Corinthians is an affront to this meaning of the Lord's meal. Paul questions whether there really can be a "Lord's meal" under such circumstances. He does not doubt that the eucharist comes about, but the sense of the whole is missed.

To give his disapproval the necessary force, Paul quotes the institution narrative, which ultimately came from Christ and which had been handed down to him in a fixed form and passed on by him on his first missionary journey in Corinth. According to the institution narrative, it is the Lord himself who determines the eucharistic action. The Corinthians are offending not only against an instruction by the apostle but against an instruction of Jesus himself.

The full significance of what the Corinthians are doing becomes clearer when we read in the pre-Pauline text (v. 27) that Christ not only speaks into the present out of the distant past through the links of tradition but is himself directly present at every celebration. The Corinthians must realize that their way of celebrating the Lord's meal has made them guilty of the body and blood of the Lord and hence worthy of judgment. The Judge is the Lord himself (v. 29). He is present in the eucharistic celebration. He is the host, and those who partake of the eucharist are the guests.

The presence of Jesus Christ is attested in the pre-Pauline formula which Paul recalls, namely the words spoken over the bread: "This is my body for you." We must not attach any special weight to the word "is." In the Aramaic language which Jesus spoke it would be of no importance. It is from the whole context that we discern the reality of the eucharist. The Greek text, however, states that the bread is the body of Christ and the wine his blood. In the language of the Old Testament the word "body" means nothing but the whole, bodily existing man. According to this, Christ said: "This is what I am for you." The reason for the pre-Pauline text saying "for you" while in Matthew and Mark we read "for many" is that it is an actualization of the words of the Lord. In the words "for you" those who are immediately involved, who are one group among many, are addressed. Thus the saving life of Jesus Christ is not limited to an exclusive circle. Christ is the bringer of salvation to all, to the whole of humanity, the whole creation. But his function of being the bringer of salvation is concentrated at the eucharistic celebration on those who are taking part in it.

The words over the cup belong with the words over the bread. The word "blood" in v. 25 refers to the violent death of Jesus Christ on Golgotha. We shall recall that in the Old Testament blood was regarded as the seat of life. Hence we can say that the word "blood" is to be understood as the whole living Jesus Christ, who has given himself for men (Deut. 12,23; Lev. 17,11-14; Gen. 4,10; Mt. 27,4. 25; Acts 5,28). If we ask if it is the glorified or the crucified Christ who is present—i.e., whether the event of Golgotha and that of Easter morning, which is indissolubly connected with it, are made present—the answer is that it is the risen Lord, who is identical with the crucified Jesus and the Christ who is to return, that is present in the eucharist.

His presence is not merely spatial, not a mere physical presentness, but rather a personal one. Jesus comes to those participating in the eucharist, bringing salvation with him. In this way the cross is made present in a salvific way. Thus the words in v. 26 about proclaiming the death of the Lord acquire a central importance for the whole text. These words, too, come, we may say, from the pre-Pauline tradition. If we ask what is the meaning of the Lord's Supper in Paul, then the answer is: the proclamation of the death of the Lord. The Lord's death is proclaimed in two ways: through words and through actions. The words can be those of a hymn, as in the manner of Phil. 2,6-11, Col. 1,12-20 (cf. also 1 Tim.

3,16; 1 Pet. 3,18-21; 1 Jn. 5,6f.; 1 Cor. 1,23; 2,3; 2 Cor. 1,19; 4,5; 11,4; Phil. 1,15; Rom. 16,25), or the eucharistic prayer. Paul emphasizes the proclamation through actions, namely the eating and drinking, the ritual meal. The proclamation is not merely speaking about Jesus but is an event in which Jesus Christ himself is present, in which he makes himself present, in order to give himself to his own people, the Christian community.

That the eucharist has a sacrificial character is not stated clearly in the text, but there are sufficient indications that it has. This is in accordance with the whole of Pauline theology. Although Paul testifies to the expiatory character of the death of Golgotha, there is still no clear and explicit statement in the main epistles (cf., though, 1 Cor. 5,7) that this expiatory death is a sacrificial one. This can be explained by the fact that Paul was engaged in a fight against pagan ritual. It was only later reflection (Ephesians, Colossians, Hebrews, and the gospels) on both the saving death of Golgotha and the making present of it in the eucharist that led to the clear insight (which we can just sense in Paul) that Golgotha was a sacrificial event; that this sacrifice is made present anew in the eucharist; and that, accordingly, the eucharist itself is a sacrifice. We find a developed view of the sacrificial character of the eucharist in the Synoptic narratives and very clearly in John.

By being celebrated in the eucharist, the saving death of Golgotha constantly gains new saving power over those present at it. The saving power of the proclamation lies both in the act and in its content, and the two cannot be separated.

The death of the Lord proclaimed in the eucharist is the basis of the new divine order. It is extremely characteristic of the Pauline text that the words over the cup do not have the same form as those over the bread. He does not say "This is my blood," but "This cup is the new covenant sealed by my blood," i.e. the blood shed, or to be shed, on the cross. Here the idea of the new covenant created by the death of Jesus is central to the Pauline understanding of the eucharist. Eucharistic realism (i.e. the real presence of the body and blood of the Lord, the identity of the bread and wine with his body and blood) takes second place. It is stated indirectly but clearly in v. 27. This relative emphasis characterizes Paul's view of the eucharist. For him the eucharistic elements are sacramental modes of appearance of the crucified Christ. This does not involve any objectification (*Verdinglichung*) of the eucharist; it is an action performed by Christ in regard to those present. This action is connected with the substantial presence of the Lord in the elements (F. Betz).

An essential element in the eucharistic text is what is said about the covenant, or the new order of God. Jeremiah (31,31ff.) had spoken of a new divine order to come. The old covenant had been broken countless times by the human partners to it. The word "covenant" (*berith*) might suggest that the relationship of God to men was a relationship of achievements and reward. The use of the word *diatheke* (i.e. disposition, testament, or order) in the New Testament in place of *berith* better expresses God's initiative and transcendence. But this new order created by God also constitutes a covenant between him and men. In this order of salvation God acts differently towards men from before, and men too are on a different footing. They are free from guilt and live in the knowledge of God and at peace with him. This freedom from sin is brought about through the expiatory death of Jesus.

When 1 Corinthians speaks of the new covenant based on the blood of Jesus, this refers to the death on Golgotha. It points back to the description of the servant of God in Second Isaiah (Is. 43) and indirectly to the sealing of the covenant at Sinai by the shedding of blood (Exod. 24,8).

Thus the fundamental gift of the eucharist is that of a share in the expiatory death of Jesus granted to the community of salvation that has been constituted through his saving death. We have seen in an earlier connection that the institution of the eucharist by Jesus Christ is fundamental to the coming into being of the new community of salvation, the Church. This is not contradicted by the statement in the eucharistic text that the death of Jesus constitutes the foundation of a new order of salvation. The Church, the new community of salvation, the new people of God, is precisely the beginning and expression of the new order of salvation. Nor is it a contradiction when in other passages Paul ascribes the incorporation in the community of salvation and in the crucified and risen Lord to baptism. Sharing in the death and resurrection of Jesus and membership in the body of Christ, the Church, are the two leading ideas of Paul's theology. Baptism imparts the life of salvation to us. The eucharist is the constantly new realization, deepening, and intensification of the community with Christ that is founded in baptism. "Baptism is the beginning of the bridge over time. The successive pylons, the eucharist, take us across the stream to the other shore, the eschatological kingdom of God. The eucharist transmits sacramentally God's saving act which is founded in baptism and carries us across the stream of time. It is the constantly new work of God."[1]

Thus we can see that the memorial celebration of Paul has nothing to do with the pagan meals for the dead. The differences are so fundamental that there is no bridge from one to the other. In the pagan meals for the dead it is the memory of a dead person that is celebrated and not, as in the eucharist, that of a living one. Nor can it be said that the early apostolic liturgical account we find in Paul's epistle is a parallel to the mystery religions. In contrast to the unhistorical nature of mythical events, the pre-Pauline eucharistic text makes a special point of the historical hour of the death of Jesus ("on the night of his arrest"). Moreover, salvation is promised not only to a particular religious community but to the whole of humanity. Above all, salvation cannot be magically assured by the performance of particular rites. Although sacramental realism is stressed, salvation is attained only through living in a way that is in accordance with the sacramental realities. What takes place in the sacramental sphere must be carried through in our lives; otherwise the sacramental element will mean a greater condemnation at the final judgment.

The idea of remembrance or memorial is found often in the Old Testament (Gen. 9,15f.; Ex. 32,13). Israel saw its history as a consequence of God's actions in the creation, in the choosing of his people and the sealing of his covenant. It constantly calls these actions to mind. The more the solemn assembly of Israel and the individual Israelite reflect upon these divine deeds, the more intensely do the promises of final salvation become present. No distinction is made between the past event of the sealing of the covenant and the ritual re-enactment of this past saving event in

[1]P. Neuenzeit, *Das Herrenmahl*, p. 231.

the present: the past event and its present saving effect are experienced as a unity. The chief Jewish memorial celebrations were the Feast of Tabernacles, the Feast of Purim, and the Feast of the Passover. The memorial is always at the same time a thanksgiving for God's saving actions (Ex. 12,27).

In the New Testament we often read that God's saving action always takes effect anew when it is manifested in the memorial of the faithful (1 Thess. 1,5; 2,1; 2,5,11; 3,3f.; 5,1). In the word of the proclamation that is spoken in the community, it is Jesus Christ himself who comes (Lk. 10,16; Mt. 10,40). It is always he himself who acts (1 Cor. 4,15; James 1,18). Without the differences between the past and the present being overlooked or underestimated, the view is expressed that the then and the now are interrelated (cf. 1 Cor. 15,22).

This view can be explained in terms of the scriptural idea of corporate personality and the Pauline doctrine of the *pneuma*. Paul's idea of the *pneuma*, according to which the Lord took on a pneumatic life in the resurrection, explains how it is that the historical Jesus, glorified in the resurrection, can here and now be salvifically—i.e. dynamically—present. A man can experience this saving presence of Jesus only as he himself enters the sphere of pneumatic life.

This saving action asks something of those who have a share in it. But the rich Corinthians fail to respond to this challenge. They do not deny the presence of Jesus Christ, but they forget two things: first, that Jesus is present as the one who gives himself for men; and, second, that his presence brought about in the sign of the meal looks forward to his future, unveiled presence. The response of those taking part to the sacrifice of Jesus must be the serving love of their brothers. It is thus that we must interpret the words in St. Luke's Gospel in connection with the pre-Lucan institution narrative (Lk. 22,26f.): "Not so with you: on the contrary, the highest among you must bear himself like the youngest, the chief of you like a servant. For who is the greater—the one who sits at table or the servant who waits on him? Surely the one who sits at table. Yet here am I among you like a servant." The account of the washing of the feet in John has the same meaning (Jn. 13,1-20).

John does not give us any formal eucharistic institution narrative, but instead he tells us of the washing of the feet. We may assume that at the time St. John's Gospel was written the eucharist was a fixed part of the Church's life. Hence it was unnecessary for John to speak of the eucharistic liturgy. But he did not think it unnecessary to speak of that helping brotherly love without which the meaning of the eucharist is not fulfilled.

Paul tells the Corinthians what they have to do at the celebration and as a result of the celebration. His idea of the eucharist is ethically orientated. There is no doubt that Paul holds to a sacramental realism, but it is ethical-sacramental in nature, just as, *vice versa*, ethics in Paul must always be regarded as sacramental ethics. The Corinthians obviously believe that possession of Jesus Christ ensures their salvation, thus falling victim to a magic sacramentalism. This is why they celebrate their eucharist as a meal of rejoicing and forget that the fulfillment is still to come. This may be connected with their doubts regarding the resurrection of the dead, which Paul answers in chapter 15 of the same epistle. Paul tells his readers that they must completely separate the meal intended to satisfy their appetite from the eucharist; they must eat in their own houses if they refuse to give the Lord's supper its real meaning. This suggestion was, in fact, followed in the second century. The eucharist was moved to the morning, and the community meal as a meal to satisfy hunger continued to be eaten in the evening. When Paul again places the memorial of the death of Jesus Christ at the center of the eucharist, the question arises what is meant by this memorial of his death.

The proclamation of the death of Jesus Christ is to continue until Christ appears. Thus in the celebration of the eucharist we are looking not only at the past and the present Christ but also towards the one to come. The pre-Pauline, i.e., the early apostolic, idea of the eucharist was eschatological, not ecstatic. It had nothing to do with mystical experience, but represented faith in redemption as part of salvation history. Just this is what Paul is trying to point out to the Corinthians. We may assume that in the earliest Christian community the eschatological tension was more important than the memorial of the crucifixion. Both had been forgotten in Corinth. Paul combines the two views. He makes the eschatological point by noting that the eucharist is celebrated only until Christ comes again. Indeed, Christ's coming is so effective in every celebration of the eucharist that his presence in it anticipates his eschatological coming: his coming is already taking place but not yet concluded. Nevertheless every eucharist is a powerful movement into the future of his final coming. The Lord's Supper is the community of Christ as it is possible "between the times"— between the age of destruction that still continues but for the Christian is rendered powerless and the future age of salvation whose reality and effect are already with us: granting us a real anticipation and yet only preparing the way and promising final and full communion (Schnackenburg).

1 Corinthians 10

Let us now consider the second text in 1 Corinthians. In chapter 10 Paul writes to the Corinthians that they cannot serve two masters. They cannot participate in both the pagan sacrificial meals and the eucharist. In the eucharist Christ identifies himself to some degree with those taking part. If, despite this, they turn to the gods (who do not, in fact, even exist), they are doing something very dangerous, namely provoking the anger of the living and powerful God. Those who take part in the eucharist are sharing at God's altar, but they must not flatter themselves with the hope that taking part in the eucharist safeguards them from every danger to salvation—any more than the old order of salvation was a safeguard against dangers to salvation for the members of the Israelite people without the necessary right moral behavior. The climax of the text in chapter 10 is the pre-Pauline verse (16) which says that the "cup of blessing" is a means of sharing in the blood of Christ and that the "bread of blessing" is a sharing in his body. The expressions "cup of blessing" and "bread of blessing" are technical liturgical expressions. Paul is not telling the Corinthians about this sharing of the body and blood of Jesus Christ for the first time. They know it so well that only a reminder is necessary, an appeal to their insight. It is this sharing in the body and blood of Jesus Christ, i.e. the sharing of the life of the crucified and risen

Lord, that should restrain them from taking part in pagan sacrificial meals.

Here we can see clearly the sacramental realism of the pre-Pauline concept of the eucharist. The accent here also, however, is on the sharing of the death (the "blood") of Jesus Christ, but the static element emerges more strongly than in chapter 11. The nature of this realism is not further explained. The question that occupied medieval theology and was answered in an authoritative way at the Council of Trent, namely whether the Lord becomes present in the eucharist through a change of substance or in some other way, was still beyond the horizon of the faithful. The important thing for them is the saving presence itself, and fellowship with Jesus in the symbolic signs of the meal.

According to this passage, fellowship with Jesus Christ is achieved in particular intensity through the sharing of the one bread, i.e. through the many becoming themselves one body through the body of Jesus Christ. It should, however, be emphasized that Paul speaks of a sharing both in the body, i.e. the whole life of Jesus Christ, and in the saving action. Through his presence Christ gives those taking part a share in his saving action. It is worth mentioning that in 1 Cor. 10,17 Paul connects the saving relationship between Christ and the Church with the taking of the bread, and in 1 Cor. 11,23ff. speaks of the new order of salvation as following from the taking of the cup. It should be said of this sharing in the presence of Jesus Christ what we have already pointed out: the body of Jesus Christ or the bodily existing risen Christ himself is present, not only spatially but personally, so that he brings about a saving encounter between himself and those who take part. Jesus Christ gives himself to them. They are incorporated in him, the corporate saving person, without losing their own personal self in the process. Although it is not clearly expressed in the text, it is Paul's teaching that this sharing through partaking of the bread and wine takes place in faith, not just through being physically present at the celebration or through the sheer act of eating and drinking. This incorporation in the glorified Christ within history is an impulse towards that future form of life in which Christ lives, namely what we call "glory."

INTERPRETATION OF THE LUCAN TEXTS

There is the difficulty in the texts of St. Luke's Gospel that he speaks of two cups. A distinction is made between a Lucan or pre-Lucan long form ("long Luke") and a short form ("short Luke"). It is probable that long Luke, which presents this difficulty, is the original form. Luke first gives us an early Passover narrative (22, 15-18), perhaps the earliest. The purpose of this is not to give us the details of the Jewish Passover meal but to recall the institution of the new Passover by Christ. By saying that he has longed to eat this meal with them, Jesus is making the point that this celebration is something new and different from what has gone before. The cup mentioned in v. 17 should very probably be understood eucharistically. It is identical with the third cup of blessing in the Jewish Passover meal, to which Jesus links the institution of the eucharistic cup. The explicit description of this blessing of a cup as a *eucharistein* ("thanksgiving") and the liturgical terminology of "take this" are evidence of its being a eucharistic narrative. The Lucan account was, however, soon felt to be insufficient (there was nothing about the bread), and hence it was added to and made clearer by simply placing after the account of 22,15-18 the separate tradition of the institution verses of 19f. This mechanical addition resulted in the eucharistic intention of vv. 15-18 no longer being understood, so that the verses could be interpreted as relating to the first or the second Passover cup.

Moreover, there is a difference of content between the two passages of text. Altogether the pre-Lucan account suggests that (unlike chapter 11 of 1 Corinthians) the proclamation of the death of Jesus is not central to the understanding of the eucharist. But it shares with the pre-Pauline text the view that in the eucharist the new covenant that has come about through the expiatory death of Jesus ("blood" signifies his violent death) is celebrated and that the celebrating community receives a share in the new covenant (v. 20). With the new covenant the kingdom of God has begun. The connection between the eucharist and the eschatological kingdom of God is expressed quite clearly in vv. 15-18. The new covenant, the new order of God, is to be continually celebrated through celebrating the memory of what the Lord performed in his farewell meal. There is here in the background also the memory of the promise of a new divine order in Jeremiah 31,31ff. as well as the image of the servant of God who through his expiatory death brings about the new divine order (Is. 53; 49). There is also the memory of the institution of the old covenant, now superseded, by the shedding of blood at Sinai (Ex. 24,8).

Thus we can see that the Lucan account testifies to the dynamic character of the eucharist, though not so clearly as the Pauline text. It is, however, in its whole view of the eucharist closer to Mark and Matthew than to Paul. In Luke we see the beginning of the approach to the eucharist that appears in its mature form in Mark. It is different from the Pauline one by its emphasis on the objective, i.e. the really present body and the really present blood of Jesus Christ. Paul too takes a realist view of the eucharist, but only as the basis for the sharing by the celebrating community in the saving death of Jesus Christ. In Luke we find the start of a stronger accent on the two eucharistic gifts.

This is combined with a new idea, not yet clearly visible in the Pauline text, that the body and blood of Jesus Christ are present as the sacrificed body and blood. This is expressed in the participle added to the word "body," which is "given for you (by God)," and in that added to the cup, "poured out for you." Of course Luke is a long way from understanding the presence of the body and blood of Jesus Christ as a purely local one. The body, as we have said, always means, in Scripture, the man. Blood, in the context of the eucharistic text, refers to the violent death of Jesus. The emphasis on the eucharistic gifts, then, testifies to the presence of Jesus himself, the presence of the risen Lord, who gave himself on the cross for his own community and for all men, expiating the sins of the world by sacrificing himself to the Father. The eucharist has obviously become so different from sacrificial Jewish ritual that the pre-Lucan text does not hesitate to use sacrificial terminology.

It follows that the idea of sacrifice is understood here in an analogous sense: it is the man Jesus himself who sacrifices himself. Thus it is the Lord who brings salvation to the world, marked forever by his sacrificial death and resurrection; the Lord who, according to the pre-Lucan text, gives himself in the eucharist to the celebrating community. We can say that in the Lucan view the soteriological aspect is combined with the christological.

It is evident from a linguistic peculiarity that the Lucan or pre-Lucan text marks the transition from the Pauline to the Marcan view of the eucharist. In the text the dynamic pre-Pauline idea of the eucharist is combined with the primarily static one developed in Mark in such a way that a linguistic disharmony remains. As we shall see presently, Mark speaks of the blood that is shed. While these words are correct in Mark in terms of language and content, in Luke they refer grammatically to the cup but in content to the blood. This discrepancy is due to the words being taken out of one stream of tradition and set within another, with no attempt made to smooth the reading out linguistically.

INTERPRETATION OF THE TEXTS IN MARK AND MATTHEW

Let us now consider the institution narratives in Mark and Matthew. If these two accounts do not include the command to repeat the celebration, the reason probably is that at the time the texts were written, the eucharist was an automatic part of the life of the Church, and hence it no longer seemed necessary to point out that Jesus Christ had commanded it.

In Mark, or the pre-Marcan institution narrative, the pre-Pauline sacramental realism that Paul took up and set within the context of the eucharistic event—has a dominant place. The main difference is that in 1 Corinthians 11,25 the saving gift is the sharing in the new order of God, while for Mark (14,24) it is the blood of Christ.

The idea of the memorial of Christ's death that Paul places in the center of his interpretation of the eucharist is preserved also in the post-Pauline eucharistic texts. In Mark, however, the accent is placed on the saving eucharistic gifts, the body and blood of Jesus Christ, the body and blood being interpreted as sacrificial. The parallel with the sealing of the covenant in the Old Testament, the foreshadowing of the new covenant, in Ex. 24,8 is clear. After the proclamation of the law of the covenant Moses set up an altar at the foot of the mountain. A great burnt-offering was made for which young oxen were used. Moses took half of the blood and threw it against the altar; with the other half he sprinkled the people, saying: "Behold the blood of the covenant which the Lord has made with you in accordance with all these words." In the eucharistic texts of Mark and Matthew Christ appears as a new Moses. In Mark the eucharist is understood typologically. It is the antitype of the Old Testament sacrifices and surpasses them. But it can only be an antitype if the death of Jesus on Golgotha is seen not only as an expiatory death but also as a sacrificial one. We may say that the way to faith in the eucharist as a ritual sacrifice does not proceed from the interpretation of the death on the cross as a sacrificial one; the development was, *vice versa,* from the view of the eucharist as a ritual sacrifice to the interpretation of the expiatory death of Jesus Christ as sacrificial.

Moreover, the Marcan version points to Isaiah 53, the text concerning the servant of God. The texts of Mark and Matthew, however, do not only say that a new covenant has been brought about by the blood of Jesus Christ; it is formally stated that the blood of Jesus Christ is in the cup. This blood present in the cup is said to be the blood of the new covenant, just as the blood poured out in Ex. 24,8 was the blood of the old. In the paralleling of the bread and the wine or the body and the blood the emphasis is on the words over the wine or the words over the blood. In Mark it is the blood that is the main thing. The interpretation of the Marcan account must, then, start from the words over the wine, and interpret the words over the bread in accordance with the interpretation of the words over the blood. The blood in the cup is ritual blood of sacrifice. In the separation of one part of the sacrifice from the other (the blood from the body) the gifts of the meal are shown to be not only a symbol but a manifestation of the crucifixion.

It must also be pointed out, nevertheless, that the Marcan text is not concerned simply with the presence of dead material to be sacrificed. However different the emphases in comparison with Paul's account, with the actual gifts placed in the foreground, in Mark also the body means the bodily Christ and the shedding of the blood, the bodily sacrifice of Christ. Or rather: in the mutual relationship of the shed blood and sacrificed body the presence of the risen Christ, who is identical with the crucified Christ, is attested. A comparison between the Pauline and the Marcan account does not show us so much two different conceptions of the eucharist as rather different emphases within the one conception of it. Whereas the Pauline one is more dynamic and personal, the Marcan appears more spatial and objective. But precisely this spatial objectivity is for Mark the reason for the personal interpretation of the eucharist. Moreover, according to Mark, it is Jesus himself who gives himself to his disciples in the symbol, which is at the same time the reality (*Realsymbol*) of his body and blood. But the main emphasis falls on this symbol. When Jesus gives himself to his disciples, it takes place by his giving them his blood, which both represents and is the basis of the new covenant. As in Paul, Jesus is here also both the giver and the gift. The fundamental thought in Mark is the communion: the eating and, still more, the drinking.

According to Mark's account, Jesus uses the symbolism available in the Old Testament to describe his sacrifice of himself. It is because of this symbolism that Mark speaks of the shedding of the blood. He uses the expressions of the Old Testament, preserving its symbolism in presenting the new order that Jesus had created. The blood that is present in the cup is that blood which was shed on the cross. The use of the present tense ("shed for many") cannot be regarded as indicating that at the moment at which Jesus speaks the words over the cup his blood is shed. The difference in time does not matter. Just as the memorial rite performed by the Church after the sending of the Spirit does not take the preceding crucifixion as a present event, so at the Last Supper the event of the crucifixion, to take place on the next day, is not anticipated as an event. Rather, both in the ritual meal of farewell that preceded the events of Golgotha and in the memorial meal that followed the crucifixion, the crucifixion is made *effectively* present.

If we consider the Marcan narrative of institution against the background of Old Testament typology, we arrive at the sure result that the blood of Jesus is really present. The words over the bread obviously correspond exactly to those over the wine. Just as in the Old Testament the blood of the sacrificial animals shed at

Mount Sinai to seal the covenant and the continually shed blood of the Paschal lamb are an analogous prefiguring of the blood of Christ, so the Paschal lamb lying on the table is an analogous prefiguring of his body. The realism of the body corresponds to the realism of the blood. Jesus says that his body is given also. This sacrifice also takes place on the cross. But the body sacrificed on the cross is made present by Jesus at the celebration of the eucharist and given to the disciples. In the real twofold symbol of the body and the blood Jesus gives himself as the one who offers himself to his heavenly Father as a sacrifice in death for his disciples to expiate their sins. Thus those who partake of it come into a living fellowship with him. In this way the ultimate significance of redemption can be fulfilled, namely coming to God, the fulfillment of God's kingdom (v. 25).

The passage in Matthew has nothing that is essentially new when compared with Mark. The main difference from the Marcan text is that in reflecting on salvation Matthew has added that Jesus Christ's sacrifice takes place for the forgiveness of sins. The forgiveness of sin is, in fact, the climax of saving history, for through the forgiveness of sin the heart of salvation is achieved, namely peace with God and peace among men.

THE GOSPEL OF JOHN

The Text Itself

The interpretation of the eucharist as a ritual sacrifice that we find in the Synoptics is concluded in the New Testament in St. John's Gospel (Jn. 6,51c-56a). John replaces the word "body" with the word "flesh." Although in John the realist, objective, and spatial conception of the presence of the flesh and blood of Jesus Christ reaches its climax, on the other hand the dynamic personalist interpretation is also brought out strongly. The latter is what is most important. This is seen from the fact that according to John, man's saving encounter with Jesus takes place through faith, i.e. through the gift by Jesus of himself to man and through man's giving himself over to Jesus. The eucharist, the "flesh" and the "blood" of the Lord, is the means of bringing about this saving encounter in faith. This interpretation does not in any way impair John's realism. It gives a fuller explanation of it and frees it from all gnosticism and conceptions drawn from nature and magic.

After the great miracle of the loaves there was an important conversation between Jesus and the crowd. In this conversation Jesus sought to convince his hearers that they should not be anxious for perishable food, but for that which lasts for eternal life. He also tells them that the Son of Man will give it to them (Jn. 2,26f.). His hearers understand his words as a call to do the "works of God." But they do not know what to do in order to do God's works. Jesus helps them. The work of God is to believe in him whom God has sent (Jn. 6,28f.). From these words develops the dialogue with all its consequence. The hearers are not ready to entrust themselves to Jesus. They call for a sign; the preceding miracle of the loaves is not sufficient for them to believe in him. When Jesus tells them that they should not first desire earthly bread, but the bread that comes down from heaven and gives life to the word, they say: "Sir, give us this bread now and always." But this request is based on a fundamental misconception. Jesus goes on:

I am the bread of life. Whoever comes to me shall never be hungry, and whoever believes in me shall never be thirsty. But you, as I said, do not believe although you have seen. All that the Father gives me will come to me, and the man who comes to me I will never turn away. I have come down from heaven, not to do my own will, but the will of him who sent me. It is his will that I should not lose even one of all that he has given me, but raise them all up on the last day. For it is my Father's will that everyone who looks upon the Son and puts faith in him shall possess eternal life; and I will raise him up on the last day (Jn. 6,34-40)

The hearers are not satisfied with this answer; on the contrary, they are very disappointed. Jesus goes on: "I am the bread which came down from heaven" (Jn. 6,41). The hearers take strong exception to these words. Again Jesus emphasizes that it is faith in him that leads to eternal life. Then come the following important words:

I am the bread of life. Your forefathers ate the manna in the desert and they are dead. I am speaking of the bread that comes down from heaven, which a man may eat and never die. I am that living bread which has come down from heaven: if anyone eats this bread he shall live for ever. Moreover, the bread that I will give is my own flesh; I give it for the life of the world.

John goes on:

This led to a fierce dispute among the Jews. "How can this man give us his flesh to eat?" they said. Jesus replied, "In truth, in very truth I tell you, unless you eat the flesh of the Son of Man and drink his blood you can have no life in you. Whoever eats my flesh and drinks my blood possesses eternal life, and I will raise him up on the last day. My flesh is real food; my blood is real drink. Whoever eats my flesh and drinks my blood dwells continually in me and I dwell in him. As the living Father sent me, and I live because of the Father, so he who eats me shall live because of me. This is the bread which came down from heaven; and it is not like the bread which our fathers ate: they are dead, but whoever eats this bread shall live for ever.

John concludes his account with the words: "This was spoken in synagogue when Jesus was teaching in Capernaum." The writer is obviously concerned to emphasize the scene. According to vv. 60-66 the disciples of Jesus are amazed and terrified at the words of their master. Jesus helps their understanding as well as giving them a hint of the full reality by revealing the connection between the resurrection and the sending of the Spirit. He says:

Does this shock you? What if you see the Son of man ascending to the place where he was before? The spirit alone gives life; the flesh is of no avail; the words which I have spoken to you are both spirit and life. And yet there are some of you who have no faith.

Interpretation

In order to understand the passage quoted it is necessary to see that this discourse has two quite distinct parts. First Jesus describes himself in a series of images as the true bread of heaven which alone is able to give true and eternal life. By speaking of his person in this way as the source of true life he seeks to direct the attention and interest of his hearers away from the earthly bread that he gave them in the miracle of the loaves to the true and real bread that he is himself. For John the duality between transient life on the one hand and real, true life on the other is founded in sin. Where sin—i.e., human autonomy directed against God—rules, there rules the aeon of death. This can only be overcome by Jesus Christ, because he has no share in sin. He does not come and draw his life from below, but from above. Even the manna given to the fathers in the desert is an element in the age of death marked by sin, and hence it could communicate only transient life subject to death. Man acquires true life through faith in Jesus. Faith is the way in which the man Jesus is able to lay hold on true life.

The word of Jesus that he himself is the bread of the true life is formulated in v. 51c in a more specific way: "The bread which I will give is my own flesh; I give it for the life of the world." There is an argument about whether the eucharistic words begin in v. 51c or only in v. 53. It seems probable that v. 51c is intended chiefly as the conclusion of the preceding passage, in which Jesus says that faith in him gives true life. This interpretation of the verse is more likely because of his remark that the bread he will give is his flesh for the life of the world. In the eucharistic celebration his flesh becomes a saving gift only for those present. If this verse directly concludes what has gone before, then it is explaining that Jesus becomes the bread of salvation only through his sacrifice unto death. The incarnation was aimed at this from the very beginning.

The verse, however, is so formulated that it provokes the question of the hearers in verse 52. This again gives direct rise to the eucharistic words. Just as the whole preceding discourse on the bread constantly refers to the eucharist in a hidden way, so verse 51c constitutes indirectly the transition to the eucharistic words. The actual eucharistic words, comprising vv. 53-58, reveal a fixed eucharistic form of utterance and indicate their dependence on a traditional institution narrative. Vv. 60-66, following the eucharistic scene ending in 59, refer both to Jesus' symbolic words about the bread of true life and to the eucharistic words—the former in that the saving effect of the death is seen only after the resurrection and the sending of the Spirit; the latter, in that the glorified body becomes present in the eucharist.

By the interpretation of v. 51c as the conclusion of the preceding symbolic words, the eucharistic texts acquire greater weight and fullness of content. For the body given for the world, according to v. 51c, in expiatory and sacrificial death and the blood shed in that death are made present to be eaten and drunk. That it is not simply a question of the material "flesh" or "blood" is seen from the fact that the words "flesh" and "blood" always refer to the whole man Jesus from a particular aspect, namely both in his physical bodiliness and in his saving sacrifice. They are not to be understood in terms of the language of sacrifice, namely as flesh separated from the blood, but in terms of Semitic anthropology, as referring to the concrete man, but at the same time to the man Jesus, who through his violent death became the expiatory sacrifice for men. This is again expressed clearly when in v. 57, Jesus goes back once more to the formulation that preceded the eucharistic section (v. 51a): "I live because of the Father, so he who eats me shall live because of me." Jesus himself becomes available to men as the source of life by giving them his flesh and his blood. The faith by which man lays hold of the life of Jesus is realized in the eating of the flesh and drinking of the blood, i.e. directly in eating the bread and drinking the wine. These material things are made one with the body and blood of Jesus, i.e., with the sacrificed body and blood, and hence with the sacrificed Lord himself. Bread and wine appear as symbols, not merely in the sense of our contemporary language but in the sense of an identity between the image and the reality which is characteristic of ancient thought.

According to this way of thinking, the original is itself present in the image: the mode of the presence is not analyzed, but it is understood in a wholly real sense. The words are free of any suggestion of magic, in that even in the eating of the flesh and drinking of the blood we are concerned with a saving encounter with Jesus himself. He is present in the mode of the flesh and the blood, and the man who eats and drinks is not simply consuming power-laden things, but is giving himself to the Lord. Jesus lessens the scandal of the words concerning the eating of flesh and the drinking of blood by referring to the coming spiritual mode of being of the flesh and blood. Flesh and blood will in fact be really present and be available for man to eat and drink, but in another mode of existence. These words concerning the spiritualization of flesh and blood do not mean a weakening of their power of reality, but another condition. It is not the earthly and perishable mode of existence, but that which has been won through death, spiritualized, corresponding to the dimension of God, mysteriously changed, the mode of existence of the future. John relates the eucharist to the whole action of salvation. He sees it as a descent (katabasis) from heaven (Jn. 6,58) and as the sacramental continuation of the life-giving mission of Jesus (Jn. 6,57). The giving of life in the eucharist, however, depends on the sending of the Spirit and hence presupposes Christ's glorification (the ascension). For the life-giving element in the eucharist is not the natural flesh as such, but the flesh united with the spirit (Jn. 6,63), just as, *vice versa,* the life-giving spirit is bound to the "flesh."

SUMMARY

Although it is not possible to reach agreement concerning every single exegetical question, a general survey of the scriptural texts does yield the following results. Immediately after the descent of the Holy Spirit the Church began to celebrate the memory of Jesus, as he had told it to. This celebration was given the name of "eucharist." The memorial was of the death of Jesus as a death of expiation and sacrifice. Although there is no express mention of the resurrection, this must be included in the memorial celebration, since the saving effect of his death appeared only in his resurrection, and the resurrection cannot be separated from this saving death.

The death of Jesus became effectively present, so that those who took part could share in this saving event. A share in the death of Jesus became possible because the risen Lord, identified with the crucified Jesus, was really present in the sign of bread and wine. It is not of great importance for the content of this belief whether we agree with Paul that the real symbol of bread and wine relates to the whole Christ, or whether we see the words "body" and "blood" as referring each to a part of the total physical life of Jesus and hence indicating the separation of the body and blood, but in either case ultimately believing that it is the whole Jesus who is present. We can call this presence of Jesus a real presence. This is the basis of the actual presence. We can also say that, according to the eucharistic texts of the New Testament, the whole mystery of salvation that is called Jesus is savingly present in the eucharistic celebration.

‹ 4

The Eucharist: Theological Development

The eucharistic texts of Scripture quoted in the preceding chapter raised a large number of problems for the post-apostolic age. The main problem to be resolved was how the eucharistic reality should be understood. The questions raised concerned the mutual relation between the body and the bread, the blood and the wine; the mutual relation of the body and the blood; the connection of the body and blood with the living Christ; the relation of the real to the actual presence. This last question also included the problem of how, in spite of its historical uniqueness, the crucifixion could be made present in every eucharistic celebration. Much theological effort and many pronouncements of the Church's teaching office were concerned with the illumination of these questions. The Council of Trent marked a climax of the insights and statements of faith in the eucharistic field but not, as our contemporary discussion shows, the end of them.

GENERAL OUTLINE

Let us first consider briefly the development which the form of the memorial celebration underwent. At the beginning, probably in accordance with what Jesus himself did, the consecrated bread was received before the meal and the consecrated cup after it. According to the Synoptics, however, these two sacramental elements were soon placed together at the end of the meal proper. Later, as we have noted, they became completely separated from the meal and combined with the service of worship in the morning. We first find this order about the middle of the second century (Justin, *Apologia*, I,67), and it became generally accepted. In the period after Constantine the eucharist assumed more and more elaborate forms. Whereas in the beginning the prayers had been freely formulated by the president of the liturgy, from the fourth century on they became increasingly fixed in form, a process concluded by about 900. We find that there was such a thing as the Roman liturgy around the year 400, and it is this which subsequently became generally accepted in the Western Church.

Statements of the eucharistic faith and the understanding of that faith on the part of the early Church are to be found both in the liturgy and in the writings of the Fathers. The former kind of testimony throws light on the latter, and *vice versa*. Whereas the simple statements of faith by the Fathers show only very slight variations, great differences are found in the theological attempts at clarification. Among the Greek Fathers, those who had most to say on the subject were Chrysostom and Cyril of Alexandria, in whom the Alexandrian view of the eucharist culminates.

On the whole, the Greek theologians regard *anamnesis*, the memorial of Jesus, as the formal principle of the eucharist both with Jesus and with his saving action. (Until the fifth century their thought was strongly influenced by the Platonic theory of the image, according to which the image and the original are in a certain sense identical inasmuch as the original appears in the image.) That it is a memorial is the basis of its sacrificial character, in terms of which the real presence is explained. The latter is seen in an analogy with the historical Jesus' structure of being (*Seinsstruktur*). Following chapter 6 of the gospel of John, they conceive of the eucharist as a perpetuation of the Incarnation (e.g. Justin, *Apologia*,I,66; Irenaeus, *Adv. haer.*, V,2,3; Clement of Alexandria, *Paedog.*, II,2).

For the Alexandrian school the memorial of the death assumes less importance: here the Logos is seen as making the bread and wine his own as elements belonging to him. In this view, therefore, the eucharist is essentially the body—the flesh—of the Logos. The dignity and the saving value of the eucharistic gift are ascribed to the fact that bread and wine are the body and blood of the Logos and establish community with him.

The school of Antioch, by contrast, identifies the real body, born of Mary, crucified and risen, together with the blood which was shed, with the eucharistic Christ. In the fifth century this christological approach led many theologians of Antioch to a doctrine of consubstantiation. In this view it is held that the unchanged first state of the bread and wine of the eucharist corresponds to the unchanged human nature of Jesus: the consecration endows the bread and wine with the Holy Spirit, making it possible for them to be called the body and blood of Jesus Christ.

In the theological development of eucharistic faith, the theologians of Alexandria placed greater emphasis on the christological element, while those of Antioch put more stress on the soteriological element (the saving action of Christ). Broadly speaking, it is possible to say that in the first millennium of the Church the emphasis was more on the event-character of the eucharist, whereas through most of the second millennium, especially from the time of the Council of Trent, it has been on the objective character of the eucharist, i.e. on the reality of the body and the blood of Jesus Christ. Today a synthesis is being sought between the act and the substance, with special prominence given to the act, or event.

The Eastern Fathers

In the *Teaching of the Twelve Apostles* (the *Didache*) the faithful are told to take part in the celebration of the breaking of bread on the Lord's day and prepare themselves for it by cultivating a brotherly spirit (ch. 4). So much emphasis is placed on this brotherly spirit that those who are not at peace with their neighbors are urgently advised to make their peace beforehand or else to refrain from participating in the eucharist. It is explicitly described as a sacrifice but not as a memorial of Jesus' death. Its eschatological character manifests itself in the *Maranatha—*

Come, Lord—at the end of the celebration. The prophets are to have plenty of opportunity to speak the necessary prayers of thanksgiving in order that it should be a eucharist (chs. 9 and 10). In the middle of the second century, Justin (*Apologia,* I,80) tells us that only those who belong to the community are allowed to take part in the Sunday celebration of the eucharist. The one presiding gives thanks and speaks the words of consecration over the bread and wine. The food becomes the eucharist through a prayer recalling the Logos who came out from God. It is the flesh and blood of the incarnate Jesus (*Apologia,* I,65,66). The celebration is held in order to recall his sufferings, accepted by his own will. It involves our thanking God both for the world he created, with everything in it for the sake of man, and for conquering all the forces of evil in the world, freeing us from the sin in which we formerly lived. In the sacrifice represented by the eucharist Justin sees the fulfillment of the prophecy of Malachy 1,10f. For Irenaeus, Jesus made the eucharist the sacrifice of a new covenant by proclaiming the cup as his blood.

From the fourth century on, we find with great frequency and intensity the idea that the eucharist is a sacrifice in that it is the memorial of the sacrifice of the cross. The reality of the body and blood of Jesus is still taught, but the emphasis is on the event of the crucifixion. It is in accordance with the nature of Christian life, expressed in the words "through Christ in the Holy Spirit to the Father," that from the fourth century on the Greek and Latin Fathers, with few exceptions, declare that despite the real presence of flesh and blood the eucharist points to a higher reality, namely the Spirit, God, who sent Jesus to save mankind. Moreover, the Fathers often expressed the view that a saving share in the eucharist is gained only by the person who presents himself to God as a living and holy sacrifice in the Spirit. If a person does not make a sacrifice of praise and thanksgiving, he is not really celebrating the memory of Christ.

We find the Antiochian view of the eucharist expressed in a particularly clear way by Chrysostom. He so emphasizes the identity between the eucharist and the historical body of Jesus that his idea of the eucharist seems to leave the sacramental sphere altogether, slipping into a naturalist dimension. Chrysostom—

and Ambrose as well—fails to make sufficient distinction between the sacramental and the historical-natural mode of being, and this had important consequences for the development in the understanding of the eucharist. On the other hand, it is Chrysostom who bases the sacrificial character of the eucharist most fully on its nature as the memorial of the death of Jesus Christ. Like many other Fathers, especially Theodore of Tarsus or Theodore of Mopsuestia, he is concerned with reconciling with the frequent celebration of the eucharistic sacrifice the statements in Hebrews that Christ died once and for all, that his sacrifice is a final one, and that hence there is no need for further sacrifices as in the time before Christ. He points out that it is always one and the same sacrifice that the Church is celebrating; there is only one single act of sacrifice in the Church, namely that of Golgotha. In the Church's celebration of the eucharist it is the re-presentation of this one sacrificial act that is celebrated: the Church does not, in the eucharist, set another sacrifice beside the sacrifice of Christ.

Cyril of Alexandria speaks of the "bloodless sacrifice" of the eucharist: if we "confess" in it the death, resurrection, and ascension of Christ into heaven, we share in the sacred body and precious blood of our common salvation. For Ignatius of Antioch (*Epistle to the Philadelphians,* 4) the eucharist is the mysterious ground of the Church's unity: he uses faith in the eucharist as a weapon in his struggle against Gnosticism. Irenaeus as well is concerned with emphasizing the reality of the body and blood of Jesus Christ in opposition to Gnostic spiritualism.

The eucharistic theology of Origen, who presents a radical version of the views of Clement of Alexandria, is of special interest. The first thing to be observed is that although he regards the eating of the flesh and the drinking of the blood as the acceptance of the word in faith, he does not minimize the reality of the eucharist, making it a mere symbol. For him the reception of the true flesh and true blood is the way of faith to union with the eternal word of God. His thinking is based on the idea of the Logos eucharist developed in Alexandria. The eternal word of God is received in two ways, through the celebration of the eucharist and through hearing Scripture. The latter is, in Origen's view, so important that he says: "If you are given the body of the Lord, you exercise the most reverent care and vigilance so that none of it may fall to the ground, so that nothing may be lost of the holy gift. But if you devote so much concern to the care of his body—and it is right to do so—how can you believe that it is a lesser wrong to neglect the word of God than to neglect his body?" (*Exodus,* 13,13).

Theodore of Mopsuestia (d. 428) is strongly influenced by Paul's theology of the eucharist and by the soteriology of Hebrews. He views the eucharist as the proclamation of the saving death of Jesus as a sacrificial death. He goes beyond Paul, however, by drawing on Platonic thought to present the eucharistic celebration as an image of the act of salvation—not only the cross of Golgotha but also the resurrection and ascension of Jesus Christ. The memorial of Christ's saving act is brought about in a symbol wherein what is represented is itself made present. He does not reflect on the way in which the original is present in the image. Theodore differs from the Platonists, however, inasmuch as he not only speaks of the real presentation of an original reality in a visible thing but also looks back from the reality to the original images of it that preceded it. This is a typological approach stemming from the Old Testament.

In Cyril of Jerusalem (*Fourth Mystagogic Catechesis*) we find an idea of the eucharist which is primarily static and objective. He speaks of the transformation of the bread into the body and the wine into the blood of Jesus Christ: the body is consumed in the form of the bread and the blood in the form of the wine. Since this view of Christ's presence is soteriological, the purely static conception tends towards the dynamic one. Those who participate in the eucharist gain a share in the body and blood of Jesus Christ and consequently a share in the divine nature.

The Western Fathers

Latin theology begins in the North African Church, with Tertullian and Cyprian. These two theologians teach the reality of the body and blood of Jesus Christ in the eucharist, but they hold that the elements of bread and wine still remain after the consecration, having become the mode of appearance of the flesh and blood of Jesus Christ. These forms of the appearance of the Lord's flesh and blood in the eucharist are different from the natural form of Jesus' appearance in history. In the eucharist, then, it is not so much the mysterious presence of the historical Jesus that we celebrate as it is the mysterious saving power of the risen Christ.

In Augustine we find a complex eucharistic theology. It is important to understand it because Augustine, with Ambrose, had the greatest influence on the eucharistic doctrine of the millennium after him. At first sight his view seems to be full of contradictions, in that he holds both that the body and blood are real and that the bread and wine are mere symbols. In fact, however, Augustine developed a doctrine which was entirely unified, basing it on the scriptural texts, especially those of John and Paul, but also drawing upon Platonic thought, which was important to him throughout his life.

For Augustine there is no question that the body and blood of Christ are really present in the eucharist, which is the center of the Church's whole life. But Christ's body and blood do not have their meaning in themselves: rather, they point beyond themselves to a higher reality, namely Jesus Christ, the Christ who is transformed by the resurrection in the Holy Spirit but is at the same time identical with the crucified Jesus. Jesus Christ is the head of the Church. Hence the content of the eucharist is the unity of the Church as the mystical body of Christ.

The Church is not merely the prerequisite and the consequence of the eucharist but, as the body of Christ, it is also the eucharistic reality, in that the whole Christ is present in the eucharist. Although this view of Augustine's is difficult to get hold of, it has scriptural foundation in 1 Corinthians 10,16.

When the Church celebrates the eucharist it is realizing itself. The eucharist is both the reality of Christ and the Church and the realization of this reality. The reality present in the eucharist realizes itself, for in the eucharist the Church is celebrating the memory of its head, a memory of his saving death, which was a sacrificial one. In this memorial celebration it confesses its Lord and constantly becomes aware again, in faith, of its own community with Christ, making it deeper and more intense. Because of the presence of Jesus Christ's flesh and blood, to celebrate the eucharist means not only to have a share in the body and blood of the Lord but also, precisely because of this, a share in the saving action accomplished by Jesus Christ. This makes it a way to God the Father, in the Holy Spirit. Hence the Church must continue to celebrate the eucharist for as long as all its members have not yet reached God. The eucharist contains the hope of this future fulfillment.

We can say of Augustine's conception of the eucharist that whereas it does not lack the objective-material aspect, its main concern is the personal encounter with Jesus Christ. Within this perspective there was no place for a eucharistic piety in the sense of adoration of the eucharist. For that, other conditions and insights were necessary which emerged in early scholasticism.

Although Augustine's interpretation of the eucharist may have been influenced by the Platonic idea of true reality as something beyond the senses and of the visible, material, and perceptible sphere as an image of the invisible, nevertheless for him as for the Greek theologians the Old Testament concept of the past event as the type of what was to come—the antitype—was probably even more important. We can see this particularly in the fact that Augustine regards the eucharist as the memorial celebration of an event and from the character of the eucharist as a memorial draws the conclusion that we can say both that Christ was sacrificed and that he is being sacrificed now in the celebration. This fusion of past and present is characteristic of the typological thinking of the New Testament. In it, however, the importance of time is by no means diminished: it is Augustine above all who places the greatest weight on the historical nature of Jesus and the Christ-event.

It is not surprising that Augustine's doctrine of the eucharist was not always understood in its structural unity during the subsequent period. Sometimes the emphasis was placed on its spiritualist, dynamic, and personalist features, and sometimes on its objective, realist ones. Augustine himself gives rise to this kind of onesided interpretation by the sharp distinction he made, during his controversy with the Donatists, between the eucharistic reality and the eucharistic effectiveness. He was forced into making this distinction by the Donatists' claim that they had the sacraments and hence were living in community with Christ like the Catholics. Augustine's reply was that although they had the sacramental signs, they did not have the Spirit to which these signs pointed. If a person did not belong to the Church, the body of Christ, then he could not participate in the Spirit of Christ, even if he was able to perform the sacramental signs validly.

The Scholastics

There is a further point to be considered in the subsequent development of the understanding of the eucharist in the period after Augustine. As we have seen, Chrysostom and Ambrose so strongly emphasized the identity between the historical and the eucharistic Christ as to run the risk of a naturalist conception of the eucharist, though it was precisely this naturalist conception, rejected by Christ himself, which had been the downfall of the Jews in Capernaum (Jn. 6,52ff.). Like every extreme, this extreme identification of the historical and the eucharistic Christ gave rise to a movement in which the undeniable distinction between the historically real and the real eucharistic modes of Christ's existence became so exaggerated that the eucharistic mode came to have less reality than the historical one. The main theological issue of the Middle Ages became the question of the real presence of Jesus.

The controversy, which had its roots in the various conceptions of the Fathers, was precipitated by the work of the Benedictine monk Paschasius Radbertus of the monastery of Corbie. His *De sanguine Domini,* the first monograph on the eucharist, appeared in 853. Paschasius took the traditional view of the Church that the eucharist contained the flesh and blood of Christ, born of Mary, crucified, and risen from the dead. But he so emphasized the identity as to refuse recognition of the fact that there was any difference in the mode of being. Like the aforementioned Church Fathers, he failed to recognize the difference between the sacramental and the historical dimensions. Thus he held that the body of Christ appears in the forms of bread and wine and can be seen and touched. This doctrine inevitably aroused opposition—the first debate concerning the eucharist. Paschasius' opinions were attacked by Rhabanus Maurus (d. 856), Ratramnus (d. 868), John Scotus Erigena (d. 877), and, in the tenth century, by Abbot Heriger (d. 1007).

For Rhabanus the eucharist is the celebration of Jesus Christ's redeeming act. Hence to share in the sacrament, in which we receive the body and blood of Christ, is to share in the passion of the Lord. Here the emphasis is on the event.

Ratramnus holds a similar view. For him the eucharist is the epitome of redemption. It is the symbol of the body and blood of Jesus Christ, but a symbol filled with the reality of what is symbolized. For him too the important thing is the personal union with Jesus Christ which is symbolized and brought about by his body and blood.

In the heat of discussion, Paschasius' views were exaggerated by some theologians. The controversy was not settled during the ninth century or the tenth. Lanfranc of Bec (d. 1089) pushed Paschasius' ideas to the extreme consequence of saying that the body and blood were subject to the laws of digestion (Stercoranism). The reaction, in the eleventh century, came in the view of Berengarius (d. 1089), the head of the school of St. Martin of Tours— the second dispute on the eucharist.

Berengarius set himself in opposition to naturalist views of the eucharist which were not in accordance with a valid conception of the sacramental. But in so doing he made the difference in the mode of existence into a difference in the reality itself. Thus, having begun by making an important point, he ended by emptying the eucharist of content, in a sense, by making it the merely symbolical presence of Christ and denying the real presence (symbolism). His doctrine was condemned by various local Church assemblies, and in 1059, under Pope Nicholas II, he assented to the formula composed by Cardinal Humbert which stated that "the true body of Christ is sensibly (*sensualiter*), not merely sacramentally but in reality *(in veritate)* touched and broken by the hands of the priest and ground by the teeth of the faithful" (DS 690). In the long run, however, Berengarius was unable to accept this formula, which contradicted the sacramental nature of the eucharist. During the years which followed there were a series of alternate submissions to the Church and attacks on the

Church's decisions. Eventually (1079) Pope Gregory VII summoned him to Rome and made him sign a profession of faith which read: "the bread and wine . . . are substantially changed into the true, proper, and life-giving flesh and blood of our Lord Jesus Christ" (DS 700).

In the twelfth and thirteenth centuries the real presence of Christ in the eucharist was denied by the Waldensians, the Catharists, and the Albigensians, and in the fourteenth century by Wyclif and Hus. The difficulty of accepting at the same time both the distinction between the historical and the sacramental modes of existence and the reality of the sacramental body of Jesus Christ led to new controversies in the Reformation.

The Reformers

The Reformers all attacked the abuses which had crept into the celebration of the mass, but with regard to the eucharist itself there were further divisions among them. Luther taught the doctrine of the real presence of Jesus Christ, but he rejected transubstantiation. In order to be able to explain the real presence, he assumed that the human nature of Jesus shared in the divine omnipresence because of its union with the Logos (ubiquity). The omnipresent body of Christ, in this view, becomes one with the bread and wine because of the words of faith spoken at the eucharist. The body of Christ is consubstantially present in, on, and under the bread and wine. In order to receive the whole Christ, there must be communion under both kinds. At times in his writings he rejected the sacrificial character of the eucharist.

Luther rightly emphasized the event-character of the eucharist, but he did it in a onesided way. He limited the presence of Christ to the moment of reception of the eucharist, firmly rejecting the idea of its continuance afterwards. Hence in his view the preservation and adoration of the consecrated host was pointless.

Zwingli regarded the celebration of the eucharist as merely symbolic; it was simply a memorial. Calvin proclaimed the reality of the eucharist but declared that it was not the body and blood themselves which were present, but only their saving power. One who received the bread and wine in faith received in them the living power proceeding from the glorified human nature of Christ in heaven: he became one with Christ through the Holy Spirit. In this way Calvin sought to make a bridge between Luther and Zwingli.

THE TEACHING OF THE CHURCH

The Church has often spoken out against erroneous conceptions of the eucharist, and most fully at the Council of Trent. It has, however, never given a full and comprehensive account of the Catholic view of the eucharist. The Church's doctrinal utterances have always been made in opposition to what is unacceptable, and hence they assert, in polemical form, only individual points, although they may be very important points. We shall consider the main issues here. But with this body of doctrine too, it must be said that many details can be considered only when we come to the systematic treatment.

A Roman synod in 1079 having taught the real presence of Christ in the eucharist, the Fourth Lateran Council in 1215 declared, against the Albigensians and the Catharists, that the body and blood of Christ are truly present in the forms of bread and wine because of the transubstantiation of the bread into the body of Christ and of the wine into his blood. This transformation is ascribed to the power of God. The purpose of the eucharist is stated to be union with Christ. The council also stated that no one could perform the eucharistic sacrifice except a consecrated priest (DS 802). The Council of Constance (1414-1418) asserted, against Wyclif and Hus, the totality of the presence of Jesus Christ (DS 1198f.; 1257). It was the Council of Trent (1545-1563) which provided the fullest definition, asserting the reality, the totality, and the permanence of Christ's presence in the eucharist and the rightness of worshipping him in it (13th session); the legitimacy of communion under one kind (21st session); and finally the sacrificial character of the eucharist (22d session). The mass is a true and real sacrifice (DS 1739-1742). The council teaches that in the holy eucharist, after the consecration of the bread and wine, our Lord Jesus Christ is truly, really, and essentially present, as true God and true man, in the form of the visible elements (DS 1636-1642), and continues so after the celebration. Jesus himself instituted this sacrament. The council quotes the words of Jesus that what he was giving to his disciples at the Last Supper was truly his body and blood and says:

Through the consecration of bread and wine there is a transformation of the whole substance of the bread into the substance of the body of Christ our Lord and of the whole substance of the wine into the substance of his blood. This transformation the Catholic Church rightly and in a true sense calls transubstantiation.

This is, for the council, the justification of the adoration of the eucharist. In the doctrinal canons of the council, the declarations of faith are stated again in detail in a clear and definite way (DS 1651-1661). Canon 1 is of particular importance:

Whoever denies that in the holy sacrament of the eucharist the body and blood of our Lord Jesus Christ, together with his soul and his divinity and hence the whole Christ, is truly, really, and essentially contained and asserts instead that he is present in the sacrament only as in a sign or in a symbol or only in his saving power, let him be anathema (DS 1651).

The emphasis of the Tridentine teaching is on the real presence. This is in fact a fundamental mystery of Christian life, and something at the same time that lies beyond all experience, so it is understandable if the Church constantly emphasizes the presence of the body and blood in face of any attempt to reduce the full significance of the eucharist.

TRANSUBSTANTIATION

The doctrine of transubstantiation, taught with great emphasis at the Council of Trent, has been more recently reaffirmed by Pius XII in the encyclical *Humani Generis* and by Paul VI in the encyclical *Mysterium Fidei*. In Paul VI's encyclical the terms "transsignification" (the transformation of meaning) and "trans-finalization" (the transformation of the purpose), are not wholly excluded, but it is pointed out that they are inadequate to the reality. It is a failure to do justice to the eucharistic mystery, says the encyclical, if the miraculous transformation of the whole substance of the bread into the body of Christ and of the whole substance of the wine into his blood, as it is defined by the Council of Trent, is not accepted. We may also cite a passage from the Constitution on the Sacred Liturgy of the Second Vatican Council, for though this document did not seek to make any formal statements of faith, it nevertheless expresses the Church's conviction. The passage indicates the development from a more static to a more dynamic conception of the eucharist: in it the emphasis has shifted from the adoration of the Lord present in the eucharist, stressed in the Middle Ages and still in modern times, to the celebration of the memory of his sacrificial death.

At the Last Supper, on the night when he was betrayed, our Savior instituted the Eucharistic Sacrifice of His Body and Blood. He did this in order to perpetuate the sacrifice of the Cross throughout the centuries until He should come again, and so to entrust to His beloved spouse, the Church, a memorial of His death and resurrection: a sacrament of love, a sign of unity, a bond of charity, a paschal banquet in which Christ is consumed, the mind is filled with grace, and a pledge of future glory is given to us. (No. 47)

It is undeniable that there is a real transformation. How is it to be explained?

The term "transubstantiation" goes back to the period of controversy concerning the eucharist. The formula that Berengarius accepted in 1059 was obviously untenable because it did not do justice to the sacramental nature of the sacrament. It was necessary to find a solution that not only recognized the reality and the totality of the presence of Jesus Christ in the eucharist but also did justice to its sacramental character.

The distinction between substance and accidents was found helpful here. This distinction led to the view that in the eucharist the substance of the bread and wine was changed into the sub-

stance of the body and blood of Jesus Christ but that the forms
of the bread and wine remain; hence the form of the body and
blood of Jesus Christ was not made present.

In the twelfth century this explanation began to be more and
more widely held, although the terms "impanation" and "consubstantiation" were also in use. Peter of Poitiers (d. 1161) declared that there was no better formulation of what took place
in the eucharist than that of "transubstantiation." The word itself
was used for the first time by Roland Bandinelli, later Pope
Alexander III (1140-1142). St. Thomas elaborated its implications
in great detail. Duns Scotus, on the other hand, was more sceptical
about the term: he said that although he found no basis for it in
Scripture, he was ready to accept it because of the Church's
teaching. William of Ockham was even more critical of it. The
term was rejected by the Reformation, as it had already been
by Wyclif and Hus. The Council of Trent used it, without giving
any detailed explanation, in order to express the real presence
of the body and blood of Jesus Christ.

The word "substance" played an important part in Aristotelian
philosophy. But it was by no means the intention of the Council
of Trent to settle, by its definition, a question of Aristotelian
philosophy. Rather, it used the language and concepts of philosophy as a tool in the expression of the faith attested in Scripture
and developed in the Church's tradition. If contemporary science
criticizes Aristotle's concept of substance, the Church's teaching
on transubstantiation is not affected by this criticism. It was not
the council's intention to canonize Aristotle's philosophy. In
whatever way modern science explains the structure of matter—
even if it comes to the view that in the sphere of matter there
is no such thing as substance as distinct from accidents—the
Church's meaning, when it uses the term "transubstantiation,"
remains the same.

In explaining what the Church means by transubstantiation
it may be of value to take an everyday example. It is a matter
of ordinary observation that a person changes over the years with
respect to his coloring, his figure, and indeed his whole empirical
appearance; and yet he remains the same person. This compels
us to distinguish between substantiality—the independent being

of the person, the man—on the one hand, and the accidents, the modes of being, the variables, on the other. We may call one sphere the meta-empirical kernel of a person's being, and the other the empirical dimension of phenomena available to the senses.

We may ask whether this distinction can be made only in regard to personal being or whether it holds true with regard to material being, but the question has no direct bearing on our theological problem. For in any case we are concerned here with personal being, namely the presence of the glorified Lord. Moreover, it is probably correct to say with respect to things, that beyond what can be empirically established, it is grounded in their meta-empirical nature if we call one thing "bread," another thing "water," and still another "wood." The nature of the change brought about in the eucharist, as taught by the Church, lies beyond what chemistry, physics, or biology are able to establish. What is changed is the essence, the fundamental being, the hidden kernel, of the thing from which its particular forms of manifestation and activity arise. From this it is possible to see that the conciliar doctrine of transubstantiation, though it has borrowed an idea from Aristotelian philosophy, can be understood without this philosophy in terms of our simple everyday experience. Pope Paul VI has stressed this in his encyclical *Mysterium Fidei.*

It must be borne in mind that transubstantiation is not the sacrament itself but the process by which it is brought about. The sacrament does not wholly consist in the event of transubstantiation; rather, the eucharist is the sacramental making present of the sacrifice of Golgotha. The sacrificial body and blood of the Lord are symbolized and made present through the outward sign, namely through the word and through the objects themselves. Transubstantiation is the way in which the outward sign has its effect.

Because the empirical phenomena, which come within the purview of science, remain unaffected, bread and wine can exercise the same physical functions after the transformation as before. They retain the same quantity, weight, mass, and nourishing power. Hence if science uses the term "substance" to refer to the empirical reality, the physical presence of bread and wine, what science is talking about is precisely the area which the Church's traditional doctrine speaks of as the area of the "accidents." Inasmuch as this area, which is the object of scientific research, is not changed but remains untouched, we could accept Luther's statement that the body of Christ is present in the bread and with the bread.

However, Christ does not become present according to the mode of empirical matter. He has no extension in space and none of the qualities belonging to that extension: no weight, no particular figure or form; he cannot see or be seen. Hence he is not divided through the breaking of the host. He is wholly present in the whole host and in every part of it. The occasional accounts of miracles lie outside the Catholic faith in the eucharist: the presence of Jesus Christ cannot be tested or confirmed by any of the natural means of knowledge available to us. It can be laid hold of and affirmed only through faith in Jesus Christ himself, in the gospel, and in the saving power of his work. The Church's teaching goes beyond the interpretation which remains in the naturalist dimension, on the one hand, and the symbolist interpretation which would empty the eucharist of reality, on the other, to reach the concept of the mode of being of the spirit.

The transformation, as opposed to any evolutionary event, takes place not in a gradual transition but in a moment. It involves a profound change in the bread and wine which penetrates into their meta-empirical depths, but at the same time there is a connection with what was there before. Thomas Aquinas conceives this connection as created being embracing the bread and wine and the body and blood of Christ in a common bond.

The doctrine of transubstantiation does not exclude the view that the eucharist is the saving sign of the presence of Jesus Christ but includes it. The bread and wine have in fact a different meaning in the eucharist than they have when they are placed on a table in a nonliturgical context: in the eucharist they are signs and guarantees of the saving will of Jesus Christ. Transsignification and transfinalization also take place; but transsignification, as is appropriate to a sacramental sign, becomes transelementation: for, as we have seen earlier, through the act of signification itself the sign produces *what* it signifies.

We can go a step further. When a community gathers for the eucharist and bread and wine are placed on the altar, there takes place what Jesus Christ promised in the words: "For where two or three have met together in my name, I am there among them" (Mt. 18,20). He is not merely spatially present, as a man is in a room, but present effectively—acting, giving himself; just as, in their turn, the real meaning of the presence of the faithful would not be realized if it were merely a physical presence inside a church. Again, the participants are present in a way appropriate to the eucharistic celebration if they open themselves in faith to the saving action of Jesus Christ.

THE PERSONAL PRESENCE OF CHRIST IN THE EUCHARIST

The presence of Jesus Christ which takes place, as the Church believes, through transubstantiation is not the only mode of his presence. The Constitution on the Sacred Liturgy mentions other modes of his presence also. It states that he is present in his Church when his Church prays, since he himself is the one who, as the Constitution says, prays for us and in us; he is the one to whom we pray; he prays for us as our priest, and he prays in us as our head, and we pray to him as our God. According to the Constitution, he is present in the Church when it does the works of mercy, not only because when we do a good action for the least of his brothers we are doing it for him (Mt. 25), but also because it is Christ who does these good works through the Church, in that he is constantly helping men with his divine love. He has promised his Church that he will be present to the end of time wherever it proclaims to men his saving death and his resurrection. He lives through faith in the hearts of men. In the Holy Spirit he is constantly working salvation in those who follow him. In these cases we can speak of an effective presence, a presence that is dynamic. We can find a distant analogy in the influence that proceeds from a man and does not depend on his physical presence.

The eucharistic gifts point to a special intensity and concrete tangibility of his presence. Over and above their mere sign character, they are the media and the place of his presence. The signs operate according to the principle that they bring about what they signify; and so by signifying it, they bring about his real presence. He himself takes hold of bread and wine and makes himself present in them through so powerful an action that the meta-empirical dimension of bread and wine is done away with and his body and blood displace the meta-empirical reality of bread and wine. Through the sacramental signs there takes place a transrealization—a transformation of the intrinsic reality—which has the character of transubstantiation. It is possible to speak of an ontological presence of Christ in the eucharist. But this has saving significance only if it is not only the mere presence *(Vorhandensein)* of Christ in the sense of Heidegger's philosophy but is also the bearer of his saving action, his personal presence. The important thing is the dynamic element.

The teaching of the Council of Trent on transubstantiation produced a far-reaching change of perspective in faith concerning the eucharist. The presence of Christ in the eucharistic host outside the event of the celebration of the eucharist became so important that the tabernacle began to take precedence over the altar. The adoration of the Lord present in the eucharist and the intimate dialogue of the heart with him pushed into the background the idea of the eucharist as the re-presentation of the saving death of Jesus. Thus an element which, though it is a very important one in the life of faith, is nonetheless secondary among the many dimensions of the eucharist, came to occupy the first place held hitherto by the memorial celebration of Jesus' death. In the theological speculation of the centuries after the Council of Trent, discussion was chiefly concerned with how the sacrificial character of the mass is to be explained. Theologians started from a concept of sacrifice derived from the study of religion in general and sought to apply it to the eucharist.

It was Pius X who, by his decrees on communion, prepared a change in both the theology of the eucharist and eucharistic piety. These decrees re-emphasized the character of the eucharist as a meal. But the breakthrough was brought about by the liturgical movement (in the theological sphere by Odo Casel and in the practical sphere by Romano Guardini). The encyclicals of Pius XII gave a new impetus to the movement and also brought about a number of clarifications. It was the liturgical movement and the encyclical *Mediator Dei,* confirming and encouraging it, which renewed the idea of the sacrificial character of the eucharist and its relation to the community. The Second Vatican Council's Constitution on the Sacred Liturgy took up all these various tendencies, working them into one great whole but at the same time opening up new ways towards the understanding of the eucharist and towards its celebration in the future.

Along with the whole problem of transubstantiation and in a certain sense parallel to it, another question emerged after the first dispute concerning the eucharist and became an issue in the twelfth century in particular. The Marcan, or pre-Marcan, narrative of institution makes the point that the words "body" and "blood" each refer directly to one element of Jesus Christ as distinct from the other. Mark, of course, uses the word "blood" to refer to the whole bodily, living but crucified, Christ. The anatomical interpretation, however, was further developed by Irenaeus *(Adv. haer.,* V,2), who declared that in the cup we drink nothing but the blood of Christ and in the bread eat nothing but his body. However, this view was satisfying neither to devotion nor theology.

In the Middle Ages the problem was resolved in the doctrine of the "natural concomitance" of the two sacramental forms which was worked out in particular detail by Thomas Aquinas. He distinguished between the reality present in the eucharist as the result of the sacramental sign, the sacrament, or transubstantiation *(vi verbi, vi sacramenti, vi conversionis)* and the reality present as a natural consequence or accompaniment *(vi concomitantiae).* In this view it is only the body and only the blood of Christ that is present in the sacrament. The reason was seen in the fact that the sign brings about only what it signifies: hence we must say that the sacramental sign of the eucharist, whose celebration brings about the transubstantiation, effects in the sacramental dimension a separation between the body and blood under the forms of bread and wine. This separation is sacramental in that it belongs to the sacramental mode of being of Jesus Christ.

And yet under each form the whole of Christ is present; for the contrary view would imply that Jesus is always slain again in each celebration of the eucharist.

The sacramental separation of body and blood was accepted after the thirteenth century in the interpretation of the eucharist as a sacrifice. In dealing with the Reformers' teaching concerning the necessity of receiving the eucharist in both kinds, the Council of Trent produced the following clarification:

The Church of God has always believed that immediately after the consecration the true body and blood of our Lord, together with his soul and divinity, exist under the species of bread and wine. His body exists under the species of bread and his blood under the species of wine according to the import of the words. But his body exists under the species of wine, his blood under the species of bread, and his soul under both species in virtue of the natural connection and concomitance which unite the parts of Christ our Lord, who has risen from the dead and dies now no more (see Rom. 6,9). Moreover, Christ's divinity is present because of its admirable hypostatic union with his body and soul. It is, therefore, perfectly true that just as much is present under either species as is present under both. For Christ, whole and entire, exists under the species of bread and under any part of that species, and similarly the whole Christ exists under the species of wine and under its parts. (DS 1640)[1]

In denying the necessity of receiving under both forms (DS 1726f.), the Church's declaration finds it sufficient to say that the person receiving the eucharist under one form is not thereby deprived of any grace necessary for salvation. It does not contradict the conciliar teaching to say that to receive under both kinds realizes more fully the symbol of the eucharistic sacrament.

[1] *The Church Teaches*, p. 283.

◂ 5

The Eucharist:
A Systematic Summary

GENERAL OUTLINE

Because of the complexity of eucharistic doctrine it is necessary, if we are to grasp it as a whole and give the right place and emphasis to its various elements, to get hold first of the fundamental idea of the eucharist. A distinction has often been made in theological writing between the real presence of Christ, the eucharist as a sacrament, and the eucharist as a sacrifice; and it is not automatically evident, in such a context, that actually the eucharist as a whole is a sacrament but that its sacramentality has several levels. When the Church itself, then, at the Council of Trent distinguishes between the eucharist as a sacrament and the eucharist as a sacrifice, there are two points to be considered: in the first place, the Church's pronouncement is not concerned with presenting a systematic view but with safeguarding an endangered doctrine bearing on salvation; in the second place, it rightly emphasizes the real presence and assigns to this the greatest importance, in contrast to the other elements, because the other elements are ontologically based on the real presence.

Nevertheless if we want to see the eucharistic truth defined by the Church within a total perspective, it is the sacramentality of the eucharist that is our general framework. The sacramentality,

99

again, is marked by its character as a memorial of Christ—primarily that of his saving action and secondarily of himself. This memorial is fulfilled through the reality celebrated in it, i.e. the saving action is effectively present. He himself is really present as the bearer of the sacramental actualization of his saving action. This actualization gains its realism through the presence of the flesh and blood of Jesus Christ. The saving action that is made effectively present with and through the present Christ is to be understood primarily as his saving death, in the sense of his sacrificial death. This is the basis of the character of the eucharist as a sacrifice. The sacramental memorial takes place in the form of a meal. Hence the participation in the celebration of the memorial takes place through the eating of the sacrificed body and drinking of the sacrificed blood of Jesus. This is one form of the act of faith, of handing oneself over to Jesus. We may say that the eucharist is the sacrificial death, made sacramentally present in the sign of the meal, of the risen Lord, really present under the forms of bread and wine, so that we may share in his sacrificial death. Hence we must consider the sign, the sacrifice of the meal, the sacrificial meal, and the saving effect.

THE SACRAMENTAL SIGN

The sign consists in a meal. The meal involves the food, the act of eating and drinking, and the words that belong to the nature of all community. The fact that it is a meal Christ himself instituted distinguishes the eucharistic meal from others. Because of its institution by Jesus Christ it acquires a dimension of faith. This also determines the character of the words that belong to this meal. They are words of faith. The meal is the "Lord's Supper." Let us consider what its chief characteristic is.

If we apply the terms "form" and "matter," developed by scholastic theology, to the eucharistic sign, then we can see from the events at the Last Supper that bread and wine are the necessary matter for the celebration of the eucharist. The Church has often spoken of this—at the Fourth Lateran Council, in its Instruction to the Armenians and for the Jacobites (DS 1320ff., 1352). But this general statement raises a number of questions. Is it, for example, theological doctrine that any form of wheaten meal is sufficient for the performing of the sacrament? The Greek Church uses leavened bread, whereas the Roman Church prescribes unleavened bread. The first clear testimony for the use of unleavened bread in the Western Church is to be found in Rhabanus Maurus (d. 850). Justin, Irenaeus, and Cyprian speak of the mingling of water with the wine. In the Instruction for the Armenians at the Council of Florence (1439), this mingling was prescribed. The reason probably is that at the institution of the eucharist Jesus mixed water with the wine, according to the custom of the country.

As for the words of faith necessary to the performing of the eucharist, it has become established that those words with which Christ gave his body and his blood to the apostles at the Last Supper constitute the form of the eucharistic sacrament of sacrifice. The Church has stated this view in a number of pronouncements (Doctrinal Instruction to the Armenians; for the Jacobites; cf. in particular the Council of Trent, the 22d session). The words over the bread are fixed, for the New Testament narratives agree essentially on them. The words over the wine, however, differ in the narratives in various significant ways. Although it is established that the Pauline text presents the oldest form of the kerygma of the institution and is closest to the event, it is nevertheless impossible for us to know exactly the words that Jesus used at the Last Supper. The words of consecration used today represent a synthesis from the New Testament narratives. It has taken more than a thousand years for them to become recognized as the only necessary and also sufficient form of the eucharistic sacrament.

In the post-apostolic period the eucharist was celebrated with a great prayer of thanksgiving, for a long time freely composed in the form of Jesus' own words of blessing. From this prayer of thanksgiving there developed the term used to describe the whole event, namely thankgiving ("eucharist"), because in it the praise of the name Jesus and thanksgiving to him found objective form.

The oldest prayer of thanksgiving we have is found in the Ordo of Hippolytus, around the year 200. He praises the saving work of God in creation and redemption and then goes on to the institution narrative. This is always included in the prayers of thanksgiving. They present the eucharist as the memorial of and participation in the saving action of God. Particular types gradually emerge. We find early evidence of the epiclesis, the invoking of the Holy Spirit. Irenaeus seems to ascribe to it consecrating power (*Adv. haer.*, IV,18) and so likewise do Basil and Cyril of Jerusalem.

Although the words of institution have always been part of the eucharistic celebration, it was Ambrose, in the second half of the fourth century, who was the first to give them special emphasis within the unified whole of the thanksgiving and epiclesis. Up to the twelfth century we often find the view expressed that it is the words of the Lord alone which make present the memory of Golgotha, but only within the whole prayer of the canon and as an organic part of it. But in the twelfth century they become increasingly emphasized within the canon and regarded as the only essential words: the rest of the canon gradually comes to be seen as a framework, as a paraphrasing of what the words of the Lord bring about. By the thirteenth century the view that the real form of consecration is to be found in the words of the Lord had become fully established.

The development was different in the Eastern Church. Here, after John of Damascus, the epiclesis was seen as an essential part of the eucharistic sacrament. Moreover, according to the general view among Orthodox Christians today, the words of consecration and the invoking of the Holy Spirit constitute an indivisible whole and are both necessary for the eucharist to be performed. In this view the words of consecration bring about the mystery in an incipient and germinal way, and the invocation of the Holy Spirit completes it. Although the meal element is very clear, we would ignore an important element of the eucharist if we failed to take account of the sacrificial element represented in the sign.

THE EUCHARIST AS THE WORSHIP
SACRIFICE OF THE CHURCH

As the proclamation of the Lord's death, the eucharist is the making present of the saving action of Golgotha, i.e. the sacrificial death of Jesus Christ. The question is whether this gives the eucharist itself the character of a sacrifice. As the institution narratives show, we can find the beginnings of this view in Scripture itself. It grew increasingly important in the Church's tradition until in medieval theology—especially in the thirteenth century, and in the greatest detail in the theology of Thomas Aquinas—it appears as a central part of the Church's faith. The Reformers rejected the sacrificial character of the eucharist either entirely or from various aspects.

The Teaching of the Church

Against the Reformers, the Council of Trent states that Jesus Christ left the eucharist to the Church, his bride, as a visible sacrifice. In it, the council goes on to say, the bloody sacrifice made once for all on the cross is re-presented to us, Christ's memory is preserved until the end of time, and the saving power of his sacrifice for the forgiveness of the sins we commit daily is made available to us. Christ, at the Last Supper, appointed his apostles priests of the new covenant, the council declares. He commanded them and their successors in their priestly office to offer the eucharistic sacrifice.

The council seeks to respond to the scriptural testimony of the uniqueness of the New Testament sacrifice on Golgotha by emphasizing that it is one and the same sacrifice that is made on Golgotha and in the eucharist, and one and the same person sacrificing, both then and in every eucharistic celebration, namely Jesus Christ (DS 1739-1742; cf. also canons 1 and 2, DS 1751f.). Although the identity of the sacrificial action itself is not expressly stated by the council, it is included in its teaching on the identity of the sacrificial gift and the sacrificing priest. It is expressly taught in the *Roman Catechism* published by order of the council (II,4,76). According to the council, the only difference between the sacrifice on Golgotha and the eucharistic sacrifice consists in the way the sacrifice is offered, i.e. the difference is not an essential one but involves only the manner of the offering: on the one occasion Jesus was sacrificed through his voluntary, bloody death *(in facto);* and on the others, he is sacrificed in a bloodless way *(in mysterio).*

The eucharist is a ritual sacrifice. Since the council Fathers avoided giving a fuller definition of the nature of the eucharistic sacrifice, a number of important and difficult questions remained open within the framework of what the council defined. In particular, the questions of the relation between the crucifixion on Golgotha and the eucharist and the relation between the eucharist and the Church require theological clarification and illumination.

Scripture

According to Hebrews (Heb. 10,5-10), which does not of course itself refer to the eucharist, and to St. John's Gospel (Jn. 3,16), the entry of the Logos into the world, his acceptance of a human body, was already orientated towards the sacrifice on the cross. This means that Jesus' sacrifice begins with the Incarnation and finds its fulfillment in the crucifixion. Although in his major epistles Paul gives only an indication of the sacrificial character of Jesus' expiatory death, there is detailed testimony to it in the other New Testament narratives of institution and in the Epistle to the Ephesians (Eph. 5,2.25), and especially in Hebrews (e.g., Heb. 7,27; 9,6-14.23-26; 10,10-14), in St. John's Gospel (17,19), and in the First Epistle of Peter (1 Pet. 1,18f.). The unique sacrifice of Jesus was the sacrifice on the cross: it is the expiatory sacrifice for the sins of the world; it is the fulfillment and the end of all preceding sacrifices. As we read in Hebrews (Heb. 10,19.21f.), in his unconditional sacrifice to the Father, Jesus opened the way into the Holy of Holies, i.e. the way to God. He himself went this way, and in that he is the representative of mankind, opened it to all men. Thus through the crucifixion a completely new situation has arisen in human history. A member of the human race has achieved access to God, for himself in the first place but at the same time for all other men, his brothers. The consequence of the final arrival of the man Jesus with God was manifested in the resurrection.

According to St. John's Gospel, Jesus Christ is not merely the bringer of salvation who has opened the way to the Father but the way itself (Jn. 14,6). This means that man can reach God, the ultimate fulfillment of his being, only in communion with Christ. Hence it is of fundamental importance to achieve communion with Jesus Christ, which can take place only by a free action of man, who is called to freedom. This takes place through faith and through baptism. In baptism, as we have seen, man acquires a likeness to Christ; he is drawn into that Sonship in which Christ lives. But baptism is only a beginning. What takes place in it must be held on to through the whole life of the individual—and indeed through the whole history of the Church—and constantly reactualized. For the approach to God realized in baptism is not necessarily lasting: it is exposed to many dangers and can be preserved only if it is constantly realized afresh through faith. Daily life offers many occasions of realizing communion with Christ. The main form is through active brotherly love.

The Eucharist as the Dynamic Presence of the Death of Jesus

Jesus himself gave the people of God one way above all of realizing their communion with him, the crucified Christ, namely the celebration of the eucharist. The cross of the Lord is effective in every realization of the Christian faith, but in the eucharist its power is present not only in a particular intensity but in a particular tangible way.

As we saw earlier (see in Volume III, "The Death of Jesus"[1]), the cross of Christ can be interpreted from various aspects. It is an expiatory death, victory over sin, over transience, over our

---

[1] *Dogma: God and His Christ* (New York: Sheed and Ward, 1971).

bondage to the letter of the external law, over joylessness; it is reconciliation, the peace of men with God and hence with one another. All these aspects are summed up in the sacrificial one. On the cross Christ gave himself to the Father as a sacrifice; the cross of Christ becomes effective as a sacrifice in the eucharist.

For a period extending between the sending of the Spirit, which was the first stage in the Church's giving of itself to Christ and through Christ to the Father, and the return of the Lord, which will bring the final fulfillment, the Church, in the eucharist, shares in the crucifixion, Jesus' sacrifice of himself, and the resurrection. Until the dialogue with God of those who believe in Christ can take place "face to face," the Christian community must realize its giving of itself through Christ in the sign it performs in faith. The celebration of the eucharist by the Church is a sacrificial self-giving, realized throughout history, which Christ performed on the cross as the representative of all men. Hence the eucharistic sacrament-sacrifice belongs to the pilgrim Church: as long as the Church is a pilgrim through history it has a share, through the sacramental sign, in the sacrificial death of Christ, in order to become all the more fully incorporated into Christ himself, its head, giving itself with an ever greater intensity to the Father in Heaven and thus becoming more and more what it already is, namely the body of Christ and the people of God. Just as celebration is part of every community and is the essential expression of community, so the celebration of the saving death of Jesus belongs to the Church. In it the Church realizes itself more and more fully as the body of Christ. Jesus has made available to the Church as his bride the sacrifice he made for the salvation of men, that act of love which found supreme expression in the shedding of his blood on Calvary. He did this in such a way that just as he himself at the Last Supper made his saving action present in a real symbol, so, on the basis of his command of institution, the Church is able to make present his sacrifice on the cross in a real ritual symbol. In this way it can become part of the movement through which Christ attained to the Father. For the individual member of the Church the interim period lasts from baptism until death. Thus both for the individual and for the whole Church the eucharist is an "interim" activity. In the eucharist the sacrifice of the cross is actualized in a sacramental way; the eucharist is the sacrament of the sacrifice of the cross performed by the Church. The unique event of Golgotha acquires a saving sacramental representation and effect in the particular here-and-now of the sacrifice of the mass. The event of Golgotha is re-actualized in a ritual way. Hence the eucharist can be called the application *(applicatio)* to the Church of the saving death of Jesus Christ as a sacrificial death. In this way the sacrifice of Christ becomes a ritual sacrifice of the Church.

This needs to be explained in greater detail. First it may be useful to give a brief interpretation of the concept of sacrifice. Although the cross, and hence the eucharist as well, are sacrifices of a special kind, the general concept of sacrifice can be illuminating in some respects. It is one of the chief forms religion takes. Arising out of the experience of one's own limitations and sinfulness, it is the attempt to acknowledge God as the absolute Lord and the holy One, to obtain his favor and grace, to enter into fellowship with him and thus be liberated from one's lonely and exposed position in the world and from sin. Sacrifice, in the full sense, is the physical manifestation of one's own inner attitude of self-giving. The supreme example of this is the acceptance of a violent death in order that God should be acknowledged (a bloody martyrdom).

In general, this inner attitude is realized by offering a gift belonging to the person making the sacrifice, something which can function as representing him and is able to manifest the degree of his inner devotion. By being offered, the gift is withdrawn from the secular sphere and handed over to God. The fact that it now belongs to God can be expressed in terms of a change in its former mode of being. This indicates the passing of the sacrificial gift, and likewise of the person offering it, from the sphere of the secular into the sphere of the divine and mediates communion with God. Through this process the sacrificial gift is consecrated and made holy. The person sacrificing seeks direct contact with God in the sacrificial meal, since he partakes at God's table of this holy food dedicated to God and hence belonging to him.

The One Sacrifice of Golgotha
and the Many Eucharists

Since Jesus' death on Golgotha there is no other lawful sacrifice. It is all the more remarkable that the Church, believing in the finality of the sacrifice on the cross, still calls the eucharist a sacrifice. The apparent contradiction here is resolved if we consider the connection between the unique and final sacrifice of Golgotha, which permits no other sacrifices beside it, and the sacrifice of the eucharist. It is true that this connection involves a profound mystery which cannot ultimately be illuminated by our categories; but it can be shown that there is no contradiction between the unique finality of the event on Golgotha and the many repetitions of the eucharistic sacrifice and that, on the contrary, the uniqueness of the sacrifice on the cross is proclaimed and represented by the repeated sacrifice of the mass. The one sacrifice of Golgotha proves its inexhaustible power in the many repetitions of the eucharistic celebration.

We began by saying that the sacrifice of the cross was not a self-contained event. It has not only a vertical dimension directed upwards to God but also a horizontal dimension directed towards men throughout the whole of human history. It is related to the whole of history, to the whole of creation. It is the sacrifice of humanity. This is a central teaching of the Greek Fathers, e.g. Gregory of Nyssa. The Roman Fathers hold the same view, although they express it more cautiously. Thus Leo the Great says (Sermon 55,13): "The cross of Christ symbolizes the true altar of prophecy, on which the oblation of man's nature should be celebrated by means of a salvation-bringing Victim." The saving power of the cross of Christ reaches beyond the time and place in which it was erected and seeks, until the end of history, to draw men into its own movement towards God.

Both Augustine and Thomas state, on the basis of Paul's theology, that Christ becomes integrated, through the faith of mankind in him, to constitute that totality which the intention of his action requires. Only through mankind, bound to him in faith, does the *Christus individualis* become the *Christus totus.*

The faith of man in Christ has an integrating function. The articulation in history of this universal place of Jesus Christ means that only through the participation of man believing in Christ does the *passio Christi* become integrated into a *passio tota,* i.e. Christ's sacrifice on the cross become the total sacrifice. Only through man's participation in the resurrection of Christ does his resurrection become integrated into the total resurrection. In this continual process of integration the eucharist, the memorial celebration of Christ's sacrificial death, plays a special part. Thus we can see that the whole course of history between the death, resurrection, and sending of the Spirit, on the one hand, and Christ's second coming, on the other, has the significance of an integration towards totality. This totality that lies in the future and is to be realized in it bears the name "Jesus Christ."

In every celebration of the eucharist the Church, by giving itself over in faith to Christ as the crucified and risen Lord, takes part in the sacrifice of Golgotha and the event of Easter as the body of Christ, and thus, on behalf of the whole of mankind, takes Christ's action one stage further towards integration, until at the final eucharist the total sacrifice, at which Golgotha is aimed, will be reached. Although the whole life of the Church serves this integrating function because of its character of the body of Christ, the sacrifice of the mass represents a special instance within the whole movement. Through the creative power of the eucharistic words of consecration, the body and blood of Jesus Christ—the sacrificed body and the sacrificed blood, i.e. Jesus Christ himself as the sacrifice—become present. But this proclaims the death of Golgotha. The proclamation of the death of Golgotha brings about the effective presence of that death through the making present of the body and blood of the Lord.

The Eucharist *as* Anamnesis

In order to give a theological explanation of the identity of the sacrifice of the cross and the sacrifice of the mass we can speak of *"anamnesis,"* of "making present," of "type," of "memorial," but not of "repetition" or "renewal." Although these last two words are frequently found in Church pronouncements, they must be understood in a wider sense. The death of Golgotha cannot be repeated, nor does it need to be renewed. The death of Golgotha, perfect in its saving power, becomes present at the celebration of the eucharist. The Fathers never tire of describing the eucharist as a memorial of the sacrifice of Golgotha. They see the sacrificial character of the eucharist itself as given in its character as a memorial.

Thomas Aquinas, and with him the majority of later theologians, sees the sacrificial character of the eucharist as symbolized by the twofold consecration, in that through the sacramental words it is first only the body, and then only the blood that is made present, so that there is a separation of the body and blood in the sacramental sphere, though owing to "natural concomitance," as Thomas Aquinas puts it, the whole Christ is present in each form. However, it is not necessary to have recourse to the twofold consecration in order to understand the eucharist as a memorial sacrifice.

The view frequently taken by the Fathers is that the presence of the body as a sacrificial body and of the blood as sacrificial blood is the presence of the sacrificial event itself. In addition to the many patristic statements on this subject we have the liturgical texts. All liturgies, both those of the Western Church and the often far longer ones of the Eastern Church, express the idea that it is a memorial that is celebrated in the eucharist. This memorial is not merely a psychological remembrance of what is past, nor is it a dramatic representation of what happened once in the past. Nor is it a memorial in the sense of a monument to someone's memory. Rather it is a ritual and effective making present of what took place once in the past, a making present which does not involve the presence of the historical death itself or of the other saving events indissolubly connected with it, such as the resurrection and ascension, in the here-and-now of the eucharistic celebration. This view of the Mystery of Christian Worship *(Kultmysterium),* established by Odo Casel, strains the concept of the memorial celebration; it also risks making the eucharistic sacrifice absolute, over against the sacrifice of the cross, by according it an independence which, though based on the sacrifice of the cross, yet belongs to the eucharistic sacrifice itself. It is more correct to say that in the symbols of the eucharist the saving work of Christ, performed in the past, is represented and hence actualized. In the eucharistic event, the ritual worship of the Church, the saving power of Christ's sacrifice appears. Hence the eucharist was often called by the Fathers the type of the sacrifice of the cross.

If the eucharist is called an image of the sacrifice of the cross, the word "image" must not be understood in its everyday meaning, though even in this sense an image can exert an extraordinary influence. In theological reflection on the eucharist what is meant is that the event of Golgotha itself is at work in the image. We can call the image of the death of Christ in the sacramental event of the eucharist a reflection of the sacrifice of Golgotha that is filled with reality *(Wirklichkeitserfüllt)*. Hence it is itself an event. Just as the historical Christ was the bearer of the historical death on Golgotha, so the sacrificial body and blood of Christ present in the eucharist is the image of that event and the bearer of the saving effect of Golgotha. This, of course, raises the question of whether the effective memory of a past sacrifice can itself still be called a sacrifice. By saying that the eucharist is the memorial of the sacrifice of the cross, we have not yet, in fact, done full justice to its sacrificial character. There is still more that needs to be added.

Let us first, however, say a word concerning the extent of what is salvifically reflected in the ritual symbol of the eucharist. It is primarily the sacrificial death on Golgotha. This is what is emphasized by the institution narratives of the New Testament and the explanations of the Fathers. The resurrection and the sending of the Spirit, however, cannot be separated from the death. For together with the resurrection and the sending of the Spirit, and even with his second coming, Christ's death constitutes a single mystery. This is the reason that the liturgies praise the eucharist as a memory not only of the death but also of the resurrection, the ascension, the sending of the Spirit, and often even of the second coming of Jesus Christ.

The Eucharist as Sacrifice
of the Church

The next question is, what is the purpose of making present the sacrificial death of Golgotha in ritual symbol as a memorial celebration? The answer cannot be: to remind God of the death of Golgotha. God does not need reminding of this; he cannot forget what happened then. We must also remember that Christ lives as the risen Lord, forever marked by the wounds of his crucifixion on Golgotha. He is, as it says in Hebrews, the High Priest at the right hand of the throne of God (Heb. 8,1f.) who intercedes for us (1 Jn. 2,1). The reason for making present the event of Golgotha is rather that, in accordance with its relation to all men, those who are remote in space and time from the event can be directly confronted with it here-and-now and thus obtain access to it. The Council of Trent also states that Christ has entrusted the Church, his bride, with the mystery of his passion: she is to present it to the Father. When she celebrates the eucharist, this means that she is accepting the gift of her Lord. But this involves the Church's recognizing Jesus Christ, the one sacrificed on the cross, as the representative of the whole of humanity, in whose name he died. The Church expresses her faith in her Lord and declares herself ready to share gratefully in his own death in order to share in this way in his glory. She confesses the sacrifice of Golgotha as the salvation of the world, but this also means that she confesses the sinfulness of her members and, speaking vicariously for the whole of humanity, the sinfulness of all and their need for redemption, acknowledging Christ as the one who has brought about reconciliation with God. In this she confesses God the Father, in that he has accepted the reconciling sacrifice of Golgotha and in his Son, Jesus, has also accepted all men, but especially the members of the Church and those gathered for the eucharistic celebration as his sons and daughters. That they belong to Christ (in whom those celebrating the eucharist were incorporated in baptism) is expressed in the most intense possible way when the Church celebrates the eucharist with the words of the Lord: This is my body, this is my blood. In these words Jesus Christ himself speaks, for only he can speak them. But he speaks, in accordance with the nature of the sacramental sphere, through the mouth of the Church. The Church can proclaim these words only because they are the words of its head. Thus they can be used by it, the body, as its own words. The Church constitutes, with Christ, the total subject of sacrifice and the total object of sacrifice, according to the structural principle of the head and the body.

Hence this event expresses the depth of faith and gratitude. In the concrete act of faith that takes place in the heart of every eucharist, the Church shares in the gesture of the sacrifice of Golgotha. This sharing is made possible by grace, for it is not an automatic thing that God should grant us this participation. The awareness that we are called to this through grace is expressed in the fact that during the celebration of the sacrifice the Church several times asks that it should be accepted. It does not need to ask God to accept with love the sacrifice of his Son. The request is, rather, that the participation of the Church itself should be accepted.

The Church prays that God will be pleased to accept its sharing in the sacrifice of the cross. It has reason to pray thus, for it knows that its members are sinful. It prays that despite the sinfulness of its members it may participate in the sacrifice of its head and through this sacrifice may approach God.

Hence the sharing of the Church in the sacrifice of the cross is formally, or quasi-formally, part of the sacrifice itself, so that without this sharing there would be no sacrifice of the mass. In the eucharist the Church is performing the sacrifice and at the same time being sacrificed. It is both the subject and the object of the sacrifice; because of its own readiness, which God has made possible in grace, it is caught up in the movement of Christ's sacrifice and can thus reach the Father with and through him. Thus the sacrifice of the mass realizes in a concentrated intensity the meaning of Christian life, which is expressed in the formula: through Christ in the Holy Spirit to the Father.

It is not as if the participation of the Church were added only in the eucharist to the sacrifice of the cross, previously made sacramentally present: the making present of the sacrifice of the cross, i.e. the sacrificial body and blood of Christ, is not done in order that the Church should have a suitable gift to sacrifice. Rather, through the proclamation of the death of Christ, which it has the function of making present, the Church enters from the beginning into the sacrifice of its Lord. The proclamation of the death of Christ in the eucharist is at one and the same time the making present of it and the Church's participation in it. Seen from the point of view of Christ, he makes himself present as the sacrifice in the eucharistic sign and thus unites himself profoundly with his body, the Church. Seen from the point of view of the Church, the Church participates in the sacrificial movement of its head by making it present. In the Church's texts, therefore, we find that the eucharist is often described as the sacrifice of the Church.

We can say that the eucharist is more than the sacrifice of the cross, for it is the ritual actualization of it in order that it should take effect in the Church and that the Church should offer itself through the sacrifice of Christ on the cross to the Father. The sacrifice on the cross is a historical reality, but it is continually re-actualized in innumerable ritual celebrations as the application of the saving death of Jesus. The Church's self-sacrifice through the self-sacrificing Christ is of constitutive importance for the eucharistic sacrament of sacrifice. This is suggested by a text in Augustine (Sermon 179) that may seem surprising at first glance: "If you are the body of Christ and his members, then it is your mystery that is laid on the altar. You receive your mystery. . . ; be what you are and receive what you are." According to this, it is not only the sacrificial body and blood of Christ that is present in the eucharist, but also the Church as the body of the Lord. This presence is not, of course, an ontological one, but one that is dynamic and actualistic. The members of the body of Christ are present in the eucharistic sacrament by offering themselves to the Father in and with Christ, their head, by sharing in his sacrifice. This takes place in faith and love, that love, which Augustine calls *caritas,* that is something quite other than *cupiditas,* desire. The love in which man sacrifices himself has, for Augustine, two dimensions: one vertical and the other horizontal. In it man rises through Christ to God, but in it he also turns towards his brothers and sisters. Man is capable of this kind of ascent only because Christ has first descended, i.e. it takes place in and through Christ. He draws his mystical body to the sphere in which he already lives, because in his crucifixion he stepped out of the life that passes away to enter true life, the life of fulfillment, peace and joy. The eucharist would have no meaning if those who took part in it did not rise to the Father through Christ in love and gratitude and also turn towards their brothers. This love that rises to God and turns towards one's brothers, Augustine says, is not just an effect of the eucharist acting as a *causa efficiens,* but an essential element of its nature.

This leads to the conclusion that ultimately only those who are filled with love, those whom Augustine calls the saints—and not those separated from Christ through sin, not those who are not at peace with the Church—can celebrate the eucharist in a meaningful, i.e. salvific, way. Augustine states: "If a person receives the mystery of unity and does not preserve the bond of peace, then he does not receive the mystery, but a witness against him" (Sermon 272). Such a sacrifice is rejected by God. God calls for sacrifice—not the sacrifice of the pierced body, but that of the contrite heart. It is valueless to offer sacrifice on an altar of stone, but not on the altar of the heart. God calls for a sacrifice that is burnt for him on the altar of the heart in a freely chosen love. In that it is love inflamed by the Holy Spirit which holds together the members of the mystical body in unity, with the crucified and risen Christ as its head, Augustine is able to say (*The City of God,* X,6): "This is the sacrifice of Christians: that many should be one body in Christ." Thus every work of love, every act of mercy, every aid given, every good counsel, is a sacrifice because in all these actions man gives himself in love to God. All these actions by man pass into the eucharistic sacrifice and gain from it new impulses. In this way daily life becomes a manifestation of the crucifixion that is made present in the mass. The eucharist is seen as the center of the Church's life, towards which all life is ordered, and from which all life flows.

In every eucharist the whole Church participates in performing a sacrifice. It functions, in a sense, as a transindividual consciousness. Those taking part in any particular eucharist are the representatives of the whole Church. It depends on them, their faith and devotion, to what extent the whole Church, in its trans-individual subjectivity, becomes part of Christ's sacrifice on the cross.

The Eucharist as Relative Sacrifice

We can characterize the relation of the eucharist to the sacrifice of Golgotha and the Church by saying that it is, in a twofold sense, a relative sacrifice. The relation to Golgotha is what characterizes its innermost nature, in that it is nothing other than the salvific ritual re-presentation of Golgotha. And just as there is no eucharist without Golgotha, so there is no eucharist without the Church—not simply because the Church is the indispensable offerer of the eucharistic sacrifice, but also because without the Church it would be without point or meaning. The making present of Golgotha and its application to the Church qualify and support each other: one without the other would have no meaning. The application belongs, as an inner formal element, to the making present of the crucifixion through the word of the Church.

The Role of Christ

To speak of the making present of the sacrifice on the cross raises the question of Christ's own activity in the eucharist. Let us remember first that what applies to every gathering of those who believe in Christ applies also to the eucharist, namely that Christ is among them (Mt. 18,20). In the eucharist he is present in a particular way, in that he is the Lord and giver of the sacrificial meal and at the same time the High Priest of the eucharistic celebration. The meal plays a part in the proclamation of Jesus, in that he describes the kingdom of God proclaimed and begun by him as a royal wedding feast (Mt. 22,1-14), and also because he had a meal with his disciples, and in particular celebrated with them with eucharistic Last Supper. At this he promised that in the future also, after his death, he would have a meal with those who believed in him. It is only because Christ himself is the host that Paul can tell his readers in 1 Corinthians (ch. 10) that those who take part in the eucharistic meal become companions of Christ and hence must not take part in the ritual meals of the heathen.

The Fathers frequently testify to the salvific serving function that Christ himself performs in the eucharist. In the pre-Nicene controversies this is sometimes called a "priestly" action. The Arian confusions led to theologians such as Chrysostom or Theodore of Mopsuestia firmly rejecting a direct priestly activity of Jesus in the eucharist comparable to his priestly action on Golgotha. Their view is that Christ is active in a priestly way in the eucharist, but only in that he is at work through the ministry of the earthly priests. In the eucharist the priest or the bishop performs the role of Christ. The risen Lord makes present his sacrificed body and blood in the sacramental symbol within the Church and through the service of the Church in the Holy Spirit, in which he sacrificed himself on the cross (Heb. 9,14). This is not to say that Christ is constantly offering himself to the Father in new acts of love and obedience. This would mean that there were constantly new sacrifices. Rather, he makes present his flesh and blood, and thus himself, in the sacramental symbol, in the uninterrupted love that led him up to Golgotha, in order that the Church could participate, in faith and love, in his own gesture of sacrifice to the Father. Ultimately it is God the Father who brings about this making present, in that his eternal act of creation is also directed towards the eucharistic presence of the incarnate Logos. But this means that God himself is giving himself to men in the real making present of the eucharistic reality.

The Function of Bishop and Priest

As the Council of Trent says (DS 1708), Christ entrusted the constant actualization of his sacrifice on the cross to the Church, his bride. Thus the Church teaches that it is the whole Church community that performs the eucharist. This is not contradicted by the Church's declaration that only the validly ordained priest or bishop has the power to consecrate (DS 1739ff., 1752, 1771), for what is meant is that only the official priest can effectively speak those words in which the eucharistic sacrifice, the body and blood of Christ, is made present. The text of the Council of Trent is not exclusive but is only positive. It is, however, the explicit teaching of the Fourth Council of the Lateran (1215; DS 802) and the constant view of the Church that only priestly or episcopal ordination imparts the spiritual authority to consecrate (DS 3850; the Second Vatican Council's Constitution on the Church, ch. 3). The priest acts here as the representative of Jesus Christ. Only he can perform the role of Christ as a result of the special resemblance to Christ that was imparted to him by his ordination. Christ has set apart special members for the central action of his Church, by whom he is represented.

It is notable that Jesus invited only the apostles, but not his other disciples and friends—not even his mother—to the Last Supper. Though it might be said that it would have been considered scandalous, according to the conventions of the time, if Christ had invited a woman to the meal, we may assume that he would not have hesitated to do so if he had desired the presence of a woman there. In the early Church it was the bishop who celebrated the eucharist together with the priests and the community present (cf. the letters of Ignatius of Antioch). Justin Martyr recounts that the sacrificial gifts have to be brought to the leader of the brethren.

This rule, going back to the apostles, was probably due to considerations of order and unity. It is precisely in the eucharist, the central act of the Church, that the unity of those who believe in Christ must manifest itself, as a community gathered around him (DS 1653). At the same time, however, the bishop was regarded as the representative of the whole Church, of the Church's "we." In relation to the community he plays the role of Christ, and in relation to Christ he plays the role of a community. In him, then, the community itself speaks. Its speaker, however, is not commissioned by the community to serve it. He must be a member of the community whom Christ himself accepts as his representative. It is he, the invisible head of the community, who determines this. He commissions his representative to perform an act of consecration. But the limits of this special representation should not be forgotten. It includes the whole of the eucharistic celebration; ordination is essential for the proclamation of the words of consecration. The participating community joins in them, but they are only effective when they are pronounced by the priest. Through the proclamation of the presence of Jesus Christ by the priest, Christ himself proclaims his presence (for the priest and the community). The proclamation of the priest is, at the same time, his own response of faith—and that of the community—to Christ.

This dual role of the priest led in the course of time to those participants who were not bishops and priests being more and more clearly distinguished from those who were. The priests' representative function in regard to the community also became more and more apparent. The concept of the "layman," in the later sense, was born; henceforth "layman" no longer had the unqualified meaning of a member of the people of God but was applied to a member of the people of God distinguished from the hierarchy—someone called more to obedience than to participation.

The Eucharist as the Celebration of the Whole People of God

Nevertheless, the conviction that the eucharist is the celebration of the whole people of God was never entirely lost. Both the liturgical texts and many pronouncements by the Church as well emphasize the plural nature of the celebrating community (cf., in particular, the encyclicals of Pius XII, *Mystici Corporis* and *Mediator Dei,* as well as the Second Vatican Council). The following elements have been emphasized. Despite the authority enjoyed by the priest alone of speaking effectively the words of consecration, those faithful who are not priests take part in the eucharistic sacrifice in such a way that they too sacrifice Christ through themselves in union with the priest and through the priest. At the same time the texts of Pius XII and the Second Vatican Council point out that they, like the priest, must not be content with being simply physically present, but must make this a personal presence by entering into the spirit and the mind of

Jesus Christ. It is further emphasized that their daily life should be an expression of their participation in the sacrifice of the cross.

For the view that all the faithful, although in different ways, are active in the sacrifice of the eucharist, Pius XII refers, *inter alia,* to Innocent III: "Not only the priests offer the sacrifice, but all the faithful also, for that which is done in a particular way through the service of the priest takes place generally through the will of the faithful." The liturgical texts themselves speak clearly enough on this subject. Let us remember the often neglected words after the preparation of the gifts: "Pray, brethren, that my sacrifice and yours may be pleasing to God the Almighty Father." In the Roman canon we find: ". . . all here present . . . for whom we offer, or who offer up to thee, this sacrifice of praise" and "Be pleased to accept the sacrifice from us your servants (i.e. priests) and from your whole family." It is the same with the prayer after the consecration. The sacrifice takes place in the dialogue between the priest and the other faithful present, although the priest speaks the most important words. According to the Fathers, those present give their assent in a particularly full way through the word "amen," and especially that amen which concludes the words of praise: "Through him, in him, and with him, be to thee, Almighty Father, in the unity of the Holy Spirit, all honor and glory for ever and ever." Thus the eucharist is always a sacrifice of the whole Church. In every particular eucharist the whole Church is involved. This is especially true of the eucharist celebrated by local Churches, i.e. the parish or the diocese. (Its public character, however, is preserved even when the priest says mass by himself.) The diocese and also the parish, whether that of a particular place or that created by a particular person, are constituted in their innermost meaning as part of the Church by and around the sacrifice of the mass.

The function of all present, as a single sacrificing community, may be made clearer by the following consideration. In every celebration of the eucharist the whole Church is represented. The readiness of the Church, i.e. of those participants who represent the whole Church, with regard to the eucharist taking place here and now, is both an inner and an outer event. It is primarily an inner one: faith, gratitude, devotion to Christ and through him to the Father. What takes place interiorly is expressed externally, in gesture and word; the words of the mass are words of petition and confession of guilt, of thanksgiving, of hope. The inner attitude of mind is also expressed in the preparation of the gifts. Bread and wine are not yet themselves the eucharistic gifts of sacrifice, but their preparation is the way towards the making present of the real gift of the sacrifice and the event of Golgotha.

Hence in their preparation the intention and desire is expressed of participating in the event of Golgotha. This desire is expressed with particular clarity when the gifts of bread and wine are brought to the altar by the participants themselves or their representative. This gesture expresses the gesture of faith, being inwardly directed in faith towards the sacrifice. In the early Church the faithful provided the gifts from which those necessary for the celebration of the eucharist were chosen. The part not used in the eucharist was given to feed the poor. This bringing of the gifts was both a task and a right of those who belonged to the community of Christ. Someone who was excluded from the eucharist because of his sinfulness or his separation from the Church was also excluded from the bringing of the gifts. His gifts were not accepted.

When the giving of the natural gifts of the soil came to an end, the giving of money replaced it and has remained to the present day. Its only meaning is that the giver seeks by his action to make himself part of the sacrifice of Jesus Christ in a particularly clear and deliberate way. In these many ways the participants become part of the sacrifice of Jesus, thus offering themselves to God. Because this offering takes place through Christ, they arrive at their goal, which is God. Participation in the sacrifice of the cross, made ritually present, reveals its full depth of meaning in the acceptance of the cross in everyday life and in care for our brothers.

ᐧ 6

The Eucharist as Meal

General

In the eucharist the memory of Christ's suffering is celebrated
in the form of a meal. Christ himself gave to the Church the
memory of his death and resurrection in the form of a meal
(DS 1739ff.): it is the basic form of the eucharistic sacrifice.
The forms of bread and wine have an essential importance. Eating
and drinking, of course, is part of a meal—what is the point of
bread if not to be eaten, of wine if not to be drunk? Thus the
eucharistic sacrament of sacrifice is a sacrificial meal. The sacrificial food is essential for the meal as a sacrifice. The sacrifice
is fulfilled through the meal.

Let us call to mind the institution of the eucharist during a
meal and in the signs of a meal, those of bread and wine. The
sacrificial altar therefore is the table on which the meal is prepared.
In the making present of his sacrificed body and blood it is
Christ who prepares the meal; it is ultimately God himself who,
as host, prepares the table for his sons and daughters.

Communion

As the eucharistic sacrifice is to be understood as a meal, so,
looked at the other way around, the meal—the communion—

122

is to be seen as a fruit of the sacrifice, as sacrificial food. Without actual eating, the eucharistic sacrifice would remain incomplete, and so the Church prescribes that at least the priest must consume the sacrificial food: but it belongs to the essential intent of the eucharistic celebration that all present should consume the sacrificial gifts (provided that they are qualified to do so, of course). To celebrate without all the participants consuming the sacrificial gifts was quite foreign to the thinking of Paul when in the First Epistle to the Corinthians he spoke about the eucharist. To participate in the eucharist means to have a share in the body and blood of the Lord. It is possible to participate in these in a weaker sense through faith, without actually eating and drinking, but the actual consuming of the body and blood of the Lord signifies the sharing in the eucharistic sacrifice which is called for by the nature of the eucharist itself.

On the other hand, communion is properly understood only if it is not detached from the celebration of the eucharist but is seen as the sharing in the sacrifice of the cross ritually made present. In communion, says Paul, the communicant gains a share in the sacrificed body and blood, i.e. the sacrificial death of the Lord. Through communion the Christian becomes incorporated into Christ in a new way, in that Christ offered himself on the cross to the Father as a sacrifice. This realizes in the fullest way the participants' offering of themselves in the eucharist, which is what it calls for. It would be wrong to regard communion exclusively as a mystical union with Christ and a blissful exchange with him, for it would be to ignore the central thing, which is its relation to his historical death on Golgotha. If communion is an element of the eucharist, then it is clear why the rubrics of the Roman Missal provide for the reception of communion by all the participants and give exact instructions for it. Reception of communion by all participants is also desirable because the eucharistic sacrifice is the celebration of the community of the people of God. At every eucharist is a group representing the whole people of God in order to praise God, in memory of the passion, death, and resurrection of the Lord, with him and through him. Hence it is appropriate that all should go to the one table prepared by God and receive the bread offered by him. The eucharist is then seen as the family meal of the sons and daughters of God. Wilfully to exclude oneself from it would be like a child absenting himself from the festive family meal presided over by the father; it is a kind of behavior which gives offense to community.

Change in the Reception of Communion

In view of this, it is remarkable that from the fourth century on, there are an increasing number of complaints about fewer participants at the eucharist actually receiving communion (Ambrose, Chrysostom). The phenomenon is undoubtedly connected with the process of secularization which took place in the post-Constantine era.

But the decline in communions was also partly due to the changes of accent in the whole of the Christian faith that came about in the controversies concerning Arianism. The emphasis on the oneness of being in Christ and the Father, which had become necessary because of the Arian interpretation of Jesus, had the effect of making the idea of Jesus as mediator and brother—that is, the image of the man Jesus—fade more and more in the minds of the faithful. The attitude towards the eucharist was inevitably affected: the idea of the presence of the Divine Majesty came increasingly to dominate the understanding of faith. Hence we find expressions such as "terrible," "alarming," "dangerous," commonly used in connection with eucharistic communion in the fourth century. This attitude developed to the point that in the Middle Ages communion was received extremely seldom, and even in religious orders only a few times a year.

The idea of the eucharist as a meal became increasingly overlaid by the idea of Jesus Christ present in the eucharist in his divinity. Thus, after the twelfth century, an aspect of the total reality of the eucharist became dominant which had not been developed in Scripture itself or in the early Church—that is, the adoration of the eucharist. For the reality which, from the thirteenth century on, theologians called the natural concomitant—the soul and divinity—received greater emphasis than the strictly eucharistic elements present *vi verbi* (the body and the blood). As a result of the controversies at the time of the Reformation there was a strong emphasis on the presence of Jesus Christ after and outside the celebration as well, a presence that included body and soul, divinity and humanity, so that the adoration of the eucharist was further developed. This was noticeable also in the style in which churches and altars were built. The baroque churches are no longer rooms in which to gather to celebrate the memory of Christ but richly adorned dwelling places of God. The fact that the altar is a table became less evident; the most important thing was the tabernacle on the altar. The altars became the thrones of God present in the church. The mighty pomp of the throne of God concealed the fact that the altar was the place of sacrifice and the table for the preparation of food. The eucharistic sacrifice itself became overshadowed by the adoration, so that the monstrance became more important than the cup. The idea is frequently found in the post-Tridentine Church that the altar serves, through the creation of the eucharistic gifts, as the foundation of the throne of God and of the monstrance exposed on it.

(It would be mistaken, however, to banish adoration from the eucharist. This would contradict the idea of the real presence of Christ that remains after the celebration. The eucharist is a whole with many dimensions, from which no one element can be seized on by a blind fanaticism without impairing faith. The adoration is of the eternal Logos who has received human nature into his own existence. Since the incarnate Logos is present in the eucharist as the crucified and risen Christ, adoration of the eucharist is a way of sharing in the cross of Golgotha and the resurrection.)

The Council of Trent itself stated expressly that the normal way of participating in the eucharist included communion (DS 1747). As a result of a practice that had developed from the era of Constantine throughout the Middle Ages, it prescribed yearly communion as the minimum of complete participation in the eucharist. However, because of the legitimate and necessary teaching concerning the sacrificial character of the eucharist and also the further teaching that the ordained priest or bishop is alone able to speak effectively the words of consecration—i.e. that the priest plays the important role in the eucharist—a climate of faith developed in which the celebration of the mass became primarily the affair of the priests; whereas, for the rest of the faithful, Sunday attendance at the sacrifice was increasingly conceived as an obligation imposed by a positive Church law and no longer as the appropriate expression of their union with Christ.

The rigorous religious and moral conditions set up by the Jansenists for the reception of the body and blood of Jesus Christ pushed communion even further into the background. The reception of communion became largely detached from the eucharistic sacrifice, in two ways: the eucharist was celebrated without the faithful communicating, and communion was received apart from the sacrifice of the mass, if it was received at all. Often the sacrifice of the mass was even used as a thanksgiving for the reception of communion. At the end of the eighteenth and beginning of the nineteenth century, communion outside mass became more and more frequent.

The change with regard to the reception of communion did not come until a hundred years later, at the beginning of the twentieth century, through the decrees on communion of Pius X. As we have already seen, the new insights into the significance of the eucharist brought about by the liturgical movement, biblical scholarship, and a renewed dogmatic theology, were confirmed and further developed by the Church's teaching office in the encyclicals of Pius XII, *Mediator Dei* and *Mystici Corporis,* and in the constitutions on the Sacred Liturgy and the Church of the Second Vatican Council. We can see a remnant of this earlier, imperfectly developed, understanding of the eucharist in the fact that even today communion is often given to the faithful with hosts from an earlier mass. If this is sometimes necessary because of particular circumstances, the meaning of the eucharist nevertheless requires that as a general rule participants should consume the bread which has been consecrated at their own eucharistic celebration.

Whereas until the thirteenth century communion was usually received under both kinds (exceptions were the communion of the sick, private communion in one's own home, and the communion of children) communion in one kind thereafter became more and more customary for practical reasons. The polemical attitude towards the Reformers heightened this tendency. It will be recalled that the Council of Trent (DS 1726-1731) stated that there is no strictly binding divine command to receive communion under both kinds. In this way, what had begun solely because of practical considerations acquired a polemical and dogmatic coloring.

According to the rubrics of the Roman rite hitherto, communion could be received by the laity only under one kind: the Second Vatican Council brought a few changes here. It is true that communion under both kinds expresses more clearly its significance as a sharing in the sacrificial death of Christ and also is in accordance with the picture that the institution narratives give of the eucharist.

The Conditions for Fruitful Reception of Communion

In order that the reception of communion should be fruitful it is necessary that there should be a living union with Christ. This is brought about through baptism and a living faith. Someone who lives in mortal sin sets himself in opposition to Christ, i.e. the host at the banquet of the eucharist. He is not worthy to sit at the table that God prepares for his own through Christ. Paul regards the antisocial behavior of the rich Corinthians as showing contempt for the Lord's Supper and the Church that celebrates it. A person who offends in this way is eating and drinking unworthily and is drinking judgment to himself.

The Church has instituted the rule that a man who has committed a mortal sin can communicate again only when he has been freed from sin through the sacrament of penance. Perfect contrition is not enough for communion, according to the Church. The reason is that the sinner has put himself in the wrong not only towards God but also towards the Church community and shown himself to be an unworthy member of it. Hence he must first be received back in peace into that community. This takes place through the sacrament of Penance, which applies not only to sins that are expressly directed against the Church community, but to every mortal sin. Only a man who is living at peace with the Church, i.e. belongs to it in a full and living sense, is worthy to take part in its central celebration.

(When the Church prescribed "fasting" before communion, it was in order to differentiate the eucharistic food from the ordinary, everyday food used to satisfy hunger. The considerable changes in these prescriptions are due to cultural, economic, and social developments.)

THE SALVIFIC CHARACTER OF THE EUCHARIST

General

In applying the structure of the salvific effect of the sacrament *(sacramentum, res et sacramentum, res)* to the eucharist, we find that there is an important difference. For the reality that is called *res et sacramentum,* i.e. that which is directly brought about by the external sign—which is itself a sign and brings about the *res*— is not, as in the other sacraments, an effect on the person receiving it, but a reality that is independent of him, although related to him. This reality is the body and blood of Christ as his sacrificed body and blood, but therefore Jesus Christ himself as the crucified and risen Lord, together with the Church actually present, performing the sacrifice. Hence the *res et sacramentum* are a reality with many dimensions and forms, involving both static and dynamic elements. This again is the reason for the many saving effects of the eucharist. The first point to be noted is that although the eucharist is the making present of the sacrifice of the cross in the ritual symbol, its saving power is still not completely identical with that of the sacrifice of the cross. For the eucharist is an actualization of the sacrifice of the cross that has a saving effect in many other ways, in that it is at work in all the events of the life of the Church as the body of Christ.

The Eucharist as Adoration, Thanksgiving, and Expiation

What does the eucharist effect? It is adoration, praise, thanksgiving, and expiation. In its statement on this question the Council of Trent emphasized primarily its expiatory character (DS 1743), which had been called into question by the Reformers. The council states:

This sacrifice is truly propitiatory, so that if we draw near to God with an upright heart and true faith, with fear and reverence, with sorrow and repentance, through the Mass we may obtain mercy and find grace to help in time of need (Heb. 4,16). For by this oblation the Lord is appeased, he grants grace and the gift of repentance, and he pardons wrongdoings and sins, even grave ones. . . . Therefore the Mass may properly be offered according to apostolic tradition for the sins, punishments, satisfaction, and other necessities of the faithful on earth, as well as for those who have died in Christ and are not yet wholly cleansed.[1]

The eucharist is adoration, thanksgiving, and praise in that it constitutes the self-offering of the Church to God through Jesus Christ in the Holy Spirit. This action involves the recognition of God as the Lord and as the God of gracious mercy.

The meaning of the eucharist is expressed in its prayers. In them the Church adores God, through Jesus Christ, as the One who created the world through Jesus Christ, who made all things to serve man and has once more reconciled sinners to himself. Thus the adoration is a worshipping in spirit and in truth (Jn. 4,23). This worship embraces all the other forms of prayer, including that for salvation.

In particular the eucharist is connected with the confession of sin and the hope of God's grace. Through the kindling of love and the spirit of penance, it helps to curb the sinfulness that still remains in those who have been baptized. By coming to the encounter with God in the eucharistic sacrifice through Christ

---

[1]*The Church Teaches*, pp. 292-293.

in the Holy Spirit in a spirit of worship and prayer, praise, and thanksgiving, the Church is received more and more fully into the love of God and increasingly freed from sin. Self-love and pride continually disappear in this devotion to God. Because every generation is constantly threatened anew through sin, it is always in need again of being purified from sin, and being sanctified and made perfect in the eucharistic sacrifice.

By giving itself vicariously for the whole of humanity through Jesus Christ to God, the Church performs its worship and praise in a representative way, so that the eucharist may have effects on the whole of humanity. By suppressing the forces of hate and pride which are disruptive of community, it performs a service for the union of the whole of mankind. In particular, however, the eucharist unites the Church more closely with Christ, and the participants grow through and in Christ into fuller community. Because those celebrating the particular eucharist are the representatives of the whole Church, every eucharist unites the whole Church more perfectly with Christ. Also its unity becomes greater, for the eucharist is the sacrament of unity and of catholicity in Christ. This is why in the canon the pope is mentioned as the visible representative of the invisible head and as the representative of the whole Church.

It is equally right that, because of the missionary authority of Christ, the canon names the bishop in charge of the local Church, since he expresses the unity of the diocese that is represented and realized in the eucharist.

Remembrance of the Dead

In the third century people began to pray in the eucharist for the dead. It gradually became an established practice to offer the eucharist itself for them. This is born of that feeling of community in the people of God which embraces all its members, both living and dead. It expresses the prayer of the Church that God may grant to its dead brothers and sisters who are not wholly purified the grace of love, for the sake of the passion and

death of Jesus, free them from their faults and make them capable
of eternal dialogue with him.

When we remember the saints in the eucharist, i.e. those men
who live in the contemplation of God, this has a twofold meaning.
First we are thanking God that he has accepted into his presence
members of the people of God through the sacrifice of the cross
made present in the eucharist, that presence towards which the
pilgrim Church is still moving. Secondly, it is a request that the
pilgrim Church may be more closely united through Jesus Christ
with those who have passed to their fulfillment.

"Fruits of the Sacrifice"

A particular problem is raised by the custom of applying the
sacrifice of the mass to a particular person. Here practice preceded
theological interpretation. In post-Tridentine theology the view
developed that every mass produces a particular saving fruit and
that this can be applied to a particular person. There is no justification for this theory and it must be rejected. The saving effect
of the sacrifice of the mass is inexaustible. Its saving power takes
effect in the Church and the individual members of the Church,
especially in the participants at a particular sacrifice, in accordance with their openness to God *(fides* and *devotio),* produced
by God's grace, i.e. by God's impulses of love.

This application of a mass to a particular person or a particular
matter means that the Church asks God, in its offering of itself
to the Father which takes place in the eucharist through Jesus
Christ, to show his grace in a special way to particular people.
As we have said in another connection, this request to God is
not intended to move him to alter his plan; rather, it means that
man presents himself before God as in need of help and thus
opens himself to God so that God can give himself to him in a
saving way, without impairing human freedom. The concept of
"application" includes the Church's confidence that God gives
himself through Christ to the person concerned in his need and
helplessness. Application is often combined with the idea of a

mass stipend. The latter is to be understood as a contribution to the performance of the sacrifice of the mass and hence is an expression of faith in Christ. A person who gives it is testifying to his faith in the cross and the fact that it is made present in the eucharist. In the application of the mass to an individual, the Church is asking God to unite this person committed to him still more closely to himself in terms of the particular situation in which the person is living.

Special Salvific Character of Communion

Participating through communion in the sacrifice of the mass brings an intensification of its saving effect. This means a fuller incorporation with Jesus Christ and the Church community and a more intense union with God the Father (an increase of sanctifying grace).

Union with Christ

The consuming of the body and blood of Jesus Christ in the form of bread and wine means not only the acceptance of a material gift but an encounter with Christ: Christ gives himself to the communicant. This giving of himself by the Lord goes beyond any self-giving by one person to another that we can experience. One person can give another things he owns, in order to show him friendship, love, fidelity, and trust. He can give a share of his knowledge, his experience, his projects. He can to a certain degree, in friendship, marriage and other relationships, give himself. But this self-giving in which one person opens himself to another and becomes part of the "I" of the other has a limit beyond which it must not and indeed cannot go. For every person is ultimately and inalienably an "I" which rests within itself; to abdicate it would mean self-destruction.

Christ gives his disciples not only a share in his mind, his thoughts, his love; he gives his very self in its bodily reality. To bring about this unreserved gift of himself he chose the form of bread and wine. The communicant receives bread and wine in a direct way, and through them the sacrificed body and blood of Jesus Christ, and through these again the gift of the Lord himself. Here love achieves what it always longs for but is powerless to achieve elsewhere: full union.

The communicant responds fully to Jesus' gift of himself in the eucharist only if he performs the act of eating and drinking in faith: the eating and drinking is a form of faith in the Lord, who is giving himself (Jn. 6,35f.). To equate faith and eating does not destroy the reality of the communion: it is a physical eating of the body and drinking of the blood, but an eating and drinking which expresses faith in Jesus Christ. It is the way in which faith in Jesus Christ is brought into the sphere of the real. Eating and drinking, then, includes the giving of oneself in a living faith to the Christ who gives himself to us, opens himself to us. Ultimately, the reception in faith of Jesus Christ means that the communicant is received into the life of Jesus Christ. Through communion what Paul calls "being in Christ" is made more intense: the communicant is placed more fully within the sphere of Jesus Christ's influence; he realizes what he is, namely his Christ-reality.

Union with One Another

As the union with Christ is made more intense, the community among those sharing the eucharist becomes deeper and more inward. Owing to their baptism in the Holy Spirit, they are so closely bound to one another as to form one body, the body of Christ. The eucharistic sacrifice is the expression, the self-representation, of this close connection. But at the same time the community is united at a deeper level in the sacrifice because of the greater incorporation in Christ. Any meal exercises a unifying power: those who eat together, if they are companions, are united with one another by a living bond. But the eucharistic meal has a further effect: those who receive the eucharistic food, by becoming one with Christ their brother, become the brothers and sisters of one another on a supernatural level. Thus the eucharist is a meal of brotherly fellowship, and it is precisely the denial of this which Paul deplores in the Corinthians. As we have seen, the greatest possible stress was put on this role of communion in the early Church. It is the guiding principle of Augustine's teaching on the eucharist. The community which comes into being in the liturgical celebration at the altar of sacrifice, at the table of the eucharistic meal, must manifest itself in the life of the world, in both the individual and the collective dimension, as a fellowship of ministering love. Thus what takes place in the mystery of the eucharist has effects far beyond the circle of those who participate in it, for it informs the conduct of the whole people of God, within its subcommunities (the parish, the diocese) and towards all men and the whole historical order. Unless fellowship with Christ expresses itself in service, it is empty and vain.

THE EUCHARIST AND ESCHATOLOGY

So immense are the effects of the eucharist, it is clear that it must not be neglected by Christians. It advances all the causes in the world which are God's, everything that makes for community, and restrains all the forces which are opposed to the divine will and disruptive of community. But even the closest union of men with Christ and with one another is still not the final fulfillment towards which the eucharist tends but only a stage on the way. The final fulfillment lies in the future. Jesus directs the minds of his listeners to it when he says (Jn. 6,54): "Whoever eats my flesh and drinks my blood possesses eternal life, and I will raise him up on the last day." To look into this future is to confront an immeasurable distance, for no one can know how far off the last day is. It is all the more important, then, that the Church, hoping where hope seems impossible, should have a guarantee for the journey which seems to stretch out endlessly. For Paul, to lose hope of reaching the ultimate future is to lose salvation itself. Salvation consists precisely in having hope through Christ. However long the fulfillment may be in coming, Christians know that they have a guarantee for their hope, an earnest of what is to come, a first instalment. The Spirit and the saving action of Jesus Christ continually celebrated in the eucharist are this guarantee. Basically, they are not two guarantees but one, for the saving action of Jesus is celebrated in the eucharist in the Holy Spirit, just as Jesus underwent his sacrificial death in the Spirit of God.

The earliest of the Church Fathers often give a very realistic account of the eucharist as this guarantee. They identify salvation with resurrection from the dead into eternal life. Because the eucharist, the sacrament of the body and blood of Christ, strengthens and nourishes the union with the risen Lord established in baptism, they look upon it as the seed of bodily resurrection. In the eucharist, says Irenaeus, a seed of bodily immortality is implanted in man. Incorporation in the eucharistic Christ takes place with the resurrection in view. Ignatius of Antioch calls the eucharist the "saving means" of immortality.

In medieval theology this naturalistic realism received less emphasis, and the view took hold that the eucharist gives man, rather, a pledge of bodily resurrection. But however it is interpreted, the eucharist is ordered towards the final bodily sharing in the life of the risen Lord within the community, and thus towards the eternal fulfillment of communion with God. The eucharistic community is the root from which that heavenly community is growing wherein men, made perfect, will be gathered around God through Christ in the Holy Spirit. Hence, far from any spiritualist and individualistic interpretations, the eucharistic celebration is an image in time of a perfect humanity gathered around God. By looking from the Lord present in the eucharist towards the Lord coming in the future, the Church is preserved from an introverted mystical contemplation of the present. It cannot celebrate the eucharist without proclaiming the death of the Lord, i.e. the past; but neither can it celebrate it without proclaiming the coming of the Lord, i.e. the future. When the Lord comes, the proclamation of his death will be at an end. At every eucharist the Church proclaims not only the past of Golgotha and Easter, not only the everlasting presence of the glorified Lord, but also the future. Affirmation of the future is a constitutive element of the eucharist.

The eschatological character of the eucharist involves a number of considerations. First, it is clear that the eucharist is an event which was instituted for only as long as the world lasts: it will come to an end when the world itself, and with it the Church in its earthly form, comes to an end. It is likewise clear that precisely because the Church continually celebrates the cross of Christ in its central ritual through a sacramental symbol, it is called to share, until the end of time, in the cross of its Lord within history. This is true in a twofold sense: it is oppressed from within by the sins of its members and from without by the sins of all men; and since it is situated in history and conditioned by history, it is exposed to all the sufferings of life in the world.

The Church cannot measure the total extent of its sufferings. When it looks back into its own history, it finds great numbers of martyr-figures; and yet the extent of the sufferings which have had to be—and still have to be—borne in secret cannot be known. It is to be expected that the revolution in the whole of life that is taking place today will not only confront the Church with new, hitherto unknown, responsibilities but also bring it new sufferings, new anxieties, and new trials. But if it continually proclaims the future in the eucharist, both for its own children and for all men, the watchfulness of its heart in waiting for its Lord will preserve it from indifference and from the loss of hope; and all the time it will have a share in that foretaste of eternal joy which is a source of unshakeable fortitude in all suffering.

For in proclaiming the ultimate future it is aware that its Lord, whose memory it constantly celebrates, has journeyed before it on the way of suffering, has arrived at the final fulfillment and is waiting for his brothers who are journeying through history as pilgrims, calling to them and strengthening them on their path. From this it derives its certainty that despite all appearances, the path it is traversing will end where the risen Lord stands. It must still pass through what he did; but the time is coming when, having reached the Lord by way of suffering and martyrdom, sin and weakness, discouragement and the loss of earthly hope, it will be able to look back in joy and gratitude. In the eucharist it continually finds renewed certitude that suffering and sin have no place in that final future which will be one of love and joy alone. Thus the eucharist becomes the constant proclamation of the ultimate absolute future—not only for those who participate in it but for the whole of humanity.

But while we take comfort in the reflection that amidst the turmoil of life in the world, every eucharist means a step forward into the ultimate future, we must not forget the negative implications which are also involved. There are two, and of one of them we have already spoken: whoever eats the bread or drinks the cup of the Lord unworthily is also moving towards an absolute future, but it is the future of judgment. The other concerns the necessity of eating and drinking. Our Lord says, according to John's gospel: "In truth, in very truth I tell you, unless you eat the flesh of the Son of Man and drink his blood, you can have no life in you" (Jn. 6,53). Anyone who does not take the step towards the future offered by the eucharist will not attain the future—or rather, he will not attain the future of fulfillment. Christ himself does not say whether his flesh and blood should be consumed frequently or whether once is sufficient. However, the Church in its solicitude for our ultimate arrival at perfect fulfillment has made certain rules: it has declared that Christians must be present at the eucharistic celebration on Sundays and on specified important feast days of the Church and that they must participate at least once a year in the eucharistic sacrifice in a full way—that is, through communion (Fourth Lateran Council, 1215; DS 1437). This is not an arbitrary decree of the Church; rather, it arises from a concern to protect and realize the Christ-life. Just as natural life follows certain rhythms, so our life in Christ has rhythms corresponding, in some degree, with those of natural life. The Church's decision on this matter is not unalterable but is conditioned by man's particular historical circumstances.

The view that the eucharist is essentially a sharing in the cross of Christ can lead to an eschatological, spiritualist misconception if the cross is taken to imply remoteness from the world. Far from leading to a withdrawal from the world, the effect of the eucharist is to create those human attitudes which make for brotherhood in the social order and in all spheres of worldly life. Hence it involves an obligation for Christians to co-operate in bringing about an order which is worthy of man. It contains, further, the implication that no order is final, but each can and indeed must be replaced by one that is new (so long as, in the change, freedom is preserved), until the final form of the world, mysteriously performed in the eucharist, is brought about through the world's final transformation. Just as living faith in Christ and living encounter with him in the eucharist, and the fraternal love given us in the eucharist, provide the impulse for constant self-reformation in the Church, so these same forces impel us to reform the world-order. The solicitude for our brothers created in us by the eucharist can take both conservative and revolutionary forms. It is committed in advance to neither conservative (in the sense of preserving) nor revolutionary action. Whether it chooses one or the other will be dictated by brotherly love. Called to action, the Christian will not forget the prudence the Lord enjoins but will let himself by motivated by love in seeking to bring it about that men become more and more that community whose primary form is continually created anew in the eucharist, until, after endless human attempts, trials, and sufferings, God invites mankind to sit at his table.

◄7

Baptism

BAPTISM AS PART OF THE EVENT OF SALVATION

Baptism is the sacrament by which the Church maintains and expands its existence through the acceptance of new members. However, it is essentially more than a mere membership ceremony, although it is that too. But since it is the act of entrance into the people of God, it is a decisive act towards salvation. From the very beginning it was part of the Church's message.

This message itself is directed towards baptism; the reception of baptism is the response of faith to the hearing of the Word. In baptism the hearer of the proclamation fulfills his desire to become a member of the Church. The Church fulfills its readiness to receive him within its community. If the Church represents the constant hidden presence of the saving, risen Lord, working through the Holy Spirit, then baptism is that act in which he performs his fundamental saving action here and now.

BAPTISM IN THE EARLY CHURCH

It is of great importance for the understanding and evaluation of baptism that after the day of Pentecost, i.e. the first day of the Church's life and activity, the early Church practiced baptism and taught its necessity for salvation. When, after the coming of the Spirit, Peter gave witness to Jesus Christ before a large audience, and they asked what they had to do, he replied: "Repent and be baptized, every one of you, in the name of Jesus the Messiah for the forgiveness of your sins; and you will receive the gift of the Holy Spirit" (Acts 2,38). Two things are noteworthy about this scene: the automatic way in which Peter immediately calls for faith and baptism, and the readiness of the listeners. Obviously they knew what baptism was.

The frank, automatic, unreflective call to receive baptism and thus to join the messianic community of salvation, handing oneself over to Jesus as the Messiah and the Son of God, can be understood only if Jesus himself commissioned the apostles to baptize. Thus baptism in the early Christian Church in Jerusalem cannot be of Hellenistic origin, nor can it be understood as an element of a process of religious evolution. Its relation to Jesus as the Messiah and the bringer of salvation is so close that it can only be interpreted as coming from Jesus. We may ask, however, when and how Jesus gave the commission to baptize. This is difficult to imagine as happening before the passion. It was only the risen Christ who gave his disciples, in his call to missionary work, the authority and the command to preach the gospel of salvation to all creatures. Jesus links with this the promise: "Those who believe it and receive baptism will find salvation" (Mk. 16,16). The form of the call to missionary work that we find in Matthew contains the direct order to "make disciples of all nations," baptizing them. Apart from this, it is characteristic of Matthew's account that he puts into the mouth of Jesus the statement that the baptism should be in the name of the Father and of the Son and of the Holy Spirit (Mt. 28,19).

Despite the fact that Christian baptism goes back to an explicit command of Jesus Christ, the question still remains whether we can see it in a wider context of religious history, or at least in a scriptural perspective. Sacred washings were widespread in the ancient world outside the sphere of the Bible. The inner significance of the baptism as practiced in Christianity, however, is so utterly different from the kind of baptism we find outside it that the former cannot derive from the latter. The purification expected in the non-Christian sphere is often regarded as a magic process of nature. As far as the realm of Scripture is concerned, we find washings of a cultic nature long before Christ. With many sects— e.g., the Essenes—they even became part of religious worship. It is, however, extremely doubtful if there is any connection between these varieties of baptism and the thinking of Jesus on the subject. In the case of the Qumran community, we can find no evidence of a baptism of initiation. Nor is it likely that the Jewish baptism of proselytes, which marked the reception into the Jewish community, had any influence, especially as it is questionable whether it still existed at the time of the emergence of the early Christian Church. We can, however, regard the baptism of John as a forerunner of Christian baptism. It has messianic significance, and is a sign and fulfillment of penance and repentance (Mk. 1,4-11; 11,27-33; Jn. 1,19-33; 3,23-29; 10,40; Acts 1,5; 11,16; 13,24; 18,25; 19,4). Its purpose is to create a restored people for the coming Messiah.

Jesus underwent the baptism of John, led by the will of the Father. For him, of course, it had a different meaning than for all other men; for the others it signified a confession of sinfulness and was at the same time a sign of penitence and of hope for the coming kingdom of God. Jesus, however, lets the symbol of the divine judgment and divine grace be realized in himself, as the representative of all other men, and precisely for this reason was revealed by God as the promised Messiah (Mk. 1,10; Mt. 3,16f.). Thus the baptism of Jesus points beyond itself into the future, which was to bring man the fullness of the Spirit and life as the sons of God. Jesus himself did not, apparently, baptize anyone, but he let his disciples continue for a while to give a baptism that was similar to John's (Jn. 4,2; cf. 3,22). Sometimes he uses the word "baptism" to describe his passion and death (Mk. 10,38f.; Lk. 12,50).

The evangelist John, whose sacramental interest is also seen in the discourse on the bread of life (ch. 6), makes Jesus tell Nicodemus about the new creation of man by the Spirit of God, connecting the event of new creation with baptism. In John, Jesus says, with great emphasis: "In truth I tell you, no one can enter the kingdom of God without being born from water and Spirit"

(Jn. 3,5). Every Christian hearer or reader of the gospel would inevitably be reminded by this text in John of the baptism he knew from liturgical practice.[1]

We might also say that Jesus prepared for baptism, the act of entry into the messianic, eschatological community of salvation, as he prepared for the Church as a whole, i.e. through his whole life, his death, and his resurrection; that on the basis of a widely familiar symbol, used especially among the Jews, he instituted the ceremony of washing as an image of the new man purified from his sins and hence living in peace with God and his fellow men. This is the only explanation for the fact that from the very beginning, baptism was seen as the way in which the turning to Jesus as the Messiah and bringer of salvation and the incorporation within the community of the "saints" took place (Acts 8,12.16.36, 38; 9,18; 10,47f.; 16,5.33; 18,8; 19,5; 22,16). On the basis of the practice of baptism in the early Church in Jerusalem, Paul developed an independent theology of baptism. The question of whether the actual words of command to baptize reported by Matthew originate directly with Christ we shall discuss later on.

THE SIGN OF BAPTISM

If we want to know what the sign of baptism is, the word itself suggests that baptism is administered through immersion in water. Very early on, however, another form developed, namely baptism by pouring or sprinkling water over a person. In the *Didache,* the teaching of the Twelve Apostles from the first half of the second century, baptism is described in the following way (ch. 7):

With baptism it is as follows: when you have said all the preceding, baptize in running water in the name of the Father and the Son and the Holy Spirit. But if you have no running water, then baptize in another. If you cannot do it in cold water, then do it in warm. If you have neither, pour water on their heads three times, in the name of the Father and the Son and the Holy Spirit. The person baptizing,

---

[1]R. Schnackenburg, *Das Johannes-evangelium,* I (1965), p. 383.

the person to be baptized, and anyone else who is able to, should fast before the baptism; the person to be baptized should fast for one or two days beforehand.

The form of immersion is attested also by the account of the baptism of the chamberlain of the Queen of Ethiopia (Acts 3,36ff.). It is only this form of baptism that makes it possible to understand the symbolism of baptism developed by Paul as an image of being buried and raised again with Jesus Christ. Until far into the Middle Ages baptism was, wherever possible, administered through immersion. Thomas Aquinas prefers it to the two other ways of baptizing. The action of immersion or sprinkling, however, is constituted as the sign of baptism only through the words of faith accompanying it. This raises the question whether the words of baptism were, or must be, christological or trinitarian. In the command by Jesus to baptize the trinitarian form is used, but Acts always speaks of baptizing in the name, or on the name, of Jesus.

Are these different baptismal formulae, or is Christian baptism being distinguished from other baptismal practices? The answer is undoubtedly that these forms of words represent baptismal formulae primarily, but as such they also express the saving significance of the action, i.e. being given over to Jesus Christ or to the triune God. According to this view, baptism could be given in the early Church, and probably even later, with the words "in the name of Jesus." Ambrose held this opinion, and so did a number of medieval theologians, with various qualifications. This is all the more likely since we cannot regard the call to missionary work by Jesus Christ as reported in Matthew, who uses the trinitarian formula, as embodying the actual words of Jesus himself.

Throughout his whole life Jesus proclaimed God—the God his hearers knew from the Old Testament—as his Father. Although he promised the Holy Spirit, he still did not state clearly that the Holy Spirit is God like the Father. This would, in fact, have been completely incomprehensible to his hearers, whose thinking was entirely monotheistic. We may say that only after the resurrection of Jesus Christ did the awareness of and faith in the

trinitarian personality of God gradually take shape, through medi-
tation on the relation to God of the risen Lord and the experience
of the Holy Spirit sent by him. Hence we can rightly see the
trinitarian words used by Matthew as resulting from an interpretation of the words of Christ performed under the influence of the
Holy Spirit and constituting an element of tradition in the early
Church—a tradition of worship, not of doctrine. Matthew took
the words from their liturgical setting and thus explained in more
detail the meaning of what Christ was saying in his commission
to baptize. We may recall here again that within a sacramental
sign- or word-field, originating with Christ or with the apostles,
the Church, the expression of whose life the sacraments are,
possesses the authority to make the sign or the words more precise
or more concrete.

In the course of history a number of individual questions have
been discussed by theologians, e.g. whether baptism in the name
of the triune God is valid if the baptismal act itself is not named,
or whether the baptizer must speak in the first person or can
speak in the passive voice ("You are baptized"). After many
fluctuations the Church ruled that the act of baptism must be
mentioned in the words of baptism, even though there is no
ultimate doctrinal decision on the subject. (Cf. the Council of
Florence's Doctrinal Instruction to the Armenians, November 22,
1439; DS 1314; the decision of Pope Alexander III, 1159-1181;
DS 757; cf. also DS 2327.)

In the early Church the act of baptism was often not mentioned
in the dispensing of the sacrament. Instead, the person baptizing
asked the person to be baptized three questions concerning his
faith, in accordance with the structure of the apostolic confession
of faith, and immersed him after each answer. Whereas in early
scholasticism many theologians regarded baptism as valid without
the baptismal act being mentioned, Thomas Aquinas and most
theologians of high scholasticism, in consideration of the Decretal
of Alexander III, regarded such a baptism as invalid. It is in the
East that we first hear of the three questions concerning faith being
replaced by the formula of faith indicating the nature of the sacrament (John Chrysostom, Theodoret). Baptism took place through

immersion (Rom. 6,4; Col. 2,12; 1 Pet. 3,22). We have evidence of a brief confession of faith by the person to be baptized in Rom. 10,9f. and Acts 8,37. We also have fragments of confessions of faith and hymns (Rom. 4,25; Eph. 5,14; 1 Pet. 3,18.22). Perhaps the candidate was tested first. There was an early connection of the laying-on of hands with baptism. It was an imparting of the Holy Spirit (Acts 8,17; 19,5) but was evidently not a necessary part of the sacrament. We can find no evidence of anointing in the New Testament period.

FAITH AND BAPTISM

In Scripture, especially with Paul but also in the early Church in Jerusalem, faith and baptism are so combined that it is clear that faith without baptism and baptism without faith can have no saving effect. It is true, however, that Scripture does not clearly distinguish between the role of faith and that of the sacrament. Sometimes it speaks as if salvation is brought about through faith alone, and at other times as if it took place only through baptism (Eph. 3,17; Rom. 6,3f.; Jn. 6,26ff.). We cannot, though, divide up the importance of faith and baptism for salvation so that each of these two events would produce a particular partial effect within the totality of salvation; rather, faith and baptism constitute an indissoluble whole. In faith we take hold of Christ who is present in baptism, achieving our salvation. We can also say that the Church's faith in Christ is realized in baptism, so that baptism is to be seen as the self-realization of faith. The believer takes hold of Christ, who is stretching out his arms to man, and at the same time takes hold of the Church's community of faith that is present in the sign. This becomes clearer if we recall that the sacraments are always the tangible and concrete form and appearance of the God who is giving himself to man.

BAPTISMAL SALVATION

General

The saving effect of baptism has many levels. It includes liberation from sin; inner renewal and sanctification (sanctifying grace); being incorporated in the Church; being incorporated in Christ; receiving a share in the life of Christ, in his saving death and his resurrection; the pouring out of the Holy Spirit; the meeting with the Father in heaven as the God of our Lord Jesus Christ, as the first person in the tripersonal divine life. Although we distinguish these various elements, this does not mean that one follows the other in time. Rather, it simply indicates their inner relationship (causality). We may describe the incorporation in Christ and in the Church as the *res et sacramentum* of baptism, to use the expression we discussed earlier, insofar as incorporation in the Church and being made to resemble Christ involve this salvific sharing of his death and resurrection. Thus baptism constitutes membership of the Church. Let us remember that we can and must distinguish here between full and partial membership, according to the extent of faith and the place in the hierarchically structured community of the Church.

Membership in the Church

According to the convictions of the first Christians, baptism represented the reception into the community of salvation (Acts 2,41). There is no other way of becoming a member of the community of salvation. A man is constituted a Christian by baptism. Hence the idea of the "anonymous Christian," if taken in its literal meaning, is contrary to Scripture. Although a non-baptized person can have the state of mind which, in the case of a Christian, would make it possible for him to be baptized, this still does not make that person a Christian. As far as the Bible is concerned, there is no such thing as Christianity without the sacraments.

Baptism may be described as a *signum distinctivum*. It creates distinctions among men that are valid for ever. It confers an indelible character, a mark, as the Council of Trent calls it (DS 1600). This ecclesiological, christological mark cannot be removed even by formally leaving the Church. Through baptism the natural relationship of a man to the community is intensified and transformed from within. It becomes a continuing coexistence within the community of salvation and hence with all those who belong to it, though without any consequent loss of the natural coexistence. Reception into the community of salvation involves first a reception into the local community, the local Church; beyond this, a reception into the Church of the diocese with the bishop at the head; and again, going beyond this, it is a membership of the whole Church. Baptism, then, creates brotherhood between men.

It is chiefly Paul who stresses the ecclesiological aspect of baptism. The thought runs through all his epistles and is most strongly emphasized at those points where Paul speaks of the Church as the body of Jesus Christ. But Paul never offers teaching for the sake of teaching, he exhorts the reader of the letter to live in harmony and brotherly love, making the basis of his exhortations the unity that already exists, as it were ontologically, and which has been brought about by baptism. Thus he writes, for example, to the Corinthians, who are in danger of schism (1 Cor. 12,13f.): "For indeed we were all brought into one body by baptism, in the one Spirit, whether we are Jews or Greeks, whether slaves or free men, and that one Holy Spirit was poured out for all of us to drink. A body is not one single organ, but many." The unity created through baptism has such power that, in comparison with it, all other differences fade away (cf. Rom 10,12; Gal. 3,28). It is in Paul's ecclesiological epistle, the one addressed to the Ephesians, that he proclaims the effect of baptism as incorporation in the people of salvation. Jesus Christ has overcome the differences that divide men from one another and split them into enemy camps. They are overcome specifically for every individual through his entering, by baptism, the community of peace created by Christ (Eph. 2,13-22; 3,6). Paul knows that every man can be a burden for every other, so that membership of the community of salvation is not an unalloyed joy but carries responsibilities.

Hence the ecclesiological mark of the baptized person is also a *signum obligativum*. Paul expresses this situation in the following way in his epistle to the Ephesians (Eph. 4,1-6):

I entreat you, then—I, a prisoner for the Lord's sake: As God has called you, live up to your calling. Be humble always and gentle, and patient too. Be forbearing with one another and charitable. Spare no effort to make fast with bonds of peace the unity which the Spirit gives. There is one body and one Spirit, as there is also one hope held out in God's call to you; one Lord, one faith, one baptism; one God and Father of all, who is over all, through all, and in all.

Relationship to Christ

Incorporation in the Church includes incorporation in Christ, i.e. encounter with, and being made into the likeness of, Christ. The latter is not the result of membership of the Church, it is the form of it. The Church is the body of Christ; Christ is the head of the Church. Thus membership in the Church contains within itself a process of growth in the likeness of Christ, the Church's head. This likeness can reach such a degree that the Christian can simply be called another Christ. As we have already said, this does not involve any effacing of the personality of the man who is committed to Christ; on the contrary, through it he reaches the fullest development of his potentialities. A man becomes fully man by growing into the likeness of Christ. Thus the ecclesiological mark is seen to be at the same time the mark of Christ. It is a *signum configurativum*.

Resemblance to Christ means a resemblance to Christ in his death and resurrection: it is not a static but a dynamic element. It impels a man to make himself more and more like Christ in his sacrificial movement to the Father for the sake of his brothers. Because of this mark of Christ the baptized Christian becomes part of Jesus Christ's mission, not as an isolated individual but as a member of Christ's community. As we have seen, to be drawn into the mission of Christ means to share in his priestly, prophetic, and royal task. Christ's concerns are the concerns of every baptized Christian. To use an image from Scripture, the baptized live in that household which is entered by those who are called to salvation. Hence they are responsible for the life of the household and for its power to attract others. They are no longer aliens in a foreign land (Eph. 2,19ff.) but fellow citizens of the saints and members of God's household, which is built on the foundation of the apostles and the prophets. Jesus Christ is the cornerstone. In him the whole structure is joined together and rises up to become a holy temple in the Lord. The seal of Christ which is placed on the baptized is not merely an external distinguishing mark or an external sign of commitment; on the contrary, it is a quality which makes it possible for him to commit himself inwardly to the mind of Christ; to share in that course of sacrifice directed to God in which Jesus Christ accomplished the work of salvation and the reconciliation of all men with God; and, at the same time, to commit himself, in Christ, to the service of his brothers and sisters.

Since Adam, and all the men after him who lived under the yoke of the powers of destruction, Jesus Christ is the first man who lives in the right relationship to God; it is he who opens for all other men the way to the right relationship to God and to a right relationship with one another. The consciousness in faith of its union with Christ and the hopes which are a consequence of this union are characteristic of the life of the early Church in Jerusalem. Although Jesus' disciples never grasped what he was about during his lifetime, they were continually aware, often in a way that was strangely oppressive to them, that something new was coming into the world. After the sending of the Spirit they come to an understanding of Jesus' death and resurrection as the great mystery of this man and of the whole of mankind (Acts 1,22). They know that they have now passed into another sphere. That is why the encounter with the risen Christ produces a new attitude of mind in them. Their joy in belonging to him transcends all other feelings of anxiety and care (Acts 2,46; 5,41; 8,39; 11,23; 13,48; Lk. 23,43; 24,31-35).

Continuing, interpreting, and reflecting on what Acts reports of the early Church in Jerusalem, Paul and John see all salvation as guaranteed in the encounter with Christ and the union with him. According to Paul, man acquires a share in the glory of God through being baptized in the name of Jesus (1 Cor. 1,13; 3,23; 6,19; 2 Cor. 10,7). The formula "in the name of," used in a document, refers to the assigning of something to that person whose name is mentioned in the document. Baptism in the name of Jesus means that the baptized person is made over to Jesus. If the name Jesus is pronounced over a person, then Jesus Christ becomes his Lord. Paul expresses this connection by means of the most varied images. In the Epistle to the Galatians he describes the connection with Christ in terms of the putting on of Jesus Christ (Gal. 3,27). In baptism Christ is put on like clothing (cf. Eph. 4,22f.; 6,11-14; Col. 2,12; 3,9f.; Rom. 13,13f.; 1 Thess. 5,8). By this image Paul does not mean an external likening to Christ; he imagines the water of baptism to be like a garment into which the baptized person slips as he climbs into the water and is immersed in it. The garment is, for him, an image of the risen Christ. The baptized person is determined in his whole existence through Christ. Christ expresses himself in him and manifests himself to him. The baptized person is molded from within by Christ. Christ is the primal image *(Urbild)* of the person who is united with him. The latter is the image and, in a certain sense, the manifestation of Jesus Christ. Because Christ penetrates him wholly from within, he is endowed with the glory of the Christ event.

A special feature of Paul's theology of baptism is his use of the phrases, the "indwelling" of Christ in men, the "indwelling" of a man in Christ, and of the baptized person being "with" Christ. (For the image of the indwelling of Christ in man, cf. Rom. 8,9ff.; 2 Cor. 4,5-14; 13,2-5; Eph. 3,16f.; Gal. 2,19f.; 4,19f.; Col. 1,17; Phil. 1,21.) The passage in Romans reads:

But that is not how you live. You are on the spiritual level, if only God's Spirit dwells within you; and if a man does not possess the Spirit of Christ, he is no Christian. But if Christ is dwelling within you, then although the body is a dead thing because you sinned, yet the spirit is life itself because you have been justified. Moreover, if the Spirit of him who raised Jesus from the dead dwells within you, then the God who raised Christ Jesus from the dead will also give new life to your mortal bodies through his indwelling Spirit.

In this text Paul is telling the Romans that the baptized person is freed from the power of sin, from the reign of death, and subject to the lordship of the Spirit of God. Christ himself lives through his Spirit within him. The Spirit of Christ dwelling in man is the new life of the human spirit, so that he is able to live a just life and one pleasing to God, being at peace with him. Even such a man must die. But the death that he dies is not eternal death, but only a superficial and temporary one. In fact, this man already has a share in eternal life. In this man the life of the risen Lord is active and is made manifest. Jesus Christ is the personal ground of the existence and activity of the man who believes in him. Such a man receives the *dynamis* and the *pneuma,* the power and the spirit of the risen Christ.

According to the passage in the Epistle to the Ephesians, Jesus Christ lives in the heart of the man who believes in him in faith. In faith a man gives up his self-sufficiency, he goes beyond himself and opens himself to God. In this he acknowledges himself as a sinner who needs to be saved. At the same time he is affirming that the Father of Jesus Christ, who raised Jesus from the dead, is the only one who can save him. Thus, because of the risen Jesus Christ he puts his hope in the Father. This self-transcendence of man towards God is the human response, brought about through God (again through grace), to the proclamation bearing witness to the resurrection of Jesus Christ from the dead. It pre-supposes the proclamation through the believing words of the Church. In the proclamation the Father moves through Jesus Christ (and thus Jesus himself also moves) towards the man who hears the gospel. In the preaching of the Church the mystery of redemption opens up before the hearer, so that he can pass into its reality. By passing into this mystery in faith, he lets the saving power of Jesus take hold of him. Thus the image of Jesus Christ dwelling within the baptized man is the equivalent of the saving lordship of Jesus Christ over him. The believer is no longer governed by his own self, but by Jesus Christ. The believer is not his own lord, for Jesus Christ has become his lord.

As for the image of man being "in" Jesus Christ, this means, in fact, the same as the first image. It is simply the movement of salvation seen the other way round. Men who are ruled by Christ are penetrated by the living power of the risen Christ. Jesus takes them into his own risen life. The meaning of the life of Christ is fulfilled in a man's sharing in it. Numerically, the phrase "in Jesus Christ" occurs far more frequently in Paul than the first phrase, appearing more than 160 times. It represents one of the dominant motifs of Paul's theology of baptism and indeed of his whole theology. We can formulate it in the following way: what happened to Christ happens to the Christian. Christian life is sharing in Jesus Christ's life of salvation.

Paul sees this as symbolized in the baptismal event itself. Let us quote one of the most revealing passages for the Pauline theology of baptism. We find it in the Epistle to the Romans, ch. 6,1-11:

What are we to say, then? Shall we persist in sin, so that there may be all the more grace? No, no! We died to sin, how can we live in it any longer? Have we forgotten that when we were baptized in union with Christ Jesus we were baptized into his death? By baptism we were buried with him, and lay dead, in order that, as Christ was raised from the dead in the splendour of the Father, so also we might set our feet upon the new path of life. For if we have become incorporate with him in a death like his, we shall also be one with him in a resurrection like his. We know that the man we once were has been crucified with Christ, for the destruction of the sinful self, so that we may no longer be the slaves of sin, since a dead man is no longer answerable for his sin. But if we thus died with Christ, we believe that we shall also come to life with him. We know that Christ, once raised from the dead, is never to die again: he is no longer under the dominion of death. For in dying as he died, he died to sin, once for all, and in living as he lives, he lives to God.

In this text Paul is not saying that we gain our understanding of baptism as a sharing in the death of Jesus Christ from the liturgy, i.e. through the baptismal form of immersion. The understanding of Christian life as a sharing in the saving fate of Jesus Christ is clear to Paul from the start. On the basis of this interpretation of baptism and of the life of Christ it creates, the immersion in baptism becomes for him an image of the burial of Jesus Christ.

He uses baptism to illustrate what he firmly holds from the beginning. Immersion is a kind of burial, resembling that of Jesus Christ. Paul sees the formal resemblance with the burial of Jesus Christ only in the going down into the water, but he draws the conclusion that he who dies with Christ, namely the Christian who is dying to the old man, the Adam, also acquires a share in the resurrection of Christ, without the share in the resurrected life of Christ being itself expressed symbolically in the baptism.

The teaching of the apostle concerning the sharing not only of the life but also of the saving deeds of Jesus Christ brings us to the problem of how these saving deeds of the past can be made available to a person living in the present. The fact itself is not to be doubted. Thomas Aquinas also says *(Summa theologica,* III, 69,2): "Through baptism man is incorporated into the Passion and the death of Christ. . . . From this it is clear that the baptized Christian receives a share in the suffering of Christ as the means of salvation *(communicatur passio)*, as if he himself has suffered and he himself died" (cf. also qu. 69, 5,7). If, however, there is no doubt about the fact of this sharing, there have been many controversies about how it is possible. According to the view represented by O. Casel and his school (mystery theology), the events of the past are made present, not in their historical succession, but "pneumatically." According to another view, it is not that the past events are made present to the man living here and now, but rather that the man living here and now is made present with the past events. It is probably best to say, with F. X. Durrwell *(The Resurrection)* and other writers (cf. also R. Schnackenburg), that in baptism man is first united with the risen Christ, and only thus, through him, with the events of Christ's life. The risen Lord remains for ever marked by his death and his resurrection, in fact by the whole course of his historical life. This also determines irrevocably his life as the life of the risen Lord. In this view the events of salvation are made present not in their particular character as events, but in their effective power, in their dynamic. It is not an ontological but a dynamic presence. The baptized Christian lives within the sphere of the saving influence of the death and resurrection of Jesus Christ. Thus he is removed from the domain of the powers of destruction and placed in the domain of the powers of salvation (cf. Col. 1,11ff.; 2,4ff.; Eph. 2,4ff.; 1 Cor. 1,1f.).

Being in Christ is the guarantee of resurrection (1 Cor. 15,22f.). Even during our earthly life there is, in a hidden way, a sharing in the glorified life of the Lord. That is why there is no longer any damnation for one who is in Jesus Christ (Rom. 8,1). Being in Christ is not to be attributed to human effort, but to divine mercy (1 Cor. 1,30).

Apart from the phrases "in Christ" and "Christ in us" there is a third, namely "being with Christ." It often means the same as the first two, but frequently has also an eschatological orientation.

Possession of the Spirit

The special feature of the community of the baptized is that they possess the Spirit. Baptism imparts the Spirit. The Spirit is often spoken of in the Old Testament. It is promised as one of the chief gifts for the messianic period. Jesus himself promised his disciples the Holy Spirit. The giving of the Spirit, of which the Old Testament speaks, is fulfilled in its being received by those who, as a result of missionary preaching, confess Jesus in faith and have themselves baptized in his name (Acts 2,38; 8,15ff.; 9,17f.; 10,44f.; 19,6). Thus every baptized Christian is a bearer of the Spirit (cf. also 1 Pet. 1,1; 2; 4,14; Jude 19f.).

The Epistle to the Hebrews points out the high distinction, but also the heavy responsibility, that rests on a man endowed with the Spirit (Heb. 2,4; 6,4; 10,29). The pouring-out of the Spirit on the believers in Christ, as recounted in Acts, indicates that the Spirit has a relation to Jesus. Peter makes this clear in his preaching. The pouring-out of the Spirit is a work of the risen Lord (Acts 2,33). In the Spirit sent by him, Jesus Christ himself is present, as the one wholly penetrated by the Spirit, as the heavenly *pneuma*. This makes his presence among his disciples not an ontological one, as we believe it to be in the eucharist, but a dynamic one. It is not a presence that is any less effective, but of an intensity that is due to the power of the Spirit itself. The presence of Jesus Christ in the Holy Spirit is one that is constantly active, in that Jesus Christ himself is active through the Spirit that achieves all things. The original source of the Spirit that is given to the baptized Christian is God the Father; but it is given through the mediation of the risen Lord who sits at his right hand.

In Acts we find that all those who profess faith in Jesus and are baptized in his name receive the Holy Spirit—but they only (Acts 2,38; 10,44ff.; 19,5f.). It is one and the same divine Spirit with which Jesus is anointed (Acts 10,38) and in whose power he did his work that is now given to his disciples in baptism.

Although Paul makes the connection of the Spirit with the risen Lord more profound and more comprehensive, he still agrees with the early apostolic view that the real mark of a Christian is the possession of the Spirit.

Who or what is the Spirit that comes to men in baptism? Paul's love of symbolical language, the many personifications of forces and powers (sin, death, flesh, etc.), might, if compared with Hellenistic ideas, lead to the conjecture that Paul regarded the Spirit as an impersonal power. Those, however, who hold that in Paul's concept the Spirit is personally determined can oppose this view with a number of cogent reasons which are difficult to demolish. Above all, he says repeatedly that the *pneuma* dwells within the Christian (Rom. 8,9f.; 1 Cor. 3,16). The body of the Christian (1 Cor. 6,19) and the Church community as well (1 Cor. 3,16) are called temples of the Spirit. A number of passages ascribe personal actions to the Spirit in a way that obviously goes far beyond the personification of a force. The Spirit testifies to us that we are the children of God (Rom. 8,16). He comes to our aid in prayer, "pleading for us through our inarticulate groans" (Rom. 8,26). He cries "Father!" in the hearts of Christians (Gal. 4,6). He teaches words of divine and spiritual wisdom (1 Cor. 2,13). He searches the depths of God (1 Cor. 2,10); he produces all the gifts of the Spirit; he gives to every man his gift of the Spirit, as he desires.

However, the most important point of all is this: in two places the Spirit is mentioned as a third person beside the personal God and the personal Lord (1 Cor. 12,4-6; 2 Cor. 13,14). It is hard to imagine that Paul would have so closely juxtaposed an impersonal force with the persons of God the Father and Our Lord.[2] According to Rom. 8,1-17 it is the Spirit dwelling in man, the Spirit of God and of Christ, that makes us Christians, that creates in us the new life of justice, a life that is pleasing to God and at peace with him. He will give life to our mortal bodies. He brings about our sonship in effecting our union with Christ. In his cry in our hearts to the Father he presents the inner testimony of our sonship of God (cf. Gal. 4,4-9; Eph. 3,16-19). Paul sees the following as signs of the possession of the Spirit: the understanding of its utterances (1 Cor. 2,13f.); the confession of Christ as the Lord (1 Cor. 12,3); the charisms (1 Cor. 12,7-11); *agape* (1 Cor. 13); and the addressing of God by the familiar word Father (Rom. 8,15).

Beside the extraordinary events of the Spirit (such as glossolalia) stand, for Paul, the ethical effects that the Spirit produces. These are the higher charisms (1 Cor. 12,31) and therefore more important than the others. In them the Spirit is at work as the Spirit of sanctification (Rom. 1,4; 1 Thess. 4,7f.; Gal. 5,22f.; Rom. 8,2.9). The Spirit is the guarantee that God really grants a share in his glory. It is, as it were, the first earnest of the final encounter with God, of communion with him in the absolute future (Eph. 1,13f.; Rom. 5,5; 2 Cor. 1,22; 5,5; Gal. 3,5; 1 Thess. 4,8). The Spirit brings it about that the Christian remains the possession of God and Christ and hence is under the divine protection. He confirms the baptized Christian as the son and heir of God. He leads him into the fulfillment of the future.

The Baptized Person as Son of God

The man who has been united with Christ in the Holy Spirit through baptism is, as the brother of Christ, at the same time the son of God, the heavenly Father. Jesus Christ is the new whole man, according to the original plan and image of God (1 Cor. 15,45-49; Eph. 2,15; Heb. 1,3; Phil. 2,6f.; 2 Cor. 4,4; Col. 1,15).

---

[2] O. Kuss. *Der Brief an die Roemer* (Regensburg, 1940), pp. 72f.

In baptism we become so similar to him, the firstborn (Heb. 1,6; Col. 1,15) among many brothers (Rom. 8,29; Col. 1,18), and so transformed, that we are taken into that relationship in which he, the man Jesus, stands to the heavenly Father through the divine person of the Logos.

In the Epistle to the Romans (8,28ff.) the baptized are seen as a family whose father is God, whose eldest and model brother is Jesus Christ, whose family spirit is that love which has personal form in the Holy Spirit as the divine "we." Paul writes the following to the Corinthians in his Second Epistle (2 Cor. 3,17-18): "Now the Lord . . . is the Spirit; and where the Spirit of the Lord is, there is liberty. And because for us there is no veil over the face, we all reflect as in a mirror the splendour of the Lord; thus we are transfigured into his likeness, from splendour to splendour; such is the influence of the Lord who is Spirit" (cf. Gal. 3,15-29). God's eternal plan of salvation is to make men his children through his son Jesus Christ: "He destined us—such was his will and pleasure—to be accepted as his sons through Jesus Christ, that the glory of his gracious gift, so graciously bestowed on us in his Beloved, might redound to his praise" (Eph. 1,5f.). According to this text, the heavenly Father has only one Son, but this sonship is extended to include the sonship of innumerable adopted sons.

The sonship of the many is achieved through their receiving a share in the eternal divine Spirit, so that they are one in the Spirit with the eternal incarnate Son of God:

For all who are moved by the Spirit of God are sons of God. The spirit you have received is not a spirit of slavery leading you back into a life of fear, but a Spirit that makes us sons, enabling us to cry "Abba! Father!" In that cry the Spirit of God joins with our spirit in testifying that we are God's children, and if children, then heirs. We are God's heirs and Christ's fellow-heirs, if we share his sufferings now in order to share his splendour hereafter. (Rom. 8, 4-17; cf. Gal. 4,1-7)

According to these texts, the baptized Christian's relationship to God as that of a son gives him freedom of speech. He can presume

to call God "Father," in freedom and trust, for he is a member
of God's household. That is why "Father" stands as a term of
address at the head of the prayer Jesus himself taught his disciples (Mt. 6,9).

St. John's Gospel emphasizes that the life of sonship is a gift
of God. It is by no means automatically that man becomes God's
son. He cannot himself take the initiative; he can only receive
his acceptance into the household of the heavenly Father in
gratitude. The gospel recounts this wonderful event, which far
transcends anything of earthly origin, as follows:

The real light which enlightens every man was even then coming
into the world. He was in the world; but the world, though it owed
its being to him, did not recognize him. He entered his own realm,
and his own would not receive him. But to all who did receive him,
to those who have yielded him their allegiance, he gave the right
to become children of God, not born of any human stock, or by
the fleshly desire of a human father, but the offspring of God himself.
(Jn. 1,9-13; cf. 1 Jn. 2,29-3,10)

The life of a son commits man to a son's attitude of mind (cf.
Mt. 18,1-5; Mk. 9,33-37). This includes trust, love, sacrifice,
adulthood, maturity, freedom (1 Cor. 3,1; 13,11; Gal. 4,1ff.;
Eph. 4,14; Rom. 8,15; 1 Jn. 3,1f.; 1 Cor. 13,12; Gal. 4,9; 5,6;
Col. 3,10; 2 Cor. 3,18-4,6).

The connection with Christ necessarily also brings about a
new inner qualification of man, the forgiveness of sin, especially
original sin, the sanctifying grace, which the Council of Trent
calls the *unica causa formalis* of justification. We shall consider
this and other related problems more fully in the section on
grace (justification).

Forgiveness of Sins

Let us consider here briefly, however, the forgiveness of sins that
proceeds from the union with Christ and the inner sanctification
of man that is brought about through baptism. If we follow here

the order: community with Christ, union with God, sharing in the Holy Spirit, the forgiveness of sins, this is to bring out the priority of the personal over the nonpersonal element.

Union with Christ in the Holy Spirit opens the way to God. It includes peace with God. But this is the same thing as the forgiveness of sin. The connection between the forgiveness of sin and union with Christ is most clearly set forth in the passage from the sixth chapter of Romans quoted above. Paul proclaims the forgiveness of sins as a dying to sin, or, more exactly, as the liberation from a reign of the powers of destruction belonging to sin and the submission to the reign of salvation established through the conquest of sin. The forgiveness of sin brings with it a new life. Christ generates the new, true life. True life is a life for God in self-transcendence towards him, though without giving up one's place in the world.

Of course the forgiveness of sin does not mean that the sinful action is cancelled out. What has happened in history continues to exist, to have its effects, in history. Every action has a momentum carrying it into the future. The forgiveness of sin means that the guilt of the sinful act is removed, so that there is no longer a rift between God and man, but peace. Scripture testifies to the forgiveness of sin without reflecting on its nature.

In Christian tradition the sin forgiven through baptism is taken to be both original sin and the personal sin of the candidate. It will be recalled that in the time of Augustine the baptism of infants was taken as proof of the validity of the doctrine of original sin. There is only one place in Scripture, namely the fifth chapter of Romans, which says that the reign of death, a state of ruin deriving from Adam, has been overcome through Christ. It is through baptism that the individual gains a share in this conquest in the reign of death. Wherever else the New Testament speaks of the forgiveness of sin through baptism, it is always personal guilt that is meant. Thus, for example, in his first sermon Peter exhorts his hearers to receive baptism for the forgiveness of sins (Acts 2,38ff.; 22,16).

If we want to see the forgiveness of sin that is brought about by baptism in terms of the category of evolution, we could say that in sin a man sets himself against the stream that is moving towards the coming Christ, towards the absolute future, but that in accepting the forgiveness of his sins he is again placing himself within the whole eschatological flow. This explanation pre-supposes that the whole world is streaming towards the absolute future represented by the returning Christ. It also involves the fact that the "natural" is embraced or penetrated by the "super-natural" and exists for the sake of the supernatural, so that the history of the world take place *for* the history of salvation and finds in the latter its meaning and measure. Baptism is for the individual the beginning of the way into the endless future. At the same time, every baptism is for the community, the Church, a step, on a way that is called Christ, towards the hour of total fulfillment. Like the whole Church, baptism exists only for the sake of this future. It is the future that gives it its ultimate meaning. All the effects of baptism, accordingly, are to be seen as a liberation from the obstacles on the way and as the granting of freedom of movement towards the future.

In Scripture the forgiveness of sins is described as a washing and, in a positive sense, as rebirth, the bestowal of the sonship of God. These terms can also be found in Hellenistic thought. The Hellenistic influence, however, consists only in terminological borrowings. This is seen from the nature of the forgiveness of sin, of rebirth, from the connection of these events with Christ and the personal God. The forgiveness of sins does not mean the removal of guilt only in an abstract way, but a transformation of the whole direction of one's human life (cf. 1 Cor. 6,9ff.; 10,1f.; Gal. 3,27; 2 Cor. 5,17; Gal. 6,15).

In his Epistle to the Colossians, in which Paul warns them of the seductive power of an anti-Christian pseudo-philosophy, we find the following remarks on baptism (Col. 2,9-15):

For it is in Christ that the complete being of the Godhead dwells embodied, and in him you have been brought to completion. Every power and authority in the universe is subject to him as Head. In him also you were circumcised, not in a physical sense, but by being divested of the lower nature; this is Christ's way of circumcision.

For in baptism you were buried with him, in baptism also you were raised to life with him through your faith in the active power of God who raised him from the dead. And although you were dead because of your sins and because you were morally uncircumcised, he has made you alive with Christ. For he has forgiven us all our sins; he has cancelled the bond which pledged us to the decrees of the law. It stood against us, but he has set it aside, nailing it to the cross. On that cross he discarded the cosmic powers and authorities like a garment; he made a public spectacle of them and led them as captives in his triumphant procession.

We find another concept of baptism in the Epistle to the Ephesians. There it is interpreted as a purification through water (Eph. 5,25ff.). Paul is obviously trying to describe the saving effect of baptism in various ways. He sees it as a sharing in the death of Christ, as a purification by water, as a putting on Jesus Christ, as incorporation in the one Body. We find the same kind of thing in the First Epistle to the Corinthians (1 Cor. 6,11): "But you have been through the purifying waters; you have been dedicated to God and justified through the name of the Lord Jesus and the Spirit of our God."

It seems, however, that the idea of sharing in the death of Christ is more important than all the other statements. The idea of rebirth is stated in the Epistle to Titus. It is also found in St. Matthew's Gospel and is used here to describe the eschatological new creation of the cosmos (cf. also Jn. 3,3ff.). There are, however, many other passages attesting to the fact itself, namely, being raised into a new sphere of life that is characterized by the Spirit. Paul means precisely this when he speaks of the new creation of man through the Spirit and union with Christ (2 Cor. 5,17; Gal. 6,15; Eph. 2,15; Col. 3,10). According to the Epistle to Titus (3,3-7), God so transforms men through baptism that misunderstanding and ignorance, disorientation, weakness of will, conflicts in living together, and the whole struggle for life and power are done away with, and kindness, trust, and community spirit created in their place. Baptism is the seed of a new, higher, mysterious life in the Spirit of God (cf. Jn. 1,13; 1 Jn. 3,9f.; 5,18; Gal. 6,15; Jas. 1,18; Col. 3,10).

The Tension between Salvation as Gift and as Task

It is characteristic of Paul's teaching on baptism that there is a tension between the indicative and the imperative, between the now and the then. In order to understand this we must first realize that Paul nowhere seeks to give a theology of baptism in the sense of a doctrinal statement, but that he is always concerned with the invitation to life that proceeds from the reality of baptism, namely from community with Christ, so that he particularly emphasizes those elements which are important for Christian living. For him the existential side of baptism is all-important, the ontological less so. He speaks of the latter only for the sake of the former. Fundamental to his exhortation to us to realize the ontological is always the conviction that despite the present possession of salvation, the future fulfillment is still to come, and we can fail to achieve it. For baptism does not work by magic, and so it would be rash and a danger to salvation if we put a false trust in the sacrament (cf. 1 Cor. 10,1-6).

In the duality of the Pauline statements, that sometimes describe the salvation won, as if everything had already happened, and sometimes exhort man to ethical effort, as if everything still had to happen, we see that peculiar character of the eschatological situation, which consists in the fact that the Christian lives in two different time-scales. Salvation has been achieved, but it does not yet exist in its fulfillment. The dialectic of indicative and imperative is the necessary consequence of the fact that Easter brought the resurrection, but not the *parousia*.[3]

The First Epistle of Peter is particularly enlightening. It is regarded by many exegetes as a sermon on baptism, either as a whole or in its most important details (cf. esp. 1 Pet. 3,21-46). The epistle reminds its readers of the saving of those people who had been taken into the Ark from the waters of the flood and sees in this a type of the salvation through the water of baptism. According to this epistle, the effect of baptism is that the baptized

[3]O. Kuss, *Der Roemerbrief* (Regensburg, 1957-59), pp. 314f.

will be saved in the future judgment. Baptism is administered as a bath in pure water and with a prayer for the forgiveness of sins. The prayer is certain to be heard, because it is based on the saving action of the resurrection of Christ, and Christ as the risen Lord permeates the Church with his saving power. Like Paul the First Epistle of Peter (1 Pet. 1,13-2,25) emphatically calls the baptized to live as those whose sins are forgiven them. The Christian must live his life according to the model of the suffering Christ. The pagans, in fact, take offense because the Christians no longer share in their unbridled talk. Indeed, Christians often had to withdraw from the social circles in which they had lived hitherto if they wanted to preserve the meaning of baptism. They not only said good-bye to pagan religion and pagan vices, but often also to their previous associates. They no longer took part in the public festivals, since these generally involved ritual celebrations. The pagans were offended at this, and even enraged. Hence they invented calumnies and sowed the seeds of suspicion. Peter tells his readers not to let themselves be affected by it.

THE ESCHATOLOGICAL ORIENTATION OF BAPTISM

To understand the saving effect of baptism, i.e. the divine saving will that is manifested in the sign of baptism, we must realize that baptism represents only the beginning. With baptism man starts along the road that leads to the fulfillment of the future. It is essential for him to remain on that road. If he leaves it, then baptism not only has no saving power for him but, worse, it becomes a judgment. Thus in baptism man is taking a heavy, lifelong task upon himself. But he has the confidence and the hope that he will arrive at that place towards which his own life and the whole of human history, indeed the whole cosmos, is flowing. This hope is not, for him, a vague expectation, but an indestructible confidence, for it is based on the Holy Spirit that is present and at work in him. The movement begun in baptism is able to proceed in full confidence towards the future only because it has its firm foundation in the past, in the saving events of Golgotha and Easter morning.

Thus baptism combines a movement out of the past, which is made present in the event of baptism, and a movement towards the future. The past that is made present in baptism in the way we have described continues to have an effect in the future and brings it about. If the individual finds himself here in a great, constantly flowing stream, everyone arrives at the goal, in a provisional way, at the time ordained. This arrival is a provisional one for everyone, until the resurrection from the dead and, with it, the fulfillment of the whole of human history and the whole cosmos. From baptism on, the life of a man must be the constant practice of dialogue with God and dialogue with his brothers, both with those who are connected with him through the same faith in Christ and the one baptism, and with those who live outside the community of the baptized and to whom Christ must be proclaimed as the savior of mankind.

Man goes forward, in the total movement of the cosmos and the human history, in this constant movement, freely chosen, into the future plenitude of the community of Christ. Indeed, the baptized Christian leads in the movement towards the ultimate goal and takes everything else with him. He is not, in this, following an inescapable law of nature, but takes upon himself the task of using his freedom. If he goes contrary to his new life created through baptism—i.e. if he comes into conflict with Christ, with the Spirit of Christ, with God—then he comes into conflict with himself, but, beyond this, into conflict with the whole movement directed towards God. Sin is an obstacle to the evolutionary process of creation. On the other hand, baptism and life after baptism are powerful impulses for the forward movement into the future. The flow becomes broader and quicker. The risen Lord, who unites the baptized person to himself, calls him, from the invisible future, to ever closer and more intense fellowship; to that moment when his life reaches its fulfillment, when it finds the plenitude of fulfillment in the fulfillment of the whole.

THE TEACHING OF THE CHURCH

In many doctrinal pronouncements the Church has taught both that baptism was instituted by Jesus Christ (the Council of Trent,

7th session, canon 1, DS 1614; the decree *Lamentabili:* DS 3442) and the sign of baptism (the Council of Trent, 7th session, canon 2, DS 1615: any natural water, and only natural water, can be used) as well as teaching the saving effect of baptism (the Creed of Nicaea and Constantinople, DS 1837; the Council of Lyons, DS 830; Doctrinal Instruction to the Armenians of the Council of Florence, DS 1314; the Council of Trent, 7th session, canons 4 and 5, DS 1514f.; 6th session, ch. 7, DS 1528ff.; 7th session, canon 13, DS 1626). It should be pointed out that the council taught both the removal of original sin and of personal guilt as well as of any punishment that this guilt incurred. It is also part of the Church's declaration of faith that baptism brings about incorporation in the Church and in Christ (the Council of Florence, Doctrinal Instruction to the Armenians, as well as Canon 87 of canon law). We shall deal with individual statements by the Church when dealing with specific questions.

THE NECESSITY OF BAPTISM

As we can see from Peter's first sermon, faith and baptism were automatically regarded by the early Church in Jerusalem as *the* means of salvation. That there could be other ways to salvation lay wholly outside the mental horizon of this first Christian community. This belief was based on the instruction of Jesus himself, according to which the disciples are to preach the gospel, baptize believers, and further initiate the baptized in the mysteries of the kingdom of God (Acts 2,38; Mt. 28,20; Mk. 16,15f.; 1 Jn. 3,5).

In the time of the Fathers the teaching on the necessity of baptism was identical with teaching on the necessity of the membership of the Church. This conviction was so strong that in the third and fourth centuries baptism was often delayed until one was dying, so that one would run no risk of losing the liberation from sin and sanctification that it brought with it. In the second half of the fourth century there was energetic opposition on the part of Cyril of Jerusalem and Augustine to this practice which, though born of a genuine concern for salvation, was nevertheless mistaken.

People began to reflect on the teaching that baptism was necessary when the Pelagians maintained that there can be eternal life, if not heaven, without baptism. The Waldensians regarded the baptism of children as unnecessary. Luther regarded the baptism of children as a real means of salvation, although it was not easy for him to harmonize this view with his teaching that faith alone saves. Calvin firmly rejected infant baptism, an inevitable consequence of his theological position. It is a subject that is much discussed in contemporary Protestantism.

In its Doctrinal Instruction to the Armenians and at the Council of Trent, the Catholic Church declared that God had ordained that baptism was necessary for salvation (DS 1310f., 1514, 1618, 1625ff.).

Teaching on the necessity of baptism needs further explanation. It is clearly identical with the necessity of the Church. Since Christ, the only bringer of salvation, exists as the head of the Church, and salvation is based on sharing the Holy Spirit which was sent with Christ, only he who belongs to the Church can share in salvation. But entry to the Church is mediated through baptism. Hence the doctrine of the necessity of baptism is an expression of the doctrine of the necessity of the Church. What was said earlier must be noted here concerning full membership of, and other degrees of belonging to, the Church. It is important to note that according to the command of Jesus Christ to baptize, as formulated both in St. Matthew's Gospel and in St. Mark's, the proclamation of the gospel and the response of faith to it must precede the reception of baptism. Hence the proclamation is a necessary prerequisite for baptism. In areas where the proclamation has not yet penetrated, there is no basis for baptism. In such a situation one cannot even speak of a commitment to baptism by Christ. The reception of baptism has saving significance only where it is the fulfillment or the expression of faith. A short confession of faith as a response to the proclamation seems to have preceded, from the beginning, the administering and receiving of baptism (Rom. 10.9f.; Acts 8,37; cf. Acts 2,38; cf. also Rom. 4,25; Eph. 5,14; 1 Pet. 3,18.22). The early Christian institution of the catechumenate is in accordance with the same idea.

Men are always able to attain their salvation through Christ alone, but because of the christocentric nature of human history they always stand in some kind of relation to him even if it is often, or generally, unconscious. As a result of this orientation towards Christ, every form of faith, whatever it is like, every desire for an absolute value different from the world, becomes, in its inner nature, a movement towards Christ. In theology and in the statements of the Church, the desire for baptism is then described as a substitute for baptism by water. In his encyclical *Mystici Corporis,* Pius XII says that even the unconscious longing for God has a saving effect. (Cf. also the Letter of the Holy Office to the Archbishop of Boston of August 8, 1949: DS 3866-3873.) Scripture has many testimonies to the saving power of baptism by desire (Lk. 7,47; 10,27f.; 18,14). In Acts (10,46f.) it is pointed out that the gift of the Holy Spirit is poured out over the family of the centurion Cornelius even before he received baptism.

Let us recall what we have already said on this subject. In the faith of the great world religions (e.g., Hinduism, Buddhism, Islam) we can see baptism by desire at work. This does not mean that the proclamation of the gospel of Christ is unnecessary for them. We must realize that it is the will and commission of Jesus Christ that the salvation he brought and the divine will that all shall be saved should be proclaimed everywhere. Moreover, just as mankind increasingly grows closer together in the natural dimension, to become one vast human family, so it should grow together more and more in Christ, to become a brotherly unity. We must also remember that the saving possibilities of faith in Christ are far fuller and stronger than all other ways, and that it is a more effective force against the dangers to salvation.

A special way to salvation is testimony to Jesus Christ by the shedding of one's blood. By martyrdom we understand the unresisting acceptance of a violent death—or of maltreatment which by its nature leads to death, directly or indirectly—for the sake of Jesus Christ. The patient acceptance of death means the strongest concentration of all one's powers in the movement of faith towards Jesus Christ. To anyone who witnesses to him before the world by the sacrifice of life Christ has promised that he will bear witness for him before heaven, before the face of the Father and all the angels and saints (Mk. 8,34-38; 10, 32-39; Lk. 4,29ff.; Jn. 12,25f.). He once described his own passion as a baptism (Mk. 10,38; Lk. 12,50). In martyrdom a man shares in Jesus Christ's death to the point of the physical suffering of the actual event.

We must also say that the readiness to make an unconditional sacrifice of oneself for another person, especially in the form of loving service, is a share in the crucifixion of Jesus Christ even if the man who is ready to die in this way knows nothing of Christ.

THE FATE OF CHILDREN WHO DIE WITHOUT BAPTISM

In view of the necessity of baptism, a special problem is presented by little children, incapable of answering for themselves, who die without baptism. The Church regards their eternal destiny with great concern. Scripture itself gives no solution to the problem, but we may say the following: it would be hard to reconcile it with the saving will of God if even one child, without being able to make a personal decision for or against Christ, were to lose salvation, i.e. the fulfillment of the encounter with God, forever. The importance and urgency of the question appears when we remember that year by year millions of children of unbaptized parents have died and are dying unbaptized and that every year hundreds of thousands of children of baptized parents die without baptism, whether or not through their parents' fault. In medieval theology, especially with Thomas Aquinas, the view was developed that children who die unbaptized do not attain to the fulfillment of the "supernatural" dialogue with God, but that nevertheless they enjoy a certain natural blessedness. Augustine held that there could not be any such thing as the painless deprivation of the eternal vision of God. St. Thomas's view of a certain natural fulfillment became the common view of modern theology. According to it, a third state must be added to the two mentioned in Scripture, namely eternal fulfillment and eternal non-fulfillment; this third is the state of natural fulfillment. This view does seem to offer a way out of a very difficult problem. It suffers, however, from the fact that we find nothing about this third state either in Scripture or the earliest period of the Fathers.

The lively conviction of the universal saving will of God as well as of the suffering involved in the eternal deprivation of the vision of God, suffering that has not been deserved by the individual, has led in recent theology to many attempts to discover a possibility of salvation for little children who die without baptism. Theologians have made use of the view that God's power is not tied to the visible sacraments. The Holy Spirit blows where it will. The almighty and incomprehensible love of God knows many ways by which it can lead man to salvation.

Two principles can be brought into the discussion, namely the christocentric nature of the whole of human history and the element of representation. The Church as such has a representative function; this is a fundamental idea of Scripture. But also individual people who believe in Christ have a representative function, e.g. believing parents in regard to their children. Under these aspects we could regard a representative desire for baptism by the Church or by the parents as effective for salvation. Saving power is ascribed to the representative desire of the parents by Gregory of Nyssa, by the theologians of early scholasticism, by Bonaventure, Durandus, John Gerson, Klee, and many modern theologians. (It was pointed out by Herman Schell that the death of such a child can be regarded as a quasi-sacrament. But when Schell's *Dogmatics* was put on the Index this view was described as *audacior* and *temerarius modus loquendi*.) Some theologians assume that God so enlightens the child at the moment of death that he is given the possibility of choosing between a life of fellowship with God and a life of self-love, remote from God. Others (e.g., P. Schuler) hold that little children who die unbaptized are presented with the final decision at the general resurrection of the dead.

Perhaps we can find an approach to the solution from the article of faith that the soul is the structural law of the body. In view of the close connection between body and soul, the difficult question is raised, to which there is no satisfactory answer, of how it is possible for the spirit separated from the body after death to perform mental functions without the body, including those of the highest intensity, namely the vision of God. One might say that in the process of death the soul practices functioning without the body. In this view death is not an instantaneous event, but a process in which the soul detaches itself more and more from the body and develops its non-somatic functions increasingly. A moment could arrive when it acquired the capacity to make mental decisions without the bodily organ, the brain. At any rate, this view offers no greater difficulty than that of the survival of the bodiless soul before the general resurrection, even if no such cogent reasons can be offered for its validity as for that of the latter. However one judges these theological attempts at an explanation, there is no doubt that the fate of little children who die unbaptized is taken up into the incomprehensible mystery of the divine saving love. They too are drawn into the universal movement of salvation towards Christ as the risen Lord and, through him, to God.

THE MINISTER OF BAPTISM

The invisible chief minister of baptism is Jesus Christ, the head of the Church. Baptism is then also the concrete form of Jesus Christ's saving presence made actual here and now. Insofar as baptism is incorporation in the hierarchically ordered body of Jesus Christ, the people of God, and always in the form of the local Church, it is appropriate that the representative of the local Church should administer baptism. In conferring baptism, he takes the candidate into the local community of Christ. Accordingly, the regular minister of baptism is the parish priest. However, the priest is the assistant of the bishop, subject in his saving work to the direction of the bishop of the diocese which includes the smaller local community. Thus, inasmuch as the priest is the representative of the bishop in the parish of which he is in charge, it is ultimately the bishop who is the regular minister of baptism. In the representative of the local community, the person baptized is received by the community itself. The community accepts him in a brotherly spirit as someone who from now on belongs to it.

The idea of baptism as an act of the community lies behind Ignatius of Antioch's statement that to baptize without the bishop is not permissible *(Letter to the Smyrnians,* 8,2). According to the law in force today, the bishop and the parish priest are the regular ministers of baptism, with the deacon as the exceptional minister.

This rule, which is based on the significance of baptism as an act of reception into the community, does not affect the fact that in case of necessity or emergency, any baptized person, or even an unbaptized person, can administer baptism. On this subject, however, we have nothing more than hints in Scripture, although we do have them. The three thousand people baptized at the first Pentecost could not all have been baptized by the apostles alone. Perhaps Paul received baptism from the disciple Ananias (Acts 9,10-18). We learn that Paul *had* the family of the Centurion Cornelius baptized (Acts 10,48). Paul even seems to be glad that in Corinth he baptized nobody except Crispus and Gaius and the household of Stephanas, so that no one could boast of having been baptized by Paul. Christ sent him not to baptize but to proclaim the gospel (1 Cor. 1,14-17).

This statement by the apostle Paul is in accordance with the view expressed by the Second Vatican Council that the primary task of the bishop and the priest is the proclamation of the gospel of salvation. When a baptized person who is not a priest baptizes someone else, he is representing the Church community. It is remarkable, however, that even an unbaptized person can administer baptism. This view can be defended by pointing to the christocentric nature of history, i.e. the ordering of every man towards Christ. It is, of course, a necessary prerequisite that the person baptizing has the intention of performing a Christian sign (DS 1611). This includes the idea that he desires to assist the recipient of baptism in becoming part of the community of Christ.

THE RECIPIENT OF BAPTISM

As far as the recipient of baptism is concerned, the ordering of every man towards Jesus Christ makes it possible for everyone to receive baptism. In Scripture there is no baptism that is not preceded by faith. In particular, the two baptismal texts in Matthew and Mark, as well as the epistles of Paul, testify to the close connection between faith and baptism (cf. Gal. 3,26f.; Col. 2,12; Acts 2,38). Adults had to profess their faith before they were baptized. This was their answer to the proclamation. The profession of faith was regarded as a liturgical act which became part of the initiation rite of baptism (cf., e.g., Rom. 10,10f.; 13,11; 16,25; 1 Cor. 15,12; Phil. 2,10f.; 1 Jn. 4,1ff. and 15; Acts 8,37; Rom. 4,25; Eph. 5,14; 1 Pet. 3,18.22). For a long time the form of the profession was an answer to the questions on faith that were asked of those seeking baptism. The community had to make sure that the attitude of mind of the baptismal candidate fitted him to be received into the community of faith. In Scripture we find elements of fixed formulae for the profession of faith (Rom. 10,9; Acts 8,37; perhaps also Rom. 4,25; Eph. 5,14; 1 Pet. 3,18.22).

We have no explicit scriptural evidence for infant baptism, but we may assume that children were not excluded when whole families were baptized (Acts 10,44-48; 16,15; 16,33; 1 Cor. 1,16). Baptism has taken the place of the circumcision of the Old Testament (Col. 2,11). Perhaps Peter's sermon after the giving of the Holy Spirit is evidence of infant baptism. He says that the Holy Spirit is promised not only to his listeners but also to their children (Acts 2,38f.). Although the order given in Scripture is: the proclamation, hearing it, believing it, being baptized, and being introduced into the life of baptism, we have evidence from tradition that infants were baptized.

The earliest clear evidence of infant baptism occurs at the beginning of the third century. (Whether it was performed during the second century has been the subject of lively debate.) Tertullian (about 230) approves of the baptism of babies. Around 215 the Ordo ascribed to Hippolytus distinguishes between the baptism of adults, of children, and of babies. According to Origen, the practice of baptizing infants was apostolic. And as we remarked above, at the time of Augustine, infant baptism was such a fixed element of tradition that he thought he could use the practice of it to prove the fact of original sin.

In opposition to the Anabaptists the Council of Trent rejected the view that young children cannot be regarded, after the reception of baptism, as among believers and hence should be baptized again when they reach the years of discretion—or even that it would be better not to baptize children at all (DS 1626). It also rejected the opinion of Erasmus of Rotterdam that children who had been baptized should be asked at a riper age whether they wanted to confirm what their godparents had promised in their name at baptism. Infant baptism can be understood only if an objective order of salvation, intended by God for all men, is recognized. It is also necessary to accept the principle of representation, whether it is representation by the Church itself or by the parents of the children. Even if, contrary to the Church's tradition, one were to regard infant baptism as not rendered necessary by original sin, it would still have a profound salvific meaning in that it creates a "living" community with Christ, brings about incorporation in him and in the Church and thus in the dynamic movement towards the future.

◄ 8

Confirmation

BAPTISM AND CONFIRMATION

Baptism and confirmation taken together constitute the full initiation rite or ceremony of acceptance into the Church. To separate them by connecting one with the person of Christ and the other with the Holy Spirit is to make a false distinction between them. They are not to be related to each other by drawing an analogy between them and the two mysteries of Easter and Pentecost and maintaining that baptism confers a share in the life of the risen Christ and confirmation a share in that of the Holy Spirit. On the contrary, *all* sacraments, baptism and confirmation included, are to be seen and understood in the light of what Easter and Pentecost signify as a whole, because they are an expression of the life of the Church which is itself founded on and determined by these mysteries. The descent of the Holy Spirit on the day of Pentecost ushers in the age of the efficacy of the sacraments, an age which is to last until Christ himself returns. Of course, Christ is still present, with the Holy Spirit, in both the Church as a whole and in each of its individual members. Our connection with Christ always takes the form of a union with the Holy Spirit. The significance attached to confirmation is not to be arrived at by underestimating the importance of baptism, nor is confirmation to be construed as the coming-of-age of those who have been baptized. This has already taken place at baptism. The idea that baptism is a children's sacrament and confirmation a sacrament for those who have reached maturity probably owes its origin more to the introduction of infant baptism at a particular moment in history than to any conclusion arrived at by theological reasoning. It has no foundation in the theology of the New Testament, the Church Fathers, or the Middle Ages. In fact, it contradicts the whole testimony of both the Scriptures and the Church Fathers regarding the efficacy of baptism.

That the Holy Spirit is received with the sacrament of baptism is a clear and indisputable fact. This is stated quite unambiguously by Peter in his Pentecostal sermon. For Paul it follows automatically that those who have been baptized are in possession of the Spirit (cf. Acts 2,38). There is, however, a difference between baptism and confirmation which corresponds to a difference within the realm of what is worked by the Spirit, and this distinction becomes clear from a reading of the first epistle to the Christian community at Corinth, according to which the Spirit works in various ways (cf. 1 Cor. 12). The question therefore arises as to what we are to understand by the working of a spirit which is different from that received at baptism inasmuch as it is conferred by means of a separate sacrament.

SCRIPTURE, FATHERS, TEACHING OF THE CHURCH

The Scriptures do little more than hint at an answer to this question. Sufficient, however, for the development of a doctrine of confirmation as distinct from that of baptism was the account to be found in the Acts of the Apostles, that above and beyond the Spirit conferred at baptism those who were united with Christ in the Holy Spirit received a further gift of spiritual power. There then remained the task of developing the distinction between baptism and confirmation until it could be made the subject of the Church's teaching and proclamation. Even the conferring of spiritual gifts above and beyond those received at baptism is vouched for by signs which made their power manifest. When Philip the deacon preached the message of salvation of the kingdom of heaven to the men and women in Samaria, they accepted his teaching and received baptism; and joy, that gift of the Spirit which the Scriptures never tire of mentioning, filled their hearts (cf. Acts 8,39). There was still thought to be something lacking, however, for when news of this event reached Jerusalem the apostles despatched Peter and John to Samaria. On their arrival they said prayers for the new converts and asked that they should receive the Holy Spirit, which had so far not descended on any of them. They had only been baptized in the name of the Lord Jesus. The apostles then laid their hands on them, and the converts received the Holy Spirit (cf. Acts 8,4-17).

Something similar happened in Ephesus, according to this account in the Acts of the Apostles:

While Apollos was at Corinth, Paul travelled through the inland regions till he came to Ephesus. There he found a number of converts, to whom he said: "Did you receive the Holy Spirit when you became believers?" "No," they replied, "we have not even heard that there is a Holy Spirit." He said, "Then what baptism were you given?" "John's baptism," they answered. Paul then said, "The baptism that John gave was a baptism in token of repentance, and he told the people to put their trust in one who was to come after him, that is, in Jesus." On hearing this they were baptized into the name of the Lord Jesus; and when Paul had laid his hands on them, the Holy Spirit came upon them and they spoke in tongues of ecstasy and prophesied. Altogether they were about a dozen men. (Acts 19,1-7)

In these accounts of the conferring of the Spirit by the laying-on of hands, reference is obviously being made to a well-known institution by which the process of becoming a Christian was completed. Even though from a purely literal reading they would seem to attribute the conferring of the Spirit exclusively to a laying-on of hands, it would be to misinterpret them entirely if we were to assume that they were denying the efficacy of the Spirit received at baptism (cf. Acts 2,38; 1 Cor. 12,13, etc.). In order to do justice to them we must regard them as testimonies to the workings of the Spirit which were considered to be of a very special kind. That they *were* considered as such may be gathered from the story about Simon the magician, who was so impressed by what he saw that he wished to acquire for himself the gift of conferring the Spirit by this means, and actually offered the apostles money in the hope that they would transmit to him the power they possessed (Acts 8,7-19).

It is clear from these accounts that the Spirit conferred by the laying-on of hands surpasses in its efficacy that which is received at baptism. It gave the disciples on whom it was bestowed added strength for bearing witness to their faith (cf. Lk. 24,19; Acts 1,8), a deeper understanding of what this faith meant, and a more firmly founded belief in it (cf. Jn. 14,26; 16,13). In the Epistle to the Hebrews the laying-on of hands is considered alongside baptism, the resurrection, and the last judgment as belonging to the fundamental principles of Christian doctrine (cf. Heb. 6,2).

In the age of the Church Fathers there is ample testimony to the laying-on of hands and also to anointing, as a ceremony that followed immediately upon baptism. However, it is not always easy to determine whether this was simply part of the baptismal rite or whether it constituted a separate sacrament. In general, the latter may well have been the case.

More than a thousand years were to elapse before the idea that confirmation was a sacrament in its own right was fully realized. In fact, it was not clearly arrived at until the twelfth century. The Reformers rejected the idea of confirmation as a separate sacrament, interpreting it as simply a confirmation of the sacrament of baptism. The Church, however, had already defined it as a sacrament in its own right at the Council of Florence, and in the ecclesiastical disputes with the Reformers which followed soon after this council the sacramental nature of the confirmation rite was given particular stress (cf. DS 215, 789, 793, 860, 1259, 1317, 1601, 1609, 1628ff., 1777).

THE SIGN

In Scripture confirmation is administered by the sacramental actions of the laying-on of hands and calling upon the Holy Spirit to descend from heaven. There is no mention of the practice of anointing. This is all the more surprising because the conferring of the Spirit is frequently referred to as an anointing (cf. 1 Jn. 2,27;

2 Cor. 1,21; Lk. 4,18). In particular, Christ is spoken of as being anointed with the Holy Spirit.

In the post-apostolic age, at the beginning of the third century, there is evidence for both the saying of prayers and the laying-on of hands, and in the Western Church right up to the fifth century confirmation was administered by these same means, but with the addition that the sign of the cross was made. Hippolytus of Rome provides an exception, inasmuch as he employed not only the laying-on of hands and the sign of the cross but also the act of anointing. In this respect he was probably influenced by the theology which had developed in Alexandria, where all three acts had been combined and treated as one at an early date. Theophilus of Antioch is the first to testify to the practice of anointing in the Eastern Church (cf. *ad Autolicum,* 1,12), and the testimonies of the Alexandrians, Clement and Origen, follow soon afterwards. During the time of Cyril of Jerusalem anointing took precedence over the laying-on of hands and actually thrust it into the background. Even in the Western Church, the practice of anointing on the forehead grew in importance from the fifth century onwards. Early scholasticism attempted to bring about a synthesis by declaring that the laying-on of hands was already comprehended in the anointing of the forehead. Pope Benedict XIV (1740-1758) was the first to stress anew the importance of the laying-on of hands as an act in its own right. Today theologians in general support the view that the outward sign of the act of confirmation consists as much in the anointing *together with* the accompanying act of the laying-on of hands as in the accompanying act of prayer. It is true, however, that in the Eastern Orthodox Church the practice of the laying-on of hands as part of the administrative rite is losing its importance (cf. DS 793).

The inclusion of the anointing with oil as a symbolic act in the performance of the sacrament may be claimed to have a scriptural foundation insofar as the plenary pouring forth of the Spirit is described in the New Testament as a holy anointing. Kings, and also priests and prophets, were anointed with oil to signify that they were men to whom the gifts of the Spirit were assumed to be vouchsafed in a specially high measure. It is also probable that the widespread use of oil for anointing in classical antiquity

contributed to the adoption of the symbolic act of anointing which
we find implicitly mentioned in Scripture. The practice was particularly suitable for making clear to all those believers who
lived in the Hellenistic world, and were acquainted with its customs
and modes of thought, the saving nature of the act of confirmation.
As a Christian rite, however, it naturally acquired a meaning and
significance quite different from that attributed to its use in the
pagan world. The consecration of oil for purposes of anointing
dates from the very earliest times. It is mentioned in Cyprian as
being an ancient custom of the Church. The consecration was
performed by the bishop, and in many cases was attended with
the most solemn ceremonies.

CONFIRMATION AND SALVATION

On the question of the saving nature of confirmation, it is generally
agreed that confirmation is the completion of baptism. The question is whether this completion is only an intensification of the
saving gifts received in baptism or whether it signifies another
orientation of these saving gifts. It is clear that confirmation
brings about an increase of sanctifying grace, i.e. it makes the
baptized person more like the triune God. If, however, this saving
effect were the important thing, it would be hard to understand
why a separate sacrament is necessary for it. There must be a
new element involved, some new effect of grace (sacramental
grace). We can move a step further by analyzing an expression
that was popular at the time of the Church Fathers, namely the
word "sealing." In confirmation the baptized person is "sealed"
with the Holy Spirit. A special mark is conferred on him and,
like the mark of baptism, it is indelible (DS 1628f.). It has both
a christological and an ecclesiological element and is a further
development of the mark conferred in baptism. It signifies a new
position in the Church and at the same time a new resemblance
to Christ.

The christological and ecclesiological orientation of this mark
of the Church involves special rights and special obligations. It is
here that we can see most clearly the special nature of confirmation

as distinct from baptism. It is the nature of the mark, in particular, that shows the place of baptism in the life of the Church and the life of the individual. With regard to this point, we can turn to Thomas Aquinas, who quotes with approval a statement by Rhabanus Maurus to the effect that in confirmation the baptized person receives the Holy Spirit in order to be given the strength to bear witness to Christ. The nature of the struggle against evil is determined by the nature of the struggle of Christ, to whom a resemblance is produced in the confirmed person. Christ conquered the sin of the world through his sacrifice even unto death. The same conclusion is to be drawn from the fact that the sealing with the Holy Spirit produces a likeness to Christ, for sealing with the Holy Spirit is sealing with love. At the same time, the mark of Christ received in confirmation indicates the sphere into which the confirmed person is called: he is made like Christ with respect to Christ's challenge to evil before the whole world through his death on the cross—that expiatory death which conquered sin and created newness of life.

It is entirely incorrect, as we have said, to regard confirmation as the sacrament of maturity, for the implication would then be that baptism was the sacrament of immaturity. This view clearly contradicts the teaching of Paul: baptized persons are also mature, and he exhorts them to conduct themselves as adults. However, confirmation does give a particular orientation to the man who believes in Christ: it gives him both the power and the commitment to hold fast to his faith in Christ in the midst of all life's hazards, the temptations and threats arising both from within and from without. This means that confirmation emphasizes strongly and clearly the fact that the Christian's life is lived within a particular situation. Confirmation is, in a special way, the sacrament of situation ethics—not of an ethics that neglects the commands of God but of one that involves the insight and energy necessary to the right application of those commands in complicated situations of personal life and of history, situations which sometimes cannot be grasped in all their dimensions and from which there seems no way out. The Holy Spirit leads a man to grasp what is essential to his Christian life in a situation which seems dominated by sin and evil as if by a mysterious power. Thus confirmation is the sacrament of encouragement, of fidelity to one's faith, to the degree that a man is ready to seal his witness to Christ with death.

It is in this way that we can understand the increase of sanctifying grace that confirmation gives. Every Christian must prove his Christian life in the world and endeavor to impose on that world a form deriving from his Christian faith; or rather, he must make a contribution towards establishing in the world an order worthy of man. The way to perfection leads through the midst of the world, not away from it. To the Christian who is confirmed special inner potentialities are given for the accomplishment of those undertakings which are incumbent on every baptized Christian. They consist in an ability to discern the essentials of a particular situation in the world, and in addition a capacity and a readiness to respond to the challenge of the situation, however difficult or unusual it is. In terms of the present time, we could say that the confirmed Christian has the capacity and the responsibility of collaborating in the transformation of the world through that insight and energy which will make its technical achievements a means of bringing about an order worthy of human beings, instead of a means of man's destruction; which, through the force of initiative and a knowledge of social conditions, undeterred by the popular opinions of the day, will set itself in opposition to error, ignorance, tyranny, anxiety, cowardice, facile solutions, indifference, irresponsibility, in coming to grips with the world problems of hunger, unemployment, and war. Of course, the individual fulfills these tasks first of all within his own particular situation, but at the same time he is serving the Church of God itself, not only the local Church but also the whole Church. It is, after all, the Church's mission increasingly to overcome the destructive powers of the world through its word and through its signs and to call forth the truly human forces of fraternal love, willing service, and self-sacrifice.

This saving significance of confirmation helps us to answer the question whether it is necessary. If a person failed to receive it out of pure indifference, it would amount to despising a sign of salvation.

THE MINISTER OF CONFIRMATION

The ecclesiological significance of confirmation indicates that the regular minister of it is the bishop (Council of Trent, 7th session, canon 3, DS 1630; cf. DS 215, 608, 794, 1318). However, the Council of Trent, out of consideration for the Eastern Churches, left the question open in one sense: it rejected only the view that the bishop was not the regular minister of confirmation, i.e. that the bishops had only the same power to confirm as priests (DS 1630).

There is evidence for this in Scripture—as, for example, when it is said that those baptized in Samaria by Philip were confirmed by John and Peter, not by Philip himself (Acts 8,14f.). Similarly, it was Paul who in Ephesus confirmed those baptized by others (Acts 19,4f.).

In the earliest times, baptism and confirmation were administered on the same occasion by the bishop. When baptism became separated from confirmation and was administered by priests, the Western Church reserved confirmation to the bishop. The reason for this is that the public character of the Church is represented in the bishop, and confirmation is the sacrament of completion and of fearless testimony to Christ before the world.

From the fourth century onwards, priests appear as the regular ministers of confirmation in the Eastern Church. The priest performs the confirmation immediately after baptism. However, the oil of confirmation—obviously the most important element for the Eastern Church—is consecrated by the bishop (Serapion of Thmuis).

In the Western Church also confirmation was sometimes, on special authority of the pope, performed by simple priests; and the Spanish bishops allowed priests to confirm in exceptional cases (cf. First Council of Toledo). Today canon law allows certain priests the right to confirm in view of their particular situations and special pastoral tasks. A papal decree of September 14, 1946, gives authority to all parish priests and all those vicars and deputies who have full priestly rights to administer an emergency confirmation to mortally sick members of the faithful within their parish if a bishop is not available. The reason for this permission given by the Church is not far to seek. In death a man is robbed of all power of self-disposal; hence death involves an invitation to man to hand himself over unreservedly in readiness and obedience to God. Confirmation confers a special inner strengthening to help the mortally ill person to overcome human selfishness and self-love.

In order to understand the power of priests to confirm, we must consider the following: as we saw in Volume IV of this work, the power of orders (consecrating power) and the power of jurisdiction (pastoral power) are the two expressions of the one missionary authority Christ gave the Church which have emerged in history. Despite their division, however, the two powers remained closely connected, so that it is not possible for one to be effective without the other. In the case of individual sacraments, the place of the Church's power of jurisdiction is especially clear. Baptism, for example, imparts to the baptized person important rights in the Church. It makes him a member of it and hence gives him all the rights of a member of the Church except where their exercise is restricted. Thus although anyone can baptize in an emergency, it is understandable that the Church has laid down particular rules for the regular administering of baptism. Confirmation is closely connected with baptism in that it is its completion and hence is subject to rules that serve the life of the community.

There is also the following point to be made. The Church is aware of the authority and responsibility imparted to it by Christ to serve the tasks that Christ has set it. It can impart the one missionary authority in different degrees of intensity—the authority of a deacon, that of a priest, or that of a bishop. The extent of the bishop's authority was established, in its essentials, by Christ. All powers can be exercised only in the name of the Church as the representative of Christ. The Church can set up particular conditions for the performance of the sacraments, because all its sacraments are expressions of its life. These prescriptions differ for the individual sacraments according to their necessity and importance for the fulfillment of the Church's mission and for salvation. The particular situation of the individual member of the Church or the general world situation can result in the Church, on its own authority, making it easier to receive confirmation and therefore giving to priests who are not bishops the authority to administer it. In this case the authority to confirm is an expression both of the Church's power to consecrate and of its pastoral authority.

Confirmation in the Eastern Church by priests who are not bishops has greatly exercised Western theologians. It has been thought, however, that a solution can be found in the view that there is tacit papal authority for this.

◂ 9

Ordination to the Priesthood

THE SACRAMENT OF DIFFERENTIATION

Baptism and confirmation open the way into the people of God. The ordination of priests is the sacrament of differentiation within the people of God. For the ordering of its life, different kinds of services are necessary which cannot be done by all members of the people in the same way: there are tasks whose fulfillment requires special authority. We have discussed this in the ecclesiological parts of this work.

We have already discussed the division of the Church's authority into the power of orders and the power of jurisdiction. Here our concern will not be with the factuality of these powers; we shall merely consider in what way they are acquired, namely through sacramental ordination and canonically imparted mission. However, we shall not be treating the latter in this context. As for sacramental ordination, we have already made a number of fundamental points concerning it, but for the sake of the systematic whole we shall reconsider the relevant points here and elaborate them.

It is fundamental to the understanding of the people of God to realize that it exists as the Body of Christ. This means that it has a share in the nature and the tasks of Christ, and hence the whole people has a priestly quality. But although the share in the priestly, prophetic, and royal task of Christ is common to all members of his people, there is apart from this shared quality a special sharing in the priesthood of Christ, namely that of the bishops, the priests, and the deacons. This special sharing is imparted through a special sacred rite. It is not difficult to understand why it is imparted by an act of consecration, and not simply by a decree of the Church. For if the whole Church is sacramental in nature, then it is clear that those acts which are of particular importance for its life bear within themselves in a particular way the Church's basic sacramental character.

THE THREE STAGES

The sacrament of priestly ordination is formally different from all the other sacraments in that it is performed in three stages. We distinguish the consecration of a bishop, the consecration of a priest, and the consecration of a deacon, into which the one sacrament of ordination is articulated. These successive stages also indicate that there is an order of importance: the norm and criterion of the whole sacrament of ordination is the consecration of a bishop. While in the Middle Ages many theologians thought that the consecration of a bishop was only a sacramental and that it was the consecration of a priest, in a narrower sense, that was the real sacrament of ordination, we have only to look at the early apostolic Church, the theology of the Church Fathers, the liturgy of the Church, and the duties incumbent on a bishop to see that if ordination is a sacrament at all, this character must be ascribed primarily to the consecration of a bishop. The other view, however, which was often expressed in the Middle Ages, was justified by the argument that ordination primarily transmitted the power to consecrate the elements of the celebration of the eucharist and that any simple priest could do this. It was overlooked that it is the bishop's task to impart to members of God's people the power to consecrate; that, further, the priest is entitled to carry out his priestly functions only by the bishop's authority; and, finally, that the office of the priest is a development from the episcopal office that alone existed in the early Church.

Hence the Second Vatican Council rightly defined the sacramentality of the consecration of a bishop. The Council of Trent had taught that a priest was subject to a bishop, but left open the question of the sacramentality of episcopal consecration. Through the ordination of priests the bishop is able to preserve the capacity of the Church to celebrate the eucharist, and he has to see that it is celebrated properly in that part of the Church which is under his leadership. The bishop is the indispensable condition for the celebration of that sacrament in which the unity of the Church is especially grounded.

The consecration of priests shares in the sacramentality of the consecration of a bishop in that it bestows a part of the total authority held by the bishop.

That the diaconate is also imparted by means of a sacramental rite is seen from the way it was given in the scriptural accounts and in the early Church. The same sign was used as that for the consecration of bishops and priests: the laying-on of hands and prayer.

Apart from the three stages of ordination attested in Scripture, further offices developed in the course of time: subdeacon, acolyte, exorcist, doorkeeper, lector. They represented special tasks and today the orders of subdeacon, acolyte, exorcist, door-keeper, and lector have been suppressed or radically revised. By an indult of September 14, 1972, Pope Paul VI abolished the orders of porter, exorcist, and subdeacon. The indult went on to say that laymen as well as clerical candidates were to be installed rather than ordained in the ministries of acolyte and lector.

THE EXTERNAL SIGN

The external sign is in all cases the laying-on of hands and prayer, but this should not prevent us from seeing that different stages of ordination are involved; for we must take account not only of the external sign but of the intention of the particular conse-cration. As we have already seen, the sign must be understood not merely in its material content but also in a sense that is intended, and must be interpreted, in faith. Jesus himself laid nothing down concerning the external sign, but we learn from the pastoral epistles that the consecration of a bishop was imparted through the laying-on of hands and prayer (1 Tim. 4,14; 2 Tim. 1,6). In the time of the Church Fathers we often hear of anointing as well.

The choice of the laying-on of hands and prayer as the external sign in apostolic times was in accordance with a practice familiar to the Old Testament and to the Jews. The laying-on of hands was also very important outside the Bible, both in the secular sphere and in that of religious ritual. In the Old Testament we find it chiefly in the initiation of the Levites. When someone else was to lead the people of God into the land of Canaan in place of Moses, namely Joshua, this charge was committed to him through the laying-on of hands (Num. 27,18ff.; 22f.; Deut. 34,8). Following this Old Testament practice, we find in later Judaism the institution of the giving of an office through the laying-on of hands. This was always one unique, unrepeatable authorization. Hence the apostles could feel all the more justified in passing on the responsibilities and authority they had received from Christ to their successors by means of this rite with which they were familiar, because Christ himself used an Old Testament institution, namely that of the *shaliach,* in order to impart his mission to the apostles. Although he simply called his apostles to him by name and sent them out to their tasks, it is still probable that these men whom he had appointed his *sheluchim* used a practice connected with this institution in order themselves to entrust others with the tasks of the Church.

The anointing of the hands, which came in gradually from the eighth century onwards, became a generally adopted element of the consecrating rite. Until the twelfth century it was regarded as a separate form of consecration. The handing over of the Church's instruments, which probably developed from the Gallican mode of conferring minor orders and was influenced by the Germanic legal form of granting possession in feudalism, developed in the ninth century and was initially used by some bishops to demonstrate the powers imparted in the consecration. These two elements soon became so prominent that in the thirteenth century they were widely regarded as the most important part of the action.

For a long time there was a lively theological discussion about whether the anointing and the handing over of the instruments were essential parts of the external sign. They were prescribed by the Church, but that still did not decide the question (cf. DS 1765, 1326).

Pope Pius XII removed all doubt and obscurity when he declared, in the Apostolic Constitution of November 30, 1947:

> By virtue of our supreme apostolic authority and from certain knowledge we declare and, should it be necessary, ordain that the matter of the sacred consecration of deacons, priests and bishops is solely the laying-on of hands. Similarly, the only form consists of the words that determine the meaning of the performance of this matter, the words from which the sacramental effects—namely the authority imparted through the consecration and the grace of the Holy Spirit— are clearly specified and that are understood and used by the Church as such. Accordingly . . . we pronounce . . . and ordain, in case there has ever been a legally valid ordinance to the contrary: the handing over of the instruments is, at least from now on, not necessary for the validity of the sacred consecration of a deacon, priest or bishop.

In the Eastern Churches to the present day, ordination is generally performed only through the laying-on of hands and prayer, not through the handing over of the implements.

THE MINISTER

According to what we know of the early Church, the minister of the sacrament of ordination is always the bishop (1 Tim. 3,1-13; 4,14; 5,22; 2 Tim. 1,6; Tit. 1,5-9). In the *Apostolic Constitutions* (I,27), from the end of the fourth century, we read:

> The bishop is consecrated by two or three bishops through the laying-on of hands . . . . The bishop blesses, but is not blessed. He lays on his hands and sacrifices. He receives the blessings from bishops, but never from a priest. The bishop dismisses any cleric who deserves to be dismissed, but not the bishop, for he cannot do that by himself. The priest blesses and is blessed; he receives the blessings from the bishop and from another priest, which is why he gives his blessing to the other priest. He lays on his hands, but does not consecrate; he

does not dismiss, but he excommunicates those who are subordinate to him if they deserve such punishment.

(Cf. also the *Apostolic Canons,* 1.) According to the Council of Trent, the consecrated bishop is the regular minister of ordination in all its stages (23d session, canon 7, DS 1777). Canon law requires the presence of three bishops for the consecration of a bishop. For the validity of the consecration only one is necessary.

Simple priests who have received the authority by law or by special permission can be the extraordinary ministers of particular orders, especially of minor orders. In the Middle Ages we some-times find the view that the pope can empower priests to consecrate deacons and other priests. On February 1, 1400, Pope Boniface IX gave the abbot of St. Osyth Priory in Essex and his successors—that is, priests—permission to consecrate members of his monastery as deacons and priests; but after three years he withdrew this permission. If this incident is not to be regarded as just an error on the pope's part, later retracted, we could explain what he did by saying that in priestly ordination the priest receives the power to ordain, but that because of an ordinance based on the Church's authority he is not able to exercise it. In other words, the papal permission actualized what was in fact imparted in the priestly ordination. The imparting of priestly ordination, then, would appear—like the sacrament of penance—as a combination of consecrating power and pastoral authority. Without the pastoral authority which only the pope can bestow, the priest is unable to realize this combination.

The laying-on of hands, which the priests present at the ordina-tion do together with the bishop (the presbyterium, the body of priests) is explained by Thomas Aquinas as a sign of the fullness of grace that is called down on the ordinand. There is nothing to prevent seeing this ancient custom, which is attested in the pastoral epistles, as meaning that simple priests can never perform an ordination without the bishop, but that their laying-on of hands has an integrating function. According to this view, the bishop speaks the sacramental form as the leader of the presby-terium and in the name of all the priests present, but their coopera-tion is neither sufficient nor necessary by itself. It can, however, be an efficacious accompaniment to the bishop's action.

In the Eastern Churches also ordination is performed by the bishop. Its validity has never been doubted. Anglican orders were declared invalid by Leo XIII in the decree *Apostolicae Curae* of September 13, 1896, because of the abbreviation of the form of consecration and the imperfect intention, which is closely bound up with the form. It seems, however, that a re-examination of this question is due.

THE RECIPIENT

As for the recipient of the sacrament of ordination, canon law (Canon 9) stipulates that only male baptized persons can receive the sacrament. In the whole history of the Church there have been no female priests, although they are well-known outside Christianity. This is all the more remarkable in view of the fact that women play a large part in the gospel, from the mother of the Lord to Mary Magdalene, who was the first witness of Christ's resurrection, so that for a long time she was called in Church tradition the *apostola apostolorum*. The low social and cultural position of women at that time makes the attitude of Jesus to women all the more notable. Although he made no woman one of his apostles, he opened the way to the kingdom of God for men and women alike. It was to a woman, namely Martha, that, according to St. John's Gospel, he revealed, in a way both profound and comprehensive, the saving mystery of his life for all men (Jn. 11,25). Martha's answer reminds us in some sense of Peter's response (Jn. 11,27 and Mt. 16,16). Women were also present when Jesus performed the great saving action of his death on Golgotha (Mt. 27,55f.; Jn. 19,25). They were the first to come to the empty grave of the Lord (Mt. 28,1-10; Mk. 16,6-8; Lk. 24,1-11; Jn. 20,1f.; 11-18). According to St. John, the women who had come with Jesus from Galilee told the eleven and everyone else of their experience of the empty tomb. Luke says explicitly that it was Mary Magdalene, John and Mary, the Mother of James, and with them the others, who told the apostles. It is true that what the women told them seemed to them like idle talk—this is understandable, not only because of the overwhelming nature of what they said but also because of the status of women at that time—but what they said was still true. Even if the apostles were the foundation of the hierarchic structure of the Church, it cannot be denied that the most important fact of Christianity was first revealed to women and passed on from women to the apostles. This retains its importance even when we know that it was primarily through the appearances of the Lord to themselves that the apostles gained their faith in the risen Christ.

It is clear, at any rate, that women were made part of the proclamation. According to Acts, the 120 believers in Christ who were gathered together in prayer after his ascension were all involved in the election of a new apostle to replace Judas. Among those present there were women, in particular Mary, the mother of Jesus. According to the context of Acts, they also seem to have voted (Acts 1,14.15). In any case, the Holy Spirit was poured out over all the members of the new people of God, both men and women without distinction (Acts 2,17f.). Paul says something worthy of note on the subject in Romans. He recommends Phoebe and says that she has worked as a deacon. He also sends greetings to Prisca and Aquila and calls these women his fellow workers in Christ (Rom. 16,1.3). There is a remarkable scene recounted in chapter 18 of Acts. There we read that a Jew from Alexandria called Apollos had come to Ephesus. He was a man well-versed in Scripture, instructed, as we read, in the way of the Lord and teaching with a fervent spirit and devotion concerning Jesus, although he had only the baptism of John. When Prisca and Aquila heard him, they invited him to their house and explained the way of the Lord further to him. Here, then, women took it upon themselves to introduce more fully into the mystery of the Lord someone who was obviously theologically interested and to some degree an educated disciple and preacher of Jesus (Acts 18,23-26).

Moreover, the women mentioned among the deacons in 1 Tim. 3,11 must have been deaconesses, in some sense a counterpart to the deacons. Paul lays down particular rules for them. It is doubtful if they are identical with the widows, for whom Paul also lays down particular rules (1 Tim. 5,3-16). At any rate, there are widows who need the help of the community, those who can live without support, and those who are in the service of the community.

It seems that the early Church offered a wide area of service to women. There were two particular forms of this service, namely private instruction at home and prayer in the Church assemblies. We find evidence of the latter in Acts 21,9. Here we read that Philip, one of the seven, had four daughters, virgins who had the gift of prophecy. Prophecy is a charism, which according to the promises of the Old Testament and the preaching of Peter was to come upon all members of the people of God after the descent of the Holy Spirit. Prophecy took place within the Church assembly and had the significance of a prayer. Women were not allowed to teach in the assemblies (1 Cor. 14,34; 11,16; 1 Tim. 2,11.12). This would indeed have been a scandalous thing, given the social and cultural views of the time. On the other hand, however, despite these prohibitions by Paul, he can still say that Prisca and Aquila were his fellow workers.

In the post-apostolic age also deaconesses (often identical with widows) performed many tasks in the community: helping in the baptism of adult women; instructing women in the faith; acting as emissaries between the bishop and women, and to the women who lived in pagan surroundings or could not attend the eucharist because of sickness or age; the care of the poor and the sick. In the third century, in Syria, the office of deaconess was put on a legal basis. At the same time its tasks were extended, especially in the liturgy (the anointing of women in baptism, acting as door-keeper). In the general intercessions, the reception of communion, the order of consecration, the deaconesses follow the deacons. They also have permission to take communion to sick women (the *Testament of Our Lord Jesus Christ,* 2,26). Nevertheless they were not until the middle of the fourth century regarded as members of the clergy. This follows from Canon 19 of the Council of Nicaea (325). The picture changes, however, by the end of the fourth century. From then on, deaconesses receive a consecration that is a counterpart to the consecration of deacons. According to the *Apostolic Constitutions* (19,20), the consecration of deaconesses is performed in the same way as that of deacons, namely through the laying-on of hands and prayer. This shows that deaconesses were regarded as part of the clergy. But the way in which their duties are described shows that the consecration of deaconesses was regarded as among the minor orders. It does seem, however, to have been at the head of these, in view of the fact that the task of the deaconesses is discussed immediately after that of the deacons *(Apostolic Constitutions,* 8,17-20,28). In imperial law (especially at the time of Justinian) deaconesses were regarded as part of the clergy. As the Church grew more and more out of its missionary stage and there was less and less baptism of adults, the office of deaconess gradually faded away.

The inner reason for the tradition of the Church reserving the order of the priesthood to baptized men is not that men are better endowed to fulfill the priestly tasks or that women are held in low opinion. In the discussions on this question many reasons have been presented based on the analysis of the nature of man or woman. Their cogency depends on whether it is possible to establish with some degree of certainty the different social and cultural functions performed within human society by men and women. Whereas in earlier times it was thought that this question could be answered with confidence, social development in our scientific and technical age has led to many uncertainties in this area. Many views formerly held must now be regarded as inadequate.

If, however, many of the reasons previously adduced for the priesthood of men alone are now no longer valid, this still does not mean that the whole tradition of the Church and its practice as it continues today is mistaken. Even if the cultural and social conditions of his time would have made it appear scandalous for Jesus to have had women among the twelve and invited women to the Last Supper, the whole style of his preaching and his life show that he would not have hesitated to provoke an outcry if he had wanted to have women as apostles, in the technical sense of the word. Moreover, we must not forget that the priesthood which is common to all opens up such endless possibilities that they could hardly ever be completely exhausted. In particular, let us remember that the Christian man who is empowered by his consecration as a bishop or a priest to perform particular services has quite specific, clearly defined tasks, whereas all the other tasks in the Church can be performed by any baptized Christian. The practical extent of the work of the laity in the Church will be realized more and more as those members of the Church who fill the office of a bishop or a priest limit themselves to the activity which is possible only for those members of the people of God who have received the special priestly consecration.

We would be approaching a whole problem with the wrong criteria, namely earthly ones, if we did not keep constantly before our eyes the goal of all the Church's activity, namely the kingdom of God. All the structural elements of the Church are subordinate to its law. Jesus himself pointed out the important thing: "Whoever does the will of my heavenly Father is my brother, my sister, my mother" (Mt. 12,50). And there were his other words: "Whoever wants to be the first must be the willing slave of all" (Mk. 10,44). Let us also remember the words of 1 Cor. 13,13: "There are three things that last for ever: faith, hope, and love; but the greatest of them all is love."

ORDINATION AND SALVATION

The saving effect of the sacrament is determined by its purpose of making possible particular saving services in the people of God. It consists in a particular indelible likening to Christ (the mark of Christ) and a particular ecclesiological position. This double effect includes the giving of the inner capacity to perform particular services which cannot be performed without the consecration (i.e. the *res et sacramentum*). With this there is connected a self-communication of Christ and God the Father, which gives to the person who has received this authority those insights and impulses that serve the proper use of it.

◄ 10

The Sacrament of Penance:
Its Place in the Church

THE PLACE OF THE SACRAMENT IN
THE LIFE OF THE CHURCH

The sacrament of penance is the concrete form of the constant penance which is asked of the Church. In Christ and through Christ man has been promised salvation by God in an ultimate and unretractable way. The salvation Christ brought remains present and attainable in history, in the Church as the concrete sign of salvation, until the return of the Lord. The community of the baptized has received Christ's salvation. It constitutes the people of God, i.e. the people chosen by God and belonging to him as his possession. The Church is the people of God in that it exists as the body of Christ, and all its members have access to God in the Holy Spirit because of their brotherly fellowship with Christ. As those who are called to the community of salvation, the members of the Church are called in Scripture "saints," i.e. those who belong to God. Although Christ signifies God's ultimate promise of salvation to man and hence universal salvation history culminates in him, the salvation history of the individual is not concluded when he is received into the community of salvation: membership in this community is not an absolute and unconditional guarantee that every individual man will eventually attain to

God and the eternal gift of himself. On the contrary, the members of the Church are still assailed by the temptation to sin and constantly succumb to it.

Incorporation in the Church and in its head, Jesus Christ, is the beginning of that movement of salvation which is directed towards the absolute future, but this movement does not constitute an inevitable evolutionary process. On the one hand, man's beginning in the way of salvation, its continuance and fulfillment depend on the gratuitous initiative of God, who in his mercy lays hold of the individual man and places him within the saving situation created by Christ, into the stream of salvation he set flowing (cf. Jn. 6,44). On the other hand, however, man's liberation from the forces of destruction into the sphere of salvation depends on his response, which, although it is made possible and called forth by grace, is nevertheless free. There is no doubt that God's freely operating will to save endures beyond the beginning of man's course; but in order that the dialogue of man with God shall not be interrupted, it is necessary that man's will also should persevere. This presents a constant challenge to a person living in the community of salvation; for although the guilt of his sin has been removed, he is still subject to the spiritual and mental pull of sin, i.e. the self-love and pride which draw him away from God. There is also the temptation to use the creation which environs him for the purposes of self-love and pride. Thus, despite his membership in the people of God and the body of Christ, the Christian is prey to temptations from within and without. The danger is that, yielding, he will establish a system of values in which it is no longer God who stands at the center of his willing and thinking but a creature, whether a person or a thing—money, property, power. Such a man leaves his Father's house, as Scripture says, to live his life in complete independence from him (Lk. 15,11ff.). This gives rise to that event which theology calls mortal (i.e. grave) sin.

This sin can take the particular form of a man's formal rebellion against God, but in general it is an offense against the works of God. Here a further distinction must be made: between offense to a person and offense to a thing. The dignity of man, residing in the fact that he is a person, requires that he shall acknowledge and accept as a person any human being he encounters—that is, that he shall not treat him as a thing, an object, approaching him in the mode of a subject-object relationship. Every encounter with another person must be an I-Thou encounter. One of the purposes of God's commandments is to protect and safeguard the dignity of man, his life and his freedom of action in the world. Personal dignity is injured through inconsiderateness, insults and contempt; through lies and hatred; through the use of violence, brutality, and murder. God created the world of things for man's sake and entrusted them to him. He intended them to serve man without any violation of their nature. The misuse of things, their destruction without reason, the failure to observe their right order—i.e. that which serves man—is an offense against the meaning of the material world.

Because men and things came into being through God's creative will, to injure them constitutes resistance to, rebellion against, God himself. Hence sin is not only a direct and formal rebellion against God but also, and generally, an offense against God's creation. In sin man establishes that autonomy which Scripture calls the striving for the knowledge of good and evil: it is the thrust of man's will, contrary to the will of God, which seeks to establish the norms of life and to live according to them in complete independence of God.

This sin is something quite other than that weakness and laziness wherein a man, though he acknowledges God as the absolute and unique personal value to which he relates everything and by which every thing is determined, does not realize his devotion to him with the necessary intensity in every situation of life. This is sin in an analogous sense. Our daily weaknesses and failures are not a lesser form of mortal sin: mortal and venial sin are two quite different categories.

Members of the people of God offend by every sin which opposes itself to their close relation to God and their membership in the body of Christ. This offense varies greatly according to the kind of sin. In mortal sin, membership in the body of Christ is not completely destroyed, but it is robbed of its efficacy. In so-called venial sin, the efficacy of the person's membership is weakened. In any event, the sinner comes into conflict with God, with the human community, and with himself. Indeed the sin of a baptized person constitutes a fourfold conflict: with God, with the unity of creation, with the Church as the community of the saints, and with the sinner's own life. These four elements are not parallel, but overlap and affect one another. In the case of someone who belongs to the people of God and the body of Christ the contradiction present in every sin is not only intensified but passes into a new dimension. A person in mortal sin turns away from the saving powers given to him in baptism and returns to his former subjection to the powers of destruction. Both the Epistle to the Hebrews and the Johannine epistles urgently warn us against this kind of relapse, for it robs a person of his hope of salvation (Heb. 6,4-8; 10,26-29; 1 Jn. 2,8-11; 4,11-16). By developing the image of the Church as the body of Christ, Paul has indicated the nature of this contradiction.

The sin of a baptized person should not be judged only from its individual aspect; it has a collective significance. Through the sin of its members the Church itself undergoes a diminution of its saving life and its brotherly fellowship. Since sin always involves selfishness, it isolates the sinner from the community and hence weakens the bonds within the community itself. At the same time, at the point where it exerts its effects it deflects the community from its orientation towards God, thus diminishing the community's openness to God's saving work. In eschatological terms, every sin constitutes an obstacle for the Church on the way towards the absolute future, inasmuch as it impedes the saving action whereby Jesus Christ and the Holy Spirit are leading the Church to the final fulfillment.

THE CHURCH'S RESPONSIBILITY REGARDING THE SIN OF ITS MEMBERS

The Church must not remain indifferent to this situation. If it is to remain faithful to its character as the people of God and the body of Christ, it must be constantly engaged at the core of its being in the struggle against sin. But we must not make a division in the Church between saints and sinners, ascribing holiness to the first group and sinfulness to the second and committing the first to fight against the sin of the second. Rather, all the members of the Church are called to pray daily "forgive us our trespasses," including themselves in this prayer. Similarly, all those who participate in the Church's central celebration, the eucharist, are to confess their sins before God with contrition at the beginning of the rite. The whole Church is empowered and committed to expiate the sin of all its members. But although the responsibility rests upon all, certain members of the Church have a particular responsibility for the whole Church. These are the members who represent the whole Church or the individual local Churches—the pope, the bishops, the priests—but, in addition, certain others who are called by God in a special way to expiation. Persons in the latter category have not merely a private role and responsibility but one within the Church. It is quite possible that owing to a particular charismatic vocation, a "layman" may be charged with a degree of responsibility for expiation not incumbent on the official representative of the whole Church or of a particular local Church.

The means for the conquest of sin are prayer, suffering, exhortation, and fraternal correction. If all these fail with respect to a sinner, then he must be excluded from the people of God (according to Mt. 18,17). Paul's testimony regarding this situation is particularly illuminating. Although he puts great emphasis on the holiness produced by baptism in the Church and its members, he never ceases to exhort Christians to live according to their new condition in Christ, freeing themselves from their former domination by the powers of destruction. His epistles are full of the dialectic of the imperative and the indicative. He never tires of warning his readers against sin and calling them to live in the Holy Spirit (e.g., Rom. 6,2-13; 13,14; 1 Cor. 3,3.16f.; 6,18f.; Gal. 3,17; 5,25; Col. 3,10; Eph. 4,24). He mentions a number of sins which exclude the sinner from the kingdom of God: "fornication, impurity, and indecency; idolatry and sorcery; quarrels, a contentious temper, envy, fits of rage, selfish ambitions, dissensions, party intrigues and jealousies; drinking bouts, orgies and the like" (Gal. 5,19ff.; cf. 1 Cor. 6,9f.; Col. 3,5; Eph. 5,3-7; Rom. 1,29-32). It is probable that particular abuses made him give these warnings. Sometimes he condemns particular sins which have been committed, smaller offenses such as quarrels, divisions and unkindnesses (1 Cor. 3,3; 11,18-22) as well as the gravest vices—incest, for example, which a Christian had committed in Corinth (1 Cor. 5,1-13).

THE EXCLUSION OF THE SINNER AND HIS READMISSION

When all the community's efforts towards the conversion of a sinful member have failed, Paul demands that association with him should cease, that he should be excluded from the family of the people of God (1 Cor. 5,2-5.12; 2 Tim. 3,5; Rom. 16,17; 2 Thess. 3,6.14; 1 Cor. 5,11). This procedure is prefigured under the Old Testament in the treatment of members of the people of God who had offended against the covenant. The offender was punished in various ways (by a rebuke, or by banishment, both in a simple and in an extreme form). Banishment was intended to make the guilty man realize what he had done: it was rescinded at his request if he was able to convince the others that his repentance was genuine.

We can gain some insight into the nature of banishment from the New Testament people of God through the regulations concerning banishment contained in the rule-book of the Qumran community. This community, which flourished from about 100 B.C. to 50 A.D., called itself "the saints." The members took over the concept of the "temple" and applied it to themselves, thus giving it a personalist significance. One who has given offense to holiness is excluded in order that he may be moved to contrition. There was a complicated system of banishment. If a person expressed contrition, he was again received into the community; but those who were incorrigible were excluded for ever (as was the practice of the Synagogue).

It was an alarming experience for the Christian communities to discover that despite their fellowship with the crucified and risen Lord, there were among their members, sins which equalled the worst sins of the heathen in gravity. Paul is outraged to learn that the Corinthians have not immediately cast such members out of their Church. As the father of the community he founded, he calls for strict measures.

On the other hand, however, even the worst sinners are not to be plunged into ruin by being abandoned by the community. The community is to pray for them, and if they repent and do penance they must be readmitted to the community (2 Tim. 2,25ff.; 2 Cor. 2,10; 1 Thess. 5,15; 2 Cor. 7,9-13). In considering the measures against sinners which Paul called for, we must note that he acts authoritatively only when the community itself fails to do anything about the abuses in its ranks and that the exclusion from the community is intended for the sinner's amendment, with a view to his reacceptance into the community. Moreover, all this is done in the name of Jesus Christ (1 Cor. 5,4), i.e. not simply for the sake of order in the Church but for the sake of the sinner's relation to Christ and through Christ to God the Father.

Because every action of the Church is related to salvation and hence has a sacramental quality as the visible manifestation of the divine saving action, we must ascribe sacramentality to the exclusion of the sinner from the Church (excommunication) for his own salvation and to his reacceptance into the Church's community (reconciliation). If owing to the continuing sinfulness of all its members the Church is called to constant self-reform in which its basic sacramentality expresses itself, its struggle against sin acquires a concrete institutional form in a procedure to which the Pauline epistles witness.

THE INSTITUTIONALIZATION OF PENANCE FOR SIN

The representatives of the Church are empowered and committed to undertake this procedure not only by the general sacramental nature of the Church—the fact that it belongs essentially to God and is united with Christ—and by the call to holiness: there are also the explicit words of the Lord. Two main texts are involved, one from Matthew and the other from John. We shall quote the text from Matthew together with its context. According to it, Christ says (Mt. 18,15-20):

If your brother commits a sin, go and take the matter up with him, strictly between yourselves, and if he listens to you, you have won your brother over. If he will not listen, take one or two others with you, so that all facts may be duly established on the evidence of two or three witnesses. If he refuses to listen to them, report the matter to the congregation; and if he will not listen even to the congregation, you must then treat him as you would a pagan or a tax-gatherer. I tell you this: whatever you forbid on earth shall be forbidden in heaven, and whatever you allow on earth shall be allowed in heaven. Again I tell you this: if two of you agree on earth about any request you have to make, that request will be granted by my heavenly Father. For where two or three have met together in my name, I am there among them.

What Jesus says to all his disciples according to this text (v. 18), he says to Peter alone, in connection with the promise of the power of the keys, according to Matthew 16,19b.

The text from John reads (Jn. 20,23ff.): "Jesus repeated, 'Peace be with you!' and then said, 'As the Father sent me, so I send you.' He then breathed on them, saying, 'Receive the Holy Spirit! If you forgive any man's sins, they stand forgiven; if you pronounce them unforgiven, unforgiven they remain.' "

The words of the Lord concerning "forbidding" and "allowing" (Mt. 18,18) have been placed in a context of his own by the author of the gospel. Verses 15-17 represent a rule of the early Christian Church. Through this juxtaposition the evangelist not only reports Christ's words but also gives them a certain interpretation. The form, the style, and the concepts of the words "forbidding" and "allowing" point, at any rate, to a Palestinian origin. There is no need to decide whether the words concerning "forbidding" and "allowing" in ch. 18 are to be ascribed to the historical or the risen Christ.

The words "forbidding" and "allowing" are terms which in rabbinical scholarship generally mean "declaring something forbidden or permitted"; but they can also (although more rarely) refer to "banishment or the lifting of banishment." Both actions are done with the claim to be valid before God, and the two meanings are closely connected inasmuch as every doctrinal pronouncement is orientated towards a juridical decision and, *vice versa,* every juridical decision is bound up with a doctrinal pronouncement. To understand what the words mean for the evangelist, we should note that "forbidding" and "allowing" in Matthew 16 are an explanation of the power of the keys promised to Peter. Hence "forbidding" and "allowing" refer here not only to the forgiveness or retention of sin but also to the whole authoritative proclamation and communication of salvation. This comprehensive meaning includes the authority to proclaim and apply the religious and moral conditions for entry into the kingdom of God and to declare the obstacles to it. Thus there are in Jesus' words the overtones of the rabbinical idea of banishment and the lifting of banishment. By placing the words of Jesus in juxtaposition with the rule of the community, the writer of the gospel has done no violence to them.[1]

There is no justification for taking the words "forbidding" and "allowing" as referring to the concept of bondage to the demonic powers of evil (a sense which was dominant in the East in ancient times, in the Old Testament and above all in the late Jewish apocalyptic writings).

The words of the risen Christ to his disciples reported in St. John's Gospel possibly represent a particular tradition of Jesus' words recounted by Matthew in their original form. This variant clarifies the idea of "forbidding" and "allowing" and at the same time limits it to the power to forgive sins. The forgiveness of sins played the most important part among the tasks which Christ gave his disciples the commission and the authority to fulfill. It is given particular emphasis in his missionary command.

According to this passage, the authority to forgive sins is unlimited, and no sin is excepted from it. If the apostles are promised a twofold authority, this means that they must use their power on the basis of a juridical judgment, and not in an indiscriminate and arbitrary way. The power they are given is a sacral one, and they can use it only in the Holy Spirit. That is why the relation of man to God is subject to their authority.

[1] Cf. A. Vogtle, *Lexikon für Theologie und Kirche,* I, 2d ed., pp. 478ff.

Neither in the words concerning "forbidding" and "allowing" reported by Matthew nor in the words in John concerning the retention or forgiveness of sins has Christ specified a particular form of the latter. In the rule of the community quoted by Matthew side by side with the words of Jesus concerning "forbidding" and "allowing": "If he will not listen even to the congregation, you must then treat him as you would a pagan or a tax-gatherer," we can see the rabbinical practice of punishing sin (especially sin against the honor of God, against doctrinal tradition, and against one's neighbor) by banishment, which can possibly later be revoked. The procedure against mortal sinners, attested in the epistles of Paul, indicates also that the authority to forgive sins, imparted by Christ to the apostles, was exercised in Old Testament form.

As regards the influence that the two texts have had on the approach to penance as a sacrament, it should be pointed out that since Tertullian theology has regarded the words of Matthew as bearing witness to the authority to forgive sin, but the Council of Trent referred only to the Johannine text when it spoke of penance as a sacrament. The fact that Jesus Christ was silent as to the form of the exercise of authority concerning grave sin and the adoption of Old Testament forms does not mean that outmoded and obsolete practices have crept into an important part of the Church's life. Rather, we should see that the Church's withdrawal of itself from those who despise the new order of God, like the withdrawing of any community from members who are in conflict with it, is a reaction that is appropriate to its own nature. Old Testament banishment is simply a preliminary form of it.

HISTORICAL DEVELOPMENT

Fundamentals

On the basis of these two texts and of the attitude of the early Christian community to sinners there developed the Catholic doctrine of the sacrament of penance. When the teaching concerning the seven sacraments was elaborated in the twelfth century, the sacrament of penance was automatically considered one of them. We must, however, point out again that according to the testimony of Scripture, penance cannot be limited to the sacrament. Rather, because of its eschatological place between the ascension of Christ and his return, the Church must be continually inspired by the spirit of penance. Within the total life of the Church this sacrament is a special concrete form of that spirit. Its particular sacramentality lies in the fact that a visible sign performed by the Church is the guarantee of God's receiving again into his kingdom someone who has fallen away.

Despite many variations, the development in the post-apostolic period runs, on the whole, in one clear direction. The post-apostolic Church considers that the baptized Christian lives as someone who has been snatched from the powers of destruction, someone who belongs to God, i.e. a saint. But this life is frequently impaired through both weakness and malice. As in the apostolic age, so in the post-apostolic period a distinction is made between minor everyday failures in regard to the new order of God created by Christ and grave major ones. The minor everyday offenses against the order of salvation must be expiated through prayer, penitence, and humility. In the case of more serious ones, those who offend must be admonished by the Church in brotherly love (cf. the *Didache,* 2,7; 4,3; Ignatius of Antioch; Eph. 10,1; 3,1; and the *First Epistle of Clement* (2,4.6; 56,1). If peaceful exhortation is of no avail or if the sin assumes unusual dimensions, those who are refractory or breakers of the law must be expelled from the life of the community. This expulsion does not mean that the Church is casting out undesirable elements in fanatical puritanism. Rather, it is directed towards conversion and salvation, and hence must always be undertaken in loving concern. Just as the Church cannot ignore sins out of a pseudo-tolerance, so it cannot make a judgment of condemnation on sinners out of a spiritualism that is remote from the world. It is not its task to anticipate the final judgment, but to bring back those who have strayed from the path of salvation. To neglect this task would mean to contradict the meaning of its existence; it would be a mistaken kindness to sinners.

Sacramental Penance for Grave Sin

Because exclusion from the life of the Church community and readmission to it constitute the basis of the development of the sacrament of penance, it is clear that in the early Church only those sins we call mortal or grave were expiated by the sacrament. Although mention was made of the confession of minor sins, this had another meaning, as we shall see, namely a confession involved in the direction of souls. There was no obligation to do sacramental penance for venial sins.

It was considered that every sin could be forgiven if the sinner turned away from his offense in penitence and expiation. The view that there were sins which could not be forgiven, or that the Church could not forgive every sin, came from Tertullian, who had fallen into Montanism, and from the Roman priest Novatian. Tertullian considered that the three sins of murder, apostasy, and adultery could not be forgiven. Novatian's view was rejected at the Council of Nicaea (325). But on the other hand the view was also rejected that only these three sins were subject to the sacrament of penance, while all other sins could be dealt with through personal penitence.

Sacramental Penance Only Once in Life

The belief that sacramental penance could be administered only once in a lifetime was an important stage in the development of the early Church's attitude towards it. Hermas, who wrote *The Shepherd* in Rome around 180, demands that only one repentance should be allowed a Christian who has betrayed his fellowship with Christ through a mortal sin. It cannot be definitely established whether Hermas was describing an already existing state of affairs or introducing a new practice. It is unlikely that there had been much reflection on this problem before this work was written, because apostasy from Christianity happened rarely if at all. The reason for penance being possible only once is eschatological: the Shepherd of Hermas believes that Christ will soon return. But there was also a pastoral and psychological motive: if a person was capable of relapsing into his old life, he could not be regarded as having any genuine spirit of penitence; and without this there is no forgiveness.

In the subsequent period it became a fixed principle that penance could be undertaken only once, and the practice was mitigated only towards the end of the sixth century. The result was that more and more Christians who had fallen into grave sin became accustomed to postponing their penance until the end of their life, so as not to forego the chance of obtaining the forgiveness of their sins before they died.

The Procedure

Exclusion from the Church marked the beginning of the process of penance. In order to receive forgiveness the sinner had to fulfill difficult conditions. What penance was asked of him was reserved to the judgment of the bishop, and in the various communities and provinces of the Church the practice differed widely. The Church in North Africa was marked by extreme strictness. Here the Montanist doctrine developed from an austere practice. To admit a sinner to penance is itself an act of grace; it is not the remission of his sin but opens the way to it. The duration of penance varied between a few weeks and lifelong obligations. The community assisted the sinner through its prayers and works of penance. Its intercession culminated in a service of worship, in which the prayers of all were combined into one profound cry for mercy and in which, Tertullian maintained, it was Christ himself who prayed. The desire to help the sinful member of the Church in this effective way is the reason for the community participation in penance. After a suitable period, the sinner is readmitted to the community of the Church's life (reconciliation). Again it is the bishop, as the representative of the community, who has the authority to decide whether the sinner is to be reconciled or not. It was believed (cf., in particular, Ignatius of Antioch) that reconciliation with the bishop and the Church was necessary for the remission of sin and that the Holy Spirit was restored to the penitent only through this reconciliation. However, that the Holy Spirit was indeed given again to the person readmitted to the Church was firmly held. Although there is no reflection on the relation of this reconciliation and the giving of the Spirit, it was not doubted that the key which opened the way to the visible Church also opened the way to God. Reconciliation often took place through prayer and the laying-on of hands by the bishop.

"Public" Penance

Another notable difference in the practice of sacramental penance in the early Church as compared to the modern period and the present day (apart from its being received only once) involves its public character. Although this difference is sometimes disputed, it is quite clear from the facts. No doubt it may be argued that the sacrament of penance, like the whole Church, always has a public character, since the whole Church is always involved in it. But we may ask whether this character of the sacrament is also manifested publicly today. While it was very clearly expressed in the early Church, this expression declined in the Middle Ages; and in the modern period, until today, it has appeared only obscurely. We need only recall that in the early Church there were penitential communities (though not everywhere); that the penitents often were confined to a special place in the church; that they could not partake of the eucharist and frequently were forbidden even to participate in its celebration; and that they were readmitted to the Church by the bishop during the service and before the whole community. Although this rite is still to be found in the *Pontificale Romanum,* these procedures do not play any considerable part in penance as it is practiced today. Moreover, from the early Middle Ages it became customary to receive the sacrament of penance for venial sins, with the consequence that it became a devotional practice which no longer made anyone conspicuous as a sinner. The shaming of the sinner that went with the public character of penance in the early Church increasingly disappeared. However, it should be pointed out that the confession of sin, which marked the first stage in the whole process of penance, was private in the early Church as well: the community did not know what sins the penitent was expiating unless some generally known offense was involved. Apart from individual cases, the call for the public confession of sin was firmly rejected by the Church (especially by Innocent I).

The Differences between Penance in the Early Eastern Church and the Early Western Church

In the Church's attitude to penance we can see clearly that despite the similarity of the essentials, there were two different views from the third century on. One, represented by the theologians of Alexandria—e.g., Clement of Alexandria and Origen—emphasizes the penitential effort of the sinner. This is seen primarily from a pastoral and educational aspect and regarded as a purification. The other, represented by the theologians of North Africa— e.g., Tertullian and Cyprian—emphasizes the reconciliation with the Church. The human effort of penance is interpreted, in this view, more as expiation and satisfaction than purification. Both views influenced the subsequent period, with the Alexandrian emphasis found more in the Eastern Church, and that of Cyprian more in the Western Church.

In the Eastern Church we find Origen's teaching on the direction of souls having an important influence, above all, in monasteries. Healing from sin became so important in the mind of the believer that it became detached from the sacrament of penance and developed independently. The important thing was that the efforts of penance and the direction of souls, which were aimed at healing, were naturally concerned not only with the major sins but also with the minor failings of everyday life. The direction of souls was the more effective the more often the penitent confessed his faults to his spiritual father. This form of confession became a fixed part of monastic discipline; it is not a sacramental act in the present-day sense, but a spiritual aid on the path to holiness. Absolution is never mentioned in this connection. The person who hears the confession need not be a bishop or a priest, but he must be a director of souls who has prudence, experience of life, knowledge of human nature, and a spiritual attitude of mind. Of course this kind of confession, too, takes place within the total sacramentality of the Church.

The concept of penance as satisfaction and expiation, held by the North African theologians and dominant in the Western Church, is based on the principle that the wrong which sin entails—the violation of order it contains—must be rectified. Thus there were juridical elements. Man's satisfaction for sin was viewed as having saving power, inasmuch as it is a sharing in the cross of Christ which restores the effectiveness of the cross where it had been rejected.

The Change to More Frequent and
Private Sacramental Penance:
The Sixth Century Onwards

At the end of the patristic age, the fact that penance was done only once and was public in character led to a grave crisis for the sacrament in the Western Church, calling for new formulations. In the sixth century that development began which consisted in the gradual increase in the frequency of sacramental penance and the diminution of its public character. Towards the end of the century, these tendencies seem to have been particularly strong in Spain. The Third Synod of Toledo (589) sought to call a halt to them, forbidding (in canon 11) both the repetition of the sacrament of penance and the practice of private penance. But the development proceeded independently of the synod's ruling.

However, the main impetus to the universal establishment of the practice of repeated and private penance seems to have come from the Anglo-Saxon and Irish Churches. We know very little about the practice of penance at that period, but clearly public and "once only" penance had not become established in the British Isles as it had on the Continent. In a seventh-century Anglo-Saxon penitential book by Bishop Theodore of Tarsus, who was made Archbishop of Canterbury in 668, we read that there was no ceremony of public reconciliation in the Irish and

Anglo-Saxon Churches because there was no public penance.

The absence of the public character in the Church's penance had an important influence on the way it was practiced. If penance did not involve exclusion from the life of the Church community and the obligation to perform humiliating penitential works over a long period; and if, moreover, it could be repeated, then it could be done for the minor offenses which were not subject to the sacramental penance of the early Church. The consequence was that from the seventh and eighth centuries on, minor daily offenses (which Augustine had held were expiated by the Lord's Prayer) were included in sacramental penance. This form of the sacrament was unknown in the early Church.

The form of penance customary in the Anglo-Saxon and Irish Churches was taken to the Continent by the many monks who came from Ireland towards the end of the sixth century, and later from England. In the eighth century we find the practice of repeated penance widespread all over the Continent. Many penitential works written in the seventh and eighth centuries fix the amount of satisfaction that is incumbent on penitents, thus withdrawing the right to fix the penance from the bishop or the priest. But although they contain many bizarre elements, they nevertheless indicate the seriousness of the penitential spirit. In general, the development in the practice of penance constitutes a mitigation of its severity.

Rules for the Reception of Penance

On the other hand, however, we find after the eighth and especially in the ninth century a number of prescriptions which made it generally obligatory for the faithful to receive the sacrament of penance. If penance can be done more than once, then of course the person in mortal sin is committed to receiving the sacrament of penance; and it must be repeated on each occasion of grave sin. But beyond this, all the members of the Church were advised— and, in time, obliged—to receive the sacrament of penance even when they had no serious sin to expiate.

With regard to the frequency with which the sacrament is to

be received, we find great variations in the period prescribed between the ninth and the twelfth centuries. The Fourth Lateran Council (1215) brought clarification in that it obliged all the faithful to receive the sacrament of penance at least once a year, a ruling which was reiterated by the Council of Trent and the Code of Canon Law. However, the general view (in which the belief of the early Church survives) is that this rule is, strictly speaking, binding only on those who consider that they have committed a mortal sin. Nevertheless the Church urges the rest of the faithful to receive the sacrament of penance frequently, a counsel which has resulted in the practice of confession as a devotion. The Eastern Church's practice of the direction of souls became combined with the sacramental forgiveness of sins, although without doing full justice to the element of spiritual direction.

Excommunication as a Separate Process

An important subsidiary effect of the change in practice of the sacrament of penance was the tendency we find in the sixth century of making excommunication into a punishment inflicted by the Church quite independently of the sacrament of penance. A sin which particularly affects the community but owing to the private nature of the sacrament of penance can no longer be dealt with through sacramental penance must, in the interests of the community, be performed in another way. This way is excommunication. The development of excommunication as an independent procedure became the basis of the separation between the *forum internum* and the *forum externum*. The consequence was an obscuring of the spiritual, salvific character of the Church's ban.

The Individualization of Sacramental Penance

A further consequence of the more frequent practice of penance was that its administration was no longer reserved to the bishop or to the "pardoner" he commissioned but generally passed into the hands of the priests (although they could act only on the orders of the bishop).

From the eighth century on, a stronger emphasis was placed on the act of confession, so that the sacrament became known as "confession." In the eighth century the practice began of combining confession and exclusion from the Church community, on the one hand, and reconciliation on the other, so that the treatment of the sacrament which has come to prevail in modern times developed. Compared with penance in the early Church, it is clearly a reduced form of the sacrament. All these changes made for a greater individualization of the sacrament, while its community character was increasingly lost sight of.

THE TEACHING OF THE CHURCH

In the course of the development which led, in the twelfth century, to the emergence from the total sacramentality of the Church of seven specific sacraments, penance became recognized as a sacrament carried out with the co-operation of the Church community and the authoritative participation of the Church's officials. This teaching was sustained against Wyclif and Hus at the Council of Constance (1414-1418, DS 1260ff.). Against the doubt cast upon it by the Reformers, the Council of Trent defined the existence of the sacrament of penance (14th session, ch. 1, DS 1668ff.). The council confirmed its institution by Jesus Christ, its distinction from baptism, and the witness to it of the Johannine text of 20,22:

If anyone says that these words of the Lord our Savior: "Receive the Holy Spirit; whose sins you shall forgive, they are forgiven them; and whose sins you shall retain, they are retained" (Jn. 20,22f.), ought not to be understood as referring to the power of remitting and of retaining sins in the sacrament of penance as the Catholic Church has always understood them from the beginning; and if anyone, to disprove the institution of this sacrament, twists the meaning of those words and refers them to the Church authority to preach the gospel: let him be anathema. (DS 1703; cf. also DS 3446)[2]

[2] *The Church Teaches*, p. 315.

Whereas we find the ecclesiological view of penance in the texts of the Council of Trent, in the post-Tridentine period we find increasingly greater stress on the purely individual interpretation of penance as a sacrament for a person who has fallen into sin after baptism. In the controversies with those who would reject the sacrament of penance, from Wyclif and Calvin on, its necessity for the salvation of the individual sinner was so strongly emphasized that the ecclesiological aspect, which had been the important one both in Scripture and in the patristic age, became more and more obscure. But we can see that it still retains some influence when we recall the Church's prescription that a person in mortal sin should not be satisfied with repentance alone but should submit himself to the sacrament of penance before being admitted to communion. The reason for this is that the celebration of the eucharist, and especially communion in which its full meaning is realized, presupposes full communion with the Church, and that sharing in the love of God presupposes peace with the Church. This idea, found in the Fathers and especially in Augustine, was not formally emphasized in the Tridentine decisions, but it is clearly behind the foregoing instructions with regard to communion.

The sacramentality of penance has been generally affirmed in the Eastern Church (apart from Cyrillos Lukaris, who was influenced by Calvin). The Reformers did not take a unanimous position with regard to penance. Luther's attitude, in particular, fluctuates: though he put the greatest emphasis on daily penance, we find contradictory statements in his writing so far as the sacrament is concerned. In his early days and again in the last years of his life, he not only spoke with high praise of the sacrament of penance but also received it frequently. Melanchthon as well sought to preserve individual confession *(absolutio privata):* for him, the main thing was the absolution. Luther shared this view, regarding the absolution as spoken by the priest in the place of God and at his command: it was because the absolution was the voice of God, he said, that penance could be called a sacrament. The new life imparted through absolution was expressed in good deeds, which are the fruits of penance. For true penance, in Luther's view, the important thing is faith in which man relies solely on God's redemption of the sinner through Christ and receives the word of forgiveness and God's word. Luther did not think that penance should be obligatory, but he would exclude persons who did not go to confession from communion.

According to Lutheran confessional writings, early Lutheranism regarded confession as in some sense a sacrament and took a certain amount of trouble to preserve it. Nevertheless it disappeared from Lutheran Church life around 1800 without ever having been officially abolished. The new Lutheranism of the nineteenth century tried hard to reintroduce it.

In general the Churches of the Reform are skeptical with regard to the sacrament of penance. Zwingli totally rejects individual confession, and Calvin rejects it on the whole, but he recommends it to those Christians who suffer such great anxiety owing to their sins that they cannot free themselves from them without the help of others. But absolution, in his view, is basically no different from the words of evangelization: the person who absolves is only the witness and guarantor of divine grace.

There has recently been a strong lay movement in Protestantism for the reintroduction of confession, and the Church authorities are, for the most part, satisfying this desire.

◄11

Penance: The Sacramental Sign

It is more difficult to see the external sign of the sacrament of penance than in the case of the other sacraments because there is no visible thing on which the creative word can confer a salvific meaning. It is in particular difficult to apply to the sign of the sacrament the concepts of form and matter developed by high scholasticism; thus it is not surprising that theological opinion has differed on this question.

HISTORY

The Council of Trent spoke of the sacramental sign, but it left open the problems debated by the theologians of the age. It stated (14th session, ch. 3, DS 1673ff.):

The holy council teaches, moreover, that the form of the sacrament of penance, which principally contains the power of the sacrament, is in those words of the minister: "I absolve you," etc. In accordance with a custom of the holy Church, certain prayers have commendably been added to those words of the minister. However, these added prayers do not pertain in any way to the essence of the form, and they are not necessary for the administration of the sacrament. The quasi-matter of this sacrament is the acts of the penitent, namely, contrition, confession, and satisfaction. Inasmuch as these acts are demanded of the penitent according to God's arrangement for the integrity of the sacrament and for the complete and perfect remission of sins, they are, for that reason, called the parts of penance.[1]

(Cf. also the statement of the Council of Florence in the Doctrinal Instruction for the Armenians, DS 1323.)

It is evident that in the course of history a profound change has taken place in the way the sacrament of penance is carried out; and yet the connection between the practice in the early Church and in modern times is such that we can speak of a single symbolic area, though it is a broad one. At any rate, in the practice both of the early Church and of modern times, the forgiveness of sins is effected by the Church and the penitential effort of the sinner accomplished under its authoritative guidance and through the impulse of divine grace. According to the *Didascalia Apostolorum,* from the beginning of the third century, those who intend and promise to do penance for their sins, having first been excluded from the Church, are thereafter received again by the Church, as by a merciful father. Special liturgical forms of exclusion and reconciliation developed; we find a description of the whole procedure according to the Roman rite in the fifth-century Church historian Sozomenos. Primarily, exclusion from the eucharistic table of the Church community was involved, but sometimes the sinner was excluded from the community's sacrificial celebration itself. The sinner was considered to have forfeited the right to be admitted to the eucharistic meal and sacrifice acquired in his baptism.

The exclusion was not carried out always and everywhere with the same rigor. According to a rubric of the First Council of Nicaea (325, canon 11), the sinner is to be placed among the catechumens. He has conducted himself as if he still belonged to the world and was still subject to the powers of destruction of old; and yet there is a great difference between the baptized sinner and an unbaptized person: despite his exclusion, the sinner still belongs to the Church. In order to reverse the exclusion procedure in train, the sinner had to confess his sin and thus detach himself from it. His confession was made to the bishop or to the pardoner he commissioned. The reconciliation generally took place accord-

---

[1] *The Church Teaches,* p. 307.

ing to a rite which included prayer and the laying-on of hands.

Beginning in the eighth century a practice developed (which had been generally accepted by the eleventh century) of combining confession and reconciliation.

OBJECTIVE AND SUBJECTIVE ELEMENTS

As for the relation of the personal effort of the penitent and the Church's reconciling action, the early Church believed that the individual's subjective penitential act combined with his objective reconciliation to the Church wiped out the sin, but the nature of this combination was not further analyzed. In his Montanist period, Tertullian took the view that the Holy Spirit wiped out the sin immediately through the Church's act of reconciliation. In any event, it was held that personal penance and the reconciling act of the Church (or, after the confession of sins and reconciliation had become combined, the Church's absolution) were necessary for the sin to be wiped out.

In the twelfth century, Peter Lombard said simply that both repentance and its manifestation in confession had to be considered sacramental and were in part the reason for the forgiveness of the sin. Absolution was the sign that the sin had been forgiven. Abelard took up a position of his own, rejecting any prerogative of the Church to forgive sin and categorizing absolution as only a procedural measure belonging to Church discipline: it involved the readmittance into the Church of a man already reconciled with God through repentance and confession.

Hugo of St. Victor rejected any devaluation of the Church's absolution. He saw the effects of sin as a twofold bondage: interiorly it involved the hardening of the heart; exteriorly it involved the incurring of future punishment. From the former the sinner was released by his repentance; from the latter, by the Church's absolution. Most theologians of the early Middle Ages held that the forgiveness of sin took place through the repentance which was connected with the *votum sacramenti,* but they found it difficult to explain what the effect of the absolution was.

In the period of high scholasticism, Wilhelm of Melitona and Bonaventure declared that the absolution was primarily responsible for the reconciliation of the sinner with the Church but that the forgiveness of sin itself was effected through repentance. According to these theologians, the Church's absolution is to be understood as the Church's request (which is unfailingly granted) that God shall remit the sinner's guilt. The Dominican Cardinal Hugo of Saint-Cher (d. 1233) ascribed to absolution a direct causal influence on the forgiveness of sins.

Thomas Aquinas calls the penitential act of the sinner—which for him includes repentance, confession, and satisfaction—the *matter* of the sacrament and absolution the *form*. The matter and form, in his view, function as a single cause. They combine in blotting out the guilt if the sin has already been remitted through the repentance which preceded the reception of the sacrament. In regarding this as the rule, Aquinas is in agreement with an almost unanimous earlier tradition. In the light of this interpretation, the Church's absolution works in advance: the repentance of the sinner is determined by the Church's absolution because it is ordered to it and hence has the effect of remitting sin. As to the order of importance of repentance and absolution, Aquinas says that the effect of the sacrament is to be found primarily in the absolution.

The Franciscan theologian Duns Scotus regards the Church's absolution alone as the external sign of the sacrament. In his view the subjective acts of the penitent are not an essential part of the sacrament but its prerequisite.

The Council of Trent follows Aquinas but takes into account the view of Duns Scotus (represented at the conciliar discussions chiefly by Tapper) in that it adds the words "as it were" to its definition of the matter and points out that penitential confession and satisfaction are a part of the sacrament of penance since they contribute to its integrity and to the full and total forgiveness of sin. It is further to be noted that the council states that the power of the sacrament is to be found primarily in the words of absolution.

ABSOLUTION

The formula used by the Council of Trent to describe absolution, i.e. reconciliation with the Church, has a long history. In the early Church and that of the early Middle Ages up to the Carolingian period, being received again into the community of the Church, which took place through prayer and the laying-on of hands, was regarded as the guarantee of the forgiveness of sins. There were many forms of this prayer in the early Church. We find both petitionary prayers, in the strict sense, and prayers expressed in the form of a desire. In the former, the Church turns directly to God, and in the latter indirectly, in that prayers are spoken over the sinner. From the Carolingian period on, we find indicative forms, often combined with supplicatory and optative ones. From the thirteenth century on, the supplicatory forms largely disappear, while the combination of optative and indicative forms becomes more common. Thomas Aquinas regarded the indicative form as the only form of the sacrament of penance, and he was able to cite the unanimous opinion of his contemporary colleagues in Paris in support of this view. But liturgical practice continued to combine optative and indicative forms until the Council of Florence, and finally the Council of Trent, clarified the matter. A historical survey shows that in the case of the sacrament of penance as in that of the other sacraments, the Church used its authority to give the central symbol of the sacrament, which originated with Christ, such a form that the sacrament can be performed today only by means of the symbol it has determined.

In the Eastern Church today, we find that the original deprecative form has been retained. Though indicative forms are also used, they are not found in the ritual. In many parts of the Orthodox Church, absolution contains both the request for forgiveness and the authoritative declaration of that forgiveness.

THE CONFESSION OF SINS

Confession and Faith

Let us first consider the subjective acts of the sinner which Thomas Aquinas regards as belonging to the external sign of the sacrament. We shall take them in the following order: the confession of sin, repentance, and satisfaction.

According to Scripture, it is a God-given law that the sinner shall confess his sins (Gen. 3,9-13; 4,9-15; Lev. 5,5f.; Num. 5,7; 2 Sam. 12,13; Ps. 32,1-5; Prov. 28,13; Acts 19,5; 1 Jn. 1,9; Jas. 5,16). Many of these texts refer only to a confession of sin to God. This does not, of course, mean that the sinner tells the sin to God, but rather that through his confession the sinner acknowledges his sin and thus withdraws himself from it. Sometimes Scripture expressly demands that he confess it before men (e.g., the prophets). The need for a sacramental confession of sin can also be derived from the fact that according to Jesus' authorizing words, the absolution calls for a decision on the part of the Church authorities, and this presupposes a knowledge of the sin.

The Fathers developed these scriptural indications into a teaching on the necessity of the confession of sin. They offer evidence that the confession of mortal sin was customary from the beginning. From them we learn of the whole penitential procedure in the early Church, concerning which we should otherwise know nothing. In the first instance, either the sinner went to the bishop on his own initiative and confessed his sin, or he was confronted by the bishop because of wrongdoing which had become public knowledge, and then confessed his sin. If the community knew nothing of the sin of their member, they were not, as we have noted, informed of its precise nature but only inferred his sinfulness from the fact that he had been excluded from the community. Thus the public act of penance was a confession of sin in a general sense, and therefore penance as a whole was called *exhomologesis,* or *confessio.* As a special act of humility the penitent, having made his confession to the bishop, might choose to make another in public before the community gathered for divine worship.

As we have seen, during the first six centuries it was usually only grave sins which were subject to penance in the Church through the private confession of sin, though minor offenses were confessed (primarily in monasteries) in connection with spiritual direction. At any rate, the Fathers believed that only a man who became aware of his sin and acknowledged it could obtain forgiveness: the proud and self-righteous person who is blind to his sin or denies it cannot be liberated from it.

The purpose of confession is not primarily to present a report or inventory but to accuse and condemn oneself. This is done, in the first place, before the priest as the representative of the Church community, but ultimately before the omniscient and all-holy God, in confrontation with the cross of Christ by which the Father in his mercy has judged sin. Thus confession is to be understood as contrition expressed in words. As long as the sinner contents himself with a general awareness of sinfulness, he can avoid the serious self-scrutiny which leads to contrition; for then he is able to overlook the personal sins which only he can answer for and to experience his own sinfulness simply as part of the universal imperfection deriving from the fall.

Confession and conversion from mortal sin must be expressed in a special personal confession. This is so because a man experiences contrition as a member of the Church, to which he is responsible. For the sin of the member does not remain enclosed within the sphere of the individual ego. As we have seen, it involves the whole community; it is an offense against the "we" of the Church, and must therefore be expiated before the community. By confessing his sinfulness before the community he asks forgiveness for the wrong done to the community and also for the community's intercession on his behalf. Further damage is avoided, however, and the possibility of permanent discrimination against the sinner, if the confession is made only to the community's representative, the priest, who is bound to absolute silence.

The reason for contrition being expressed in words rather than in some visible sign is that a man can make the clearest self-representation in words: words are his mode of self-expression; he is a word-being. Inasmuch as the confession is a self-accusation involving a willingness to accept the judgment of the priest (and in it the judgment of God), it is possible to regard the confession of sin as an act of personal spiritual utterance and self-development.

What we have said concerning personal confession is in no way intended to detract from the importance of the general communal confession of sin by the whole community. But the response to this communal confession is the communal absolution which does not relieve a person in mortal sin of the obligation to make a special private confession.

Mortal and Venial Sins

According to the teaching of the Council of Trent, it is the divine ordinance that all mortal sins committed since baptism must be confessed, both with respect to their nature and to the number of times they have been committed. The reason for this, the council says, is that the priest functions here as a judge. Without knowing the facts, he cannot pass judgment or determine the proper punishment. The council dismisses the objection that this obligation leads to a perpetual torture of conscience, saying that only those grave sins which can be remembered after careful reflection need be confessed. Sins which have been forgotten are blotted out along with the others. But if someone remembers such a sin after confession, it must be submitted to the Church's power of the keys at his next confession (DS 1679ff., 1706f., 1682; cf. also DS 1157, 1270).

Luther maintained that although in individual confession we should mention all those sins which we are aware of or feel in our hearts, a total confession of sin is impossible and hence unnecessary. If absolution applied only to the sins mentioned in confession, we should not, Luther thought, be helped very much. The distinction between venial and mortal sin must not, he warned, deceive us into thinking that venial sins need not be taken seriously. The danger of minimizing the importance of sin, on the one hand, and of scrupulosity, on the other, must be avoided. In the sense that Luther meant them, his theses do not contradict the Tridentine statement or the papal bull *Exsurge Domine* of June 15, 1520 (DS 1456, 1464). However, many of them were interpreted and publicized at the time of the Reformation in the sense condemned by the council. It is to be observed that the council also points out that even a grave sin can be forgotten, a statement which is only formally different from Luther's view that owing to our imperfect self-knowledge we are incapable of recounting even all our grave sins. The Tridentine definition assumes that Christians can distinguish without too much difficulty between grave and venial sins; otherwise these terms would be meaningless. Although it may not always be possible in every particular instance to decide whether a sin is grave or not, it must generally lie within the power of a conscientious average Christian to see this difference quickly, clearly, and with certainty. According to the council's statement, only those grave sins of which the Christian, after carefully examining himself, is certain need be confessed.

It is in accordance with the general view of theologians and the Church's practice that a physical or genuine moral impossibility (e.g., when vast numbers need to receive the sacrament) is recognized by the council. In such cases, general absolution can be given.

From the impenetrable darkness which constitutes the mystery of sin Scripture brings to light certain aspects which can help us to distinguish between the two kinds of sin. The man in mortal sin has turned away from God: he has become lawless, a rebel, withdrawing himself from the divine authority and acting as if he were his own master. He makes himself the norm and the center of his own life. Sin, then, is a form of lie. The sinner becomes the slave of the devil, the father of lies. Because God comes to the encounter with man in Christ, enmity towards God becomes enmity towards Christ: the sinner crucifies Christ anew. Enmity towards Christ widens into enmity towards the Church, the body of Christ. The nature of sin, realized in faith, becomes apparent through Christ and his work.

The foregoing considerations apply only to mortal sin. Scripture also speaks of sins which do not involve a betrayal of God but nevertheless indicate a careless, thoughtless attitude towards him. The Council of Trent stated that the confession of these "venial" sins is not necessary but is permitted and valuable. The sacrament of penance was instituted primarily for the forgiveness of mortal sin, and secondarily for the wiping out of daily sin, sin in an analogous sense (cf., however, the encyclical *Mystici Corporis* and the encyclical *Mediator Dei* of Pius XII).

Benedict XIV—and canon law sometime later—declared that even those mortal sins that had already been subject to the sacrament of penance could be confessed again. The reason for this is, as the Greek Fathers regularly point out, that sin is not merely a single sinful action but a whole sinful complex. Although the particular guilt is wiped out by the absolution, this does not destroy the whole complex of guilt, the punishment that sin brings with it and the whole tendency to further sin that it produces. Like the Greek theologians, we can call this whole complex "sin." It is continually reduced through fresh absolution, although the guilt itself is no longer affected by the fresh absolution, since it has already been wiped out by the earlier one.

In the history of the sacrament of penance we find many attempts to define the differences between grave and venial sin more precisely. In the period of the Fathers the emphasis is more on the objective content, whereas in the modern period and today it is more on the subjective attitude (full insight and full freedom). The history of these endeavors shows us that in regard to the objective element, i.e. the importance of an action for human life from the individual and the collective point of view, there have been many uncertainties and variations. They continue to the present day. But also in regard to the subjective element it is difficult to draw firm lines in any particular case. Moral theology has developed norms for both spheres. Their application, especially in regard to the combination of the objective and subjective elements, often leads to ambiguous results. However fundamental the difference between mortal and venial sin—so that one must not regard mortal sin as simply venial sin on a larger scale—it is difficult to state always whether a particular case is a mortal or a venial sin. Ultimately every man bears in his own conscience the responsibility for his actions and hence must make his own decisions concerning himself. This implies that conscience must be constantly formed and purified so that it does not fall victim to selfishness, frivolity, self-glorification or—at the opposite extreme—scrupulosity.

SORROW FOR SIN

Its Significance

Contrition, which in a certain sense belongs within the sign-field of the sacrament, is the expression of inner conversion, i.e.

the inward turning away from the sinful action and from the way of life inimical to God which it reveals (Council of Trent, 14th session, ch. 4, DS 1676ff.). It is a profound event in which a man turns to face another way on his journey through life and sets out in a new direction. Thus it includes the determination to live a new life.

A man's sinful action does not, so to speak, erupt from his ego in a sudden and unexpected way. Rather, it is the issue of a slowly developing movement, directed against God either consciously or unconsciously, which determines the present course of the man's life and impels him along it with increasing momentum. Since man possesses himself at every moment on the basis of his own personality, he is always free, in a moment of decision, to turn away from himself in his role of a creature in rebellion against God and—for God's sake—to turn back to God. This turning-back to God is an essential part of contrition. It is possible only if and insofar as God calls the sinner to him. The free decision of the sinner consists in listening to God's call and responding to it. The way to God is through Christ, for Christ is the mediator between man and God and the bringer of salvation. By turning to the Father the sinner discovers his true self. He gives up the self that has been falsified by sin and fallen into a life of lies and comes, in a real sense, to himself. Turning to oneself means turning to the community. Or rather, turning to Jesus Christ is turning to the head of the Church, and hence to the people of God and the body of Christ. It means, therefore, the discovery of one's own self.

Contrition is made an essential part of absolution by the Church and only in absolution does it acquire its full meaning. Together with absolution it constitutes a salvific whole, even if the contrition aroused by God in the sinner is enough to make God receive him again into the embrace of his love.

Perfect and Imperfect Contrition

Since the early period of scholasticism the distinction has been made between perfect and imperfect contrition (*contritio,* in the narrower sense, and *attritio*). This division is connected with the problem of the relation between the personal penance of the sinner and reconciliation with the Church, i.e. absolution. After Anselm of Canterbury contrition became generally known as *contritio* (it had earlier been called *compunctio*). At the beginning of the thirteenth century we find the term *attritio* being used. The distinction between *contritio* and *attritio* was at first regarded as one not of kind but of degree: it was a question of the depth of the grief felt (the sorrow involved in *contritio* being greater). But when the doctrine of *gratia informans* established itself in the course of the thirteenth century, the criterion became the relation of contrition to justifying grace. For high scholasticism, then (e.g., Thomas Aquinas), *contritio* is the contrition that is given and characterized by grace itself, whereas *attritio* is attrition that is not given by grace. Dun Scotus, however, attached greater importance to *attritio* than had preceding theologians in this sense, that he saw it as likewise orientated towards the ultimate goal of man. Even contrition which is not given by grace can, he held, proceed from a love of God.

The Council of Trent uses the word *contritio* for contrition in general, of which *attritio* is a certain kind, namely *contritio imperfecta*, imperfect contrition. The distinction it makes, in other words, is one of degree. The council calls *attritio* genuine contrition: for although it cannot of itself justify the sinner, it prepares him to receive God's grace in the sacrament of penance, and love cannot be completely excluded from it.

It is therefore incorrect to distinguish between perfect and imperfect contrition as contrition motivated by love and contrition motivated by fear. The distinction which may be made is in the kinds of love involved. Perfect contrition is that which proceeds from perfect love of God. In perfect love, God is loved for his own sake, not out of regard for the salvation he has promised to man. This love means the acknowledgment of God as Absolute Being and hence includes worship. Imperfect contrition, on the other hand, is an expression of that love whereby man gives himself to God with a view to salvation. It includes hope and longing.

Although the two kinds of contrition can be distinguished conceptually in this way, the distinction becomes less clear in practice, since both involve acts of love. In his love of God man is not capable (permanently, at any rate) of getting away from the fact that God is the One who calls him to himself and makes possible the fulfillment of his life, assuring him of blessedness in the ultimate future. This becomes still clearer when we recall that God is the Love which gives itself (1 Jn. 4,8.16). If a man loves God, he loves him as this Love. Moreover, even a man whose love is imperfect cannot fail to see that only God is able to grant him the ultimate fulfillment of his life, only he can call him into a future of blessedness. And so, inevitably, this imperfect love, too, includes an element of worship.

It becomes evident, therefore, that despite the intellectual distinction we are able to make, the difference in practical terms becomes one of accent. For granted that a man feels sorrow for his sins out of perfect love and therefore arouses perfect contrition in himself, he is still unable to suppress his hope for God. On the other hand, the man who is sorry for his sins out of imperfect love, which involves the longing and hope for salvation, is not indifferent to God himself. On the contrary: the hope for salvation includes the longing for God, who is absolute Being and perfect Love. Thus the difference between the two kinds of contrition becomes simply a difference in the degree of intensity of love. There is no borderline between the two, where one ends and the other begins.

The Council of Trent largely left open the question of the relation between perfect and imperfect contrition and the question of the relation between perfect contrition and absolution. Hence a controversy arose in post-Tridentine theology which was often conducted with passionate intensity and not without personal polemics. On the one hand, it was recognized that perfect contrition justifies even before absolution because it is perfect love. Hence the question arose of what effect, in that case, can be ascribed to absolution. But on the other hand, there was the idea that there could be no justification without perfect contrition. The Council of Trent states that in fact the sinner who turns to God in faith, placing his hope in him, begins to love him as the source of all justice, and thus turns away from sin (DS 1526). Although it speaks here only of an incipient love, this love is described as the preparation for justification. The view of the Thomist school was that this incipient love is transformed into perfect love through absolution. But here again the question is raised whether absolution means more than simply a declaration that a sin has been forgiven: for what the Thomist is saying is that justification is effected by perfect love, even if this perfect love is brought about through absolution. Imperfect contrition seems to have no meaning here.

The views held by the various theological schools, especially those of Thomas Aquinas and Duns Scotus, sometimes conflicted with one another. The theologians of Salamanca attempted a kind of reconciliation. They said that imperfect contrition necessarily involved the love of hope, if not the love of worship, and that every act of true contrition implied the love of hope: it did not need to be explicitly aroused. Later, Alphonsus of Liguori propounded this view. It may be regarded as the popular view today.

The fact that perfect contrition gives justification before absolution follows from those words in which Jesus celebrated the saving power of love (Jn. 14,21ff.; 1 Jn. 4,7f.; Lk. 7,47-50). In John's first epistle we read the following (1 Jn. 2,29-3,3):

If you know that he is righteous, you must recognize that every man who does right is his child. How great is the love that the Father has shown to us! We were called God's children, and such we are; and the reason why the godless world does not recognize us is that it has not known him. Here and now, dear friends, we are God's children; what we shall be has not yet been disclosed, but we know that when it is disclosed we shall be like him, because we shall see him as he is. Everyone who has this hope before him purifies himself, as Christ is pure. (Cf. 1 Pet. 4,8; Ez. 32,12; Is. 30,19; Ps. 32,5; Prov. 8,17; 10,12)

These passages are fully illustrative of the saving power of perfect contrition. It is possible only for someone who is already living in the friendship of God and at peace with him: it is the fruit and the sign of grace. A person who returns to God in loving sorrow for sin has already returned to God's love. God's first care is for the sheep who is lost, and his forgiveness is founded on the contrition which he himself brings about in the sinner. Contrition is the work of God in the world, reconciling it to himself through Christ (cf. 2 Cor. 5,19f.).

The fact that imperfect contrition also has a saving and justifying effect can be inferred from the words of Jesus that we are not to fear those who seek to kill the body, but are unable to kill the soul, but rather him who is able to destroy both body and soul in hell (Mt. 10,28; 5,29f.; Lk. 13,3; cf. also Mt. 3,7-12; Lk. 3,7ff.). Moreover, it will be recalled that the Council of Trent declared that imperfect contrition is good and salvific because it prepares a man for justification. For though it cannot of itself, without the sacrament of penance, lead the sinner to justification, by removing the obstacles to the entrance of divine love, it clears the way for absolution (DS 1677, 1558). However, the question upon which we touched above, with regard to what is ultimately achieved by absolution, still remains. Following Thomas Aquinas, many theologians hold that absolution does not bring about the forgiveness of sins directly but transforms the incipient love contained in imperfect contrition into perfect love and thus reconciles the sinner with God. Through imperfect contrition, the way is opened up for God to enter into a man: God gives himself and the man is transformed.

The questions left open by the Council of Trent and discussed but not solved in post-Tridentine theology are an inheritance from the theology of the patristic age. The Fathers had constantly been concerned with the problem of the relation between the sinner's subjective penance and the reconciliation with the Church, and with the further question of the relation between the reconciliation with the Church and the divine forgiveness of sins. These questions belong to the whole problem, which can never be fully resolved, of the relation of man as creature to God as creator.

What is raised here is the universal question of the interaction of God and man. If we say that God alone acts, man's independence and freedom are undermined; but if we say without further explanation that God and man work together, this makes God and man partners on the same level. An explanation must be found in terms of which, on God's side, everything which is done is accomplished through his omnipotent will; and on man's side, everything is accomplished through his own efforts, so that he remains fully responsible for his actions. If we say that all man's decisions are wrought by God, then we are confronted with the problem of how it is that the fact that everything which happens in the world owes its origin and its accomplishment to God does not compel us to say that God alone accomplishes everything—how, in other words, there is any room left for human freedom. This is a mystery we cannot solve.

The fact of the matter is that in the sacrament of penance it is God himself who speaks to man in the Church's words of absolution. As the Council of Trent says in opposition to the views of the Reformation, the absolution is not to be referred only to the Church's authority to preach the gospel; it is not a mere declaration, lacking in the power to remit sin. Nevertheless it does have the function of proclamation also, a proclamation in which the saving power of Jesus Christ and his heavenly Father itself is effective. For God the human words of the Church's absolution are the means of giving himself to man. Thus the words of proclamation are not merely declarative, they are creative as well: they produce the effect which they declare. This, of course, is characteristic of every sacramental sign. Luther himself had the same view of the word.

To return to the question raised in post-Tridentine theology concerning the question of what is achieved by absolution if perfect contrition already brings about the forgiveness of sins: in the light of the patristic concept of contrition and absolution constituting one organic whole, which we mentioned earlier, consideration should be given to the ecclesiological function of the sacrament of penance. As we have seen, after the twelfth century full justice was not done to this aspect, since it became almost completely supplanted by the individualistic approach. As a consequence no real function was seen for absolution. But conceived as constituting an organic whole with perfect contrition, absolution does have a special function within the ecclesiological context. It is then the equivalent of reconciliation, i.e. reception back into the Church community. Only through this reacceptance into the Church— not temporally but causally—is communion re-established with the Holy Spirit and in him with God the Father, inasmuch as God gives himself to the member of the Church through Christ as its head, i.e. as our firstborn brother.

SATISFACTION

We have seen that in the early Church the performing of penance was regarded as a fundamental part of the whole penitential procedure. Consequently penance was often referred to as a painful baptism. The penance done by the sinner was regarded as replacing the eternal punishment the sinner had merited (the Western Church), or at least as a means of purification (the Eastern Church). This meant that the penance had to be severe, difficult, and of long duration. Indeed the Church frequently hesitated to pronounce absolution for fear that the sinner had not done enough—but to determine what was sufficient was more or less impossible. It was believed that God determined the measure of punishment, but how much penance God requires of a man is not revealed to us. This dilemma was in some sense resolved by the teaching of Cyprian and Clement of Alexandria that what was still lacking in the penance of the sinner upon his reconciliation with the Church would have to be made up in the hereafter, whether as satisfaction and expiation or as purification. Adopting this view, the Church was able to moderate the rigors of penance, making it increasingly gentle and simple until it assumed the easy forms of satisfaction found today.

There is much evidence in Scripture, in both the Old and the New Testaments, that over and above the repentance necessary for the forgiveness of sin, God requires penance of the sinner so that the wrong he has done may be redressed and the breach of order which his sinful act produced both in himself and in the world may be healed (cf. Gen. 3,14-19; Num. 20,12; 2 Sam. 12,13f.; Col. 1,24; 1 Cor. 9,27; 2 Cor. 7,10).

Whereas the Western Church sees the forgiveness of sin as a single, self-contained action from which it is possible to distinguish satisfaction, expiation, and restitution, the Eastern Church regards forgiveness as a liberation both from guilt as such and from the passions it has engendered and the punishment it has incurred. The forgiveness of sin, in that view, must be understood as a gradual process. The meaning of this interpretation will be clear only if we recall that this theology of sin does not distinguish with any precision between guilt and punishment. Following Paul's theology as expounded in Romans 5, the Eastern Church regards sin and punishment as constituting one complex of evil. This raises the question, which it does not consider, of whether the punishment is something imposed from without on the sinner or whether it consists in an inhibition of life issuing from the sin itself; in other words, whether the punishment is inherent in the sin or is something inflicted. It is more in accordance with the approach of the theologians of the Eastern Church to regard it as the former, i.e. as a consequence of the wound inflicted by sin, as a downward tendency in the life of the individual and the life of the community which is produced by sin. But the distinction is not an important one for the theological interpretation of punishment. Even if God freely decides to judge man and punish him for his rebellion or his failure, this is always a punishment that is appropriate to the situation of sinful men. It is intended, for as long as he lives, to move him to repent, i.e. to liberate himself from his sinful way of life.

The Council of Trent speaks in the spirit of Scripture when it rejects the view that the need for satisfaction, which is part of the sacrament of penance, contradicts Scripture, diminishes the value or merit of the satisfaction made by Christ, or is a purely human institution, and states on the contrary that the priest should impose an appropriate penance on the sinner (DS 1689ff., 1699, 1712ff., 1715).

Of course, every explanation of sacramental satisfaction must have the expiatory death of Christ as its starting point. The Christian's work of purification, satisfaction, and expiation is a participation in the sacrifice of Jesus Christ on Golgotha, and only as such has it saving significance. There is only one way to God: Christ. In baptism, man acquires a share, in the Holy Spirit, in the life of the crucified and risen Christ and thus community with God the Father. Through this complex encounter he is released from the domination of the powers of destruction; but by mortal sin he withdraws from his relationship with God and returns to his former subjection to those powers. He can be freed from them again only by returning to the Way which is Christ. The likeness to Christ that is brought about through baptism and can never be lost offers the starting point for a new encounter with him. God blots out the guilt of a sinful act through the cross of Jesus Christ. This movement of God's grace towards man is paralleled by the movement of man freed from sin towards God; that, too, derives its value from the cross of Jesus Christ. There is no other way in which man can move towards God. Through sharing in the cross of Christ man seeks to repair the disorder which his sin has brought about in himself, in the Church, in the whole human community, and in the creation.

As we have already observed in an earlier context, a sinful act always takes place in a transient moment of free decision; but it transcends itself, and thus acquires a certain independence of the moment when it was committed. It brings into existence in the sinner a lasting state of self-contradiction in that he comes into conflict with himself as a creature, someone redeemed by Christ and living within the Church. The consequence is a kind of split personality: on the one hand, the sinner by his nature as a creature and by his baptism belongs to God; on the other, he is in conflict with God, and hence at the same time with his own real self. Through the power that sin has obtained over him, he is continually driven to commit new sins (the disorder of concupiscence). Moreover, he loses his sense of the right relations of men and things to one another and to God and also that capacity for self-denial which is essential if meaningful orders are to be created in political, economic, and social life. Thus sin reveals itself as not only a wrong action against God but also as a wrong action, permanent in its effects, directed against the person who does it and against all other men. We call these consequences the "punishments" of sin. Let us point out again that although we make the abstract distinction between punishment that is part of the sin itself and punishment that is imposed, every sin bears its punishment within itself. God's punishments, of which Scripture speaks, are to be understood as confirmations, concrete and specific realizations of the punishments which proceed from the sin itself as a permanent source of evil (cf., for example, Gen. 3,14-19).

Contrition for sin includes the will to make restitution for the havoc it has worked in the sinner's own life, in the life of the community, and in the whole creation. The sinful action can never be expunged from human history, nor can the consequences of sin be fully overcome. As we have said, we cannot know how far the consequences of any one sin reach. But if the sinner rejects the false values of which his sin is an expression and the self-glorification and selfishness that sin involves, he is trying to remove from the world the disorder of which he has been the cause.

The willingness of the sinner to make reparation is expressed in a concrete, tangible sharing in the saving cross of Christ through detaching himself from the things of the world which he has misused and by surrendering himself to God. In the early Church there were several more or less official forms of this detachment from the world: fasting combined with almsgiving, going without sleep, and sexual abstinence. Food, possessions, sleep, sexual intercourse—all belong to the necessities of our historical condition. In fasting and almsgiving a man detaches himself from the goods which support earthly life; in sexual abstinence he renounces the activity which is the basis of earthly life. To detach oneself from the things of the world is not the same thing as despising the world. The Christian is never called upon to do that; on the contrary, it is forbidden to him, for the forms of earthly life are part of God's creation. The Christian is called to love men and the things of this world because and insofar as he loves God. By detaching himself from things he acknowledges, on the one hand, that God is the supreme Lord; but on the other, that the world is a penultimate reality proceeding from God. The participation in the cross of Christ which is involved in detachment from the world has wide-ranging salvific consequences. In that God is acknowledged as Lord, satisfaction is made to him. In that man must demand an effort from himself, his actions are expiatory. By surrendering his autonomy with regard to the disposition of his own life, the lives of others, and the things of the world, he is purified of his self-will and pride, and thus becomes once more capable of loving again and of using things in the right way.

The acceptance of the satisfaction imposed by the confessor intensifies the expression of the sinner's penitential attitude as a sharing in the cross of Christ, in that the sinner lets another person tell him what to do and dutifully follows out this direction—a reversal of the sinful action which proceeded from pride. Thus in penance the saving cross of Christ acquires concrete power over man. Penance becomes a manifestation of the cross of Christ, which reveals its saving activity in it.

THE MINISTER OF THE SACRAMENT OF PENANCE

It must be remembered that in this, as in every other sacrament, God himself lays hold of man through Christ in the Holy Spirit and draws him into living fellowship with himself. God's action appears in the action of the Church's minister. The Council of Trent declares that the Church's minister of this sacrament is the bishop or the confessor he commissions, basing the ruling on the words of Christ in Matthew 18,18 and John 20,23.

The reason is not far to seek. The administration of the sacrament of penance includes the authoritative exclusion of the sinner from the Church community and his subsequent reconciliation with it. In both these actions the appropriate representative of the community is the bishop or the confessor deputed by him. The community itself is also involved in the action, but in a different way; namely, through its prayers and penance. Until the sixth century priests played no independent role in the administering of the sacrament: it was their task to support the bishop in various ways, admit people to penance in his name and perform the act of reconciliation. But from the sixth century on, priests acquired greater independence, a process which started in Spain. The more extensive the Church communities became, the less the bishop was able to undertake all the Church's duties himself and the more the independence of the priests grew. This process was hastened by the development of the practice of repeating the sacrament of penance which took place in the sixth and seventh centuries and by the increase in private penance.

As the confession of sin became regarded as an important expression of repentance, the view developed, first in the Eastern Church and later in the Church of the West, that the confession of sin to a Christian who was not a bishop or a priest was also of saving efficacy—namely, for the purpose of spiritual direction. Here all that was called for was that the spiritual director should have experience in such matters. As we have seen, this practice was cultivated primarily in the monasteries, but it found adherents in the outside world as well. Although this confession for the purpose of spiritual advice and direction was not sacramental in the strict sense, the situation developed in which spiritual fathers who prayed with their spiritual children for the forgiveness of their sins ended by assuring their clients that their sins were forgiven, whether these directors were priests or not. The Pseudo-Dionysius protested against this practice, which was common in the Eastern Church as early as the fifth and sixth centuries. From around 800 on, it was almost exclusively the monks who administered penance in the Eastern Church. Simeon the New Theologian (d. 1041) justified this practice by saying that whereas originally the apostles had passed on the authority received from Christ to forgive sins to the bishops, the Church hierarchy had in the course of time themselves fallen into sin and hence been abandoned by grace. This grace, he held, had passed to the monks—not to all of them but only to those who were distinguished by their holiness. After the thirteenth century we find a movement in the opposite direction in the Eastern Church. Gradually it became the ordained priest who was regarded as the exclusive minister of the sacrament. Confession to laymen never became widespread in the Russian Church.

In the West, confession to laymen went through a long development. According to the rules of the Irish and Anglo-Saxon monasteries, the monks had to confess even their most minor offenses daily before the monastic community or its leaders. This kind of confession, which was regarded as an effective means of spiritual progress, was recommended to the laity also, apart from sacramental confession. Indeed, the Venerable Bede expressly recommended the nonsacramental confession of minor sins before other lay people. It never became a general practice, however.

Nevertheless, because of the importance they attributed to the confession of sin, many theologians took the view that owing to the bond of faith and love between the members of the Church community, a layman had authority to absolve in an emergency (Albert the Great). Thomas Aquinas, although he did not ascribe any authority to the laity in the matter of absolution, stated that anyone confessing to a lay person in an emergency was absolved because it is Christ himself who blots out sin. Behind these views, which may seem strange in the light of the general development of the Church, there may have been the early Christian idea of the collective performance of the sacrament of penance. It was accepted that the bishop or the confessor he commissioned was the representative of the particular Church community whom Christ himself had chosen and who was responsible for the exclusion and reconciliation of the sinner; but the question was, What happened when such a representative was not available? Can another member of the community then responsibly assume the function of the absent member of the hierarchy? Albert and Thomas thought so, but their views were not generally adopted by the Church.

Luther went along with the tendencies which had emerged in the Middle Ages. He declared that normally the ordained priest was the proper confessor, but he accepted the idea that confession might be made to a non-ordained person, a layman. Consequently, the school of thought in Lutheranism which accepted confession to laymen was able to quote him in support of their views. It must be remembered, however, that by ordination Luther did not mean the consecration of a priest in the Catholic sense, but the commissioning by the community of a relevant authority. Like Simeon the New Theologian he believed that through the sins of the hierarchy the Church had been reduced to a state of emergency, and that therefore non-ordained Christians who had a living faith were called upon to exercise the saving functions previously performed by the hierarchy.

To administer the sacrament of penance, the priest must not only be consecrated, he must also have the necessary legal authority. This is either given with the office or specially conferred on him (ordinary or delegated authority to hear confessions). Through his consecration he has received the inner capacity to administer the sacrament, but in view of the fact that a legal judgment is involved—i.e. exclusion and reconciliation—he must also have authority over the penitent. The pope has this power over all baptized persons. Absolution, as can be seen from the history of the sacrament, is a combined action of consecrated and pastoral authority. Owing to the particular nature of the sacrament, the power imparted through consecration can be exercised only through pastoral power, and *vice versa*. Because of the legal decision involved in the administering of the sacrament, particularly grave sins can be reserved for the bishop or the pope to pronounce on. This is done in order to make the sinner aware of the gravity of his offense and move him to greater penitence.

This limiting of the power of absolution to particular members of the Church does not have the effect of dividing Christians into two groups, sinners and those who sit in judgment on them. Absolution should rather be viewed as a fraternal service done by some men for others, something that must be given and received as a gift of the love of God. Moreover, everyone who has committed grave sin, no matter what position he holds in the Church, must accept this ministry. If absolution is given and received in this attitude of mind, then there is no greater measure of interpersonal tension than is inevitably part of the transmitting of salvation by one man to another (cf. Gal. 6,1-5; Mt. 18,23-35).

◄12

Penance and Salvation

As we have repeatedly stressed, the purpose of the sacrament of penance is the forgiveness of mortal sin. There are two elements involved here, the praise of God as holy and merciful and the salvation of man: *confessio* means the praise of God as well as the confession of sin. The fact that God's saving action is represented in the sacrament emerges most clearly in the way it was performed in the early Church, i.e. through exclusion and reconciliation. That it has the character of a judgment is manifest—that is, of an act of pastoral authority directed towards the pardoning of the guilty person. It is an effective symbol of the action of God towards the sinner because the merciful judgment upon him is made by God.

As the sacrament is performed today, exclusion and reconciliation are no longer two distinctly separated acts: today's form is almost identical with what the early Church called reconciliation. And yet a vestige of the division into two distinct phases remains in that the penitent separates himself from the community's celebration of the eucharist and goes to a specially provided place for confession, thus revealing himself as a sinner and a man in need of repentance. Only after he has received absolution does he return to the eucharist. This procedure is what remains of the public character of the sacrament which was manifest in the early Church. The practice of the early Church was the fullest form of the sacrament, whereas the present-day practice is a greatly

241

reduced version. The same process can be seen at work in the case of baptism and the other sacraments.

Scripture records many judgments of God on the sin of humanity. The Old Testament prophets interpret the tribulations which come upon man as heavenly judgments. God's judgment of sinful mankind reached both its climax and its fulfillment in his merciful judgment on Jesus Christ, his Son. The death of Jesus has many aspects; one is the aspect of judgment. To return briefly here to our fuller discussion of this aspect in an earlier volume:

Through the cross of Christ, God passed judgment on man. That is to say, in a divine, sovereign act of justice and holiness he made manifest the situation into which man fell through sin. In Christ's death on the cross the abyss of sin and the existential lostness of the sinner, and at the same time the holiness and righteousness of God, are revealed.

As devastating as the judgment of the cross was, it is nevertheless a judgment of grace. God passed this judgment only once; he sent his only-begotten Son to the cross. Only this man was able, owing to his nature, to reveal the abyss of sin, because he alone was empowered to carry out God's revelation of himself as holy and righteous.

The goal of the death on the cross is not death but new life. This cannot be attained simply through the giving up of that old life which had fallen into sin; it is possible only through a renovation from within. God holds man responsible; man must answer for his acts, must bear the consequences of his decisions. Jesus, through his death on the cross, does this in the name of all men. How man is to answer for his sin God has already laid down from the beginning of his eternal plan of salvation: through Jesus' death on the cross.[1]

The sinner who receives a renewed share in the death of Jesus Christ in a revival of his faith is accepting God's judgment through Jesus. If he preserves his friendship with Christ, he need have no fear of condemnation at the final judgment. When the sinner acknowledges Jesus Christ in faith as his representative in accepting

---

[1]See Volume III of this work, *Dogma: God and His Christ* (New York: Sheed and Ward, 1971), "The Death of Jesus."

the judgment of the Father, he will become himself an image of Jesus, on whom the Father has pronounced a merciful judgment. In the sacrament of penance, the confessor takes the role of the Father and the sinner that of Jesus Christ. In the penitent sinner the cross of Jesus is actualized in that it was a judgment of God.

Since God's judgment of Jesus was a judgment of love, it had the power of creative renovation. The sinner's sharing in the judgment of the cross is productive of the same effect: he is transformed into a new man, the image not only of the crucified but also of the risen Christ. These two elements of judgment and transformation do not succeed each other in time but are interwoven. Even the imposing of penance, i.e. the acceptance of the judgment of the cross, was regarded by the early Church as a grace; and sharing in the resurrection, the new life of Jesus Christ, always includes the sharing in the judgment of the cross. God's merciful judgment is made not only visible but effective by the judgment of the Church: its judgment is a sign that has the creative power of making-present God's judgment.

The absolved sinner has a new position in the Church, in that he is a man who has passed through the judgment of God and been pardoned. It will be revealed at the Last Judgment that he has been forgiven by God (Heb. 3,13), so long as he does not abuse the absolution given him in the sacrament of penance and by fresh sins draw upon himself the fresh judgment of God.

The new place of the absolved sinner in the Church and his resemblance to Christ, because the latter accepted the judgment of the Father, constitute the *res et sacramentum* of penance. This inner sign that is brought about by the outer one is itself the sign of the *res sacramenti*. At the time when the individual approach to the sacrament increasingly overlaid the ecclesiological one, it was the *ornatus animae* that was called the *res et sacramentum*. This was identified with the *poenitentia interior* (Thomas Aquinas). This interpretation can be seen as part of the early Church's understanding of penance, in that the man who is freed from his sin in the sacrament is impelled in a special way by the spirit of penance.

There is no need to point out that the new position in the Church and the resemblance to Christ in penance lead to that way of life described in Scripture and the liturgy as "through Christ to the

Father in the Holy Spirit." The fresh self-communication of himself by Christ to the sinner which takes place in penance naturally results in a new quality in the sinner, namely what we call sanctifying grace.

It is of vital importance for the understanding of what forgiveness of sins involves in the sacrament of penance that it is only God who can forgive sins. If God uses man as mediator, man can only be a tool. Human action, in particular human words, can only be a condition or *causa sine qua non*, the guarantee and sign that God is giving himself again in merciful love to sinful man. Hence the Church's words of absolution are not formally identical with divine forgiveness. And yet it is the words of the Church that bring about the forgiveness of sins. There are, however, different levels in this effect. God pardons through the words of the Church. They have more than an informative function and are, rather, the means through which God promises himself to the sinner. They have creative power in that God works through them; they are a proclamation as well, inasmuch as God renews his promise of himself to man. By being reconciled with the Church, the body of Christ, and enabled once more to take a full share in the life of the Church and the celebration of the eucharist (communion), a man who has received forgiveness for his sins can share with renewed vigor in the movement of the Church community towards its ultimate future.

If only venial sins are to be confessed, the direct effect of the sacrament of penance is likewise a new mode of resemblance to Christ and of membership in his body, since the penitent becomes more fully incorporated with Christ and the Church community, with a consequent increase of sanctifying grace. But what is "new" here is only an intensification of what has gone before. However, this effect cannot be taken alone as the norm for the frequency of confession as a devotion, for there are many ways of increasing one's fellowship with Christ in the Church which formally serve this end, especially the celebration of the eucharist. The question of the frequency of confession as a devotion must be considered in relation to the whole meaning of the sacrament of penance. As we learn from the words of institution and the practice of the early Church, it serves to blot out mortal sin; and this essential purpose is served not only when a mortal sin has actually been committed but also when a course of action has been entered upon which, except for the grace of the sacrament, would issue in mortal sin.

SIN AND PUNISHMENT: INDULGENCES

The problem of indulgences is closely connected with the sacrament of penance. The indulgence is a sacramental which emerged from the practice of penance in the early Middle Ages as a separate entity. It is important that it should be seen as a sacramental, for then it cannot be assigned more importance than the sacrament of penance itself. History shows that there is a danger of this happening, for theological reflection on indulgences did not come until their practice had become established.

With respect to both the theology and the practice of indulgences, it is important that this point should be noted: though the forgiveness of sin as guilt takes place in a single event, this does not necessarily mean that the whole complex of sin—the act and its consequences—is eliminated. In the language of the Church, this is expressed in the distinction between sin and the punishment for sin (punishment here is, of course, to be understood analogously, like every other theological statement). Punishment for sin takes two forms: the involvement of the sinner in a sinful tendency (disordered desires, concupiscence) and the disorder among men and in the world produced by sin. Undergoing the punishment for sin involves both purification and satisfaction or expiation.

The Origin of Indulgences

When the austere early Christian practice of penance began to yield, after the sixth century, to the practice we know today, the penitential works demanded of the sinner in the early Church could no longer be retained in their old form. From that time on, the confession of sin and absolution began to be performed at the same time.

The question presently arose of how the penitential attitude of mind in the sinner could be expressed in a new form of the sacrament of penance if it were not to be realized in a period (long or short) of expulsion from the Christian community. In response to this question and as an aid to confessors, there came into being in the Irish and Anglo-Saxon Church the penitential books we have already mentioned. These set out in an exact and very detailed way the penance which was to be exacted for every sin. With penances thus established on the basis of a fixed "tariff," so to speak, obviously consideration could be given only to the external, objectively established action, with little regard for the inner attitude of mind.

The penances set out in the penitential books were often difficult and severe, and they soon met with considerable opposition. From the seventh century onwards, therefore, an elaborate system of so-called commutations and redemptions began to arise. The punishments set down in the penitential books gradually acquired the character of a norm which helped to establish the specific and reasonable penances that could be performed. To begin with, the difficult penances were simply abbreviated; but gradually they were converted into simple and brief works of penance, prayer, pilgrimage and—from the eleventh century on—penitential fines in the forms of gifts for Church purposes. The latter in particular became very widely practiced. Even these penitential works manifested a certain spirit of penance: sin was still taken seriously. Nevertheless there was the danger that some would submit to these easy penitential exercises without inwardly freeing themselves from their sin. This danger was particularly great in the case of the fines, and they played a fateful role in the origin of the Reformation. It is within the context of this whole development that indulgences have their place.

In the early Church the penance imposed on a sinner might sometimes be shortened by prayer for the intercession of a martyr. This was not regarded simply as a mechanical, partial remission of punishment; it was believed that the martyr's intercession had given the sinner a more intensely penitential attitude of mind in faith, hope and love, from which came the expiation and satisfaction as well as the purifying function of his penance.

At the end of the patristic period and the beginning of the Middle Ages, it was the practice of the Church to offer prayers asking God to remit the sinner's punishment. This intercession was carried out in two ways: by the members of the Church sharing in the sinner's penance through prayer and a sacrificial spirit and by means of official prayers instituted by the Church's hierarchy and adopted, in part, in the penitential liturgy, i.e. what were called the "absolutions." A penitential spirit in the recipient of these authoritative prayers was believed to be the necessary condition of their effectiveness. This had to be proved through appropriate actions recommended and required by the Church. The transition from these "absolutions" to indulgences took place gradually, and almost imperceptibly, in the course of the eleventh and twelfth centuries.

The new element with regard to indulgences was this: the expected effect of the Church's prayer on the afterlife was taken into consideration in measuring the penance done within the Church here on earth, so that the latter could be reduced accordingly. Thus the "absolution," formerly a prayer, became a formal remission of a particular Church punishment and hence a jurisdictional act.

When the theologians set out to offer an explanation and justification of this procedure, the doctrine of the Church's treasury of merit developed. By this was meant Jesus Christ's work of expiation and satisfaction and the expiatory works of the saints which were nourished from this source. In explaining indulgences in terms of the Church's treasury of merit, some medieval theologians stressed Jesus Christ's expiatory suffering, whereas others put the accent on the personal effort of the sinner.

The Teaching of the Church

Wyclif and Hus, and indeed the whole Reformation as well, strongly opposed this doctrine of the Church's treasury of merit and indulgences in general, especially those that could be obtained for money. These things were regarded as a cheapening and a mechanization of the whole process of salvation. That there was a danger of their having that effect cannot be denied, and history shows that many believers succumbed to it. Explaining the doctrine of the Church's treasury of merit in such a way as to banish these dangers and misunderstandings is not easy. Pope Clement IV, the first to proclaim a general indulgence in his Jubilee Bull of 1333, explained it on the basis of the Church's treasury of merit. The Council of Trent was very cautious in its statements on indulgences, stating, in reply to attacks on indulgences and in order to clarify preceding condemnations, that the Church has the authority to grant indulgences; that indulgences are valuable for salvation and hence are to be retained; but that the proper measure must be observed concerning them (DS 1835; cf. 1867).

Further elements of the Church's teaching are these: that as necessary prerequisites to receiving an indulgence one must have been baptized; one must be free of excommunication; grave sin must already have been remitted; the prescribed conditions for receiving the indulgence should be fulfilled; and one should have at least the general intention of obtaining an indulgence.

Indulgences derive from the Church's treasury of the merits of Jesus Christ and the saints. They relate not only to the Church's punishments but also to the punishment of sin before God. They can be applied to the living and the dead, to the former *per modum absolutionis* and to the latter *per modum suffragii*. They are of various kinds.

The "Treasury" of the Church

The belief concerning the Church's treasury of merit is not a defined doctrine of the Church, but it is part of the Church's general awareness of its own faith. Theologians have explained it in very different ways, and the same is true of the formula *per modum absolutionis*.

As regards this formula, the pastoral authority of the Church applies, of course, primarily to the remission of the punishment it has itself imposed. But it is difficult to understand even this remission, because the Church today no longer imposes on the sinner a punishment in the real sense, as in earlier times. We can understand this view only if we remember that the early Christian view of penance remains in the memory of the Church, as a norm that is no longer realized but is still effective as an idea. In granting indulgences, the Church states indirectly that on the basis of the authority imparted to it, it chooses to remit the exclusion from the community which, in the old penitential discipline of the Church, would have been incurred by sin, and also remits the penance connected with it. It would not do justice to the Church's teaching on indulgences, however, if we were to regard the remission of punishment as nothing but a human action by the Church. Rather, the Church holds that the remission of its punishment affects the relationship of the sinner to God and also produces the remittance of the punishment by God. We cannot, of course, know to what degree the "indulgence" affects the punishment ordained by God.

It is important to note that the remission of punishment in the next world is not formally ascribed to the Church's power. It cannot dispose of God and his plans, and such an interpretation would bring the connotation of magic into the Church's actions. Hence we can interpret the Church's jurisdictional act in regard to its effect on the next world only as a request made through Jesus Christ, its head, and in fellowship with those of its members who have already reached their home in God. This request will not be denied, since it takes place in, through, and with Christ. Thus indulgences combine the pastoral authority of the Church with its consecrated authority, the *opus operatum* with the *opus operantis*. Indeed, the *opus operatum*, namely the Church's jurisdiction in regard to earthly punishment, acquires the function of an *opus operans*, namely of prayer to God. What is asked of God is, again, not simply the mechanical suspension or shortening of the punishment—this would be to impose an earthly and human nature on God. What the Church is asking for when it prays to God is that he should give himself to the sinner in such great mercy and love that the latter is freed increasingly from his involvement in sin and prepared to make restitution (satisfaction and expiation). The recipient of the indulgence remains entirely free, so that the effect of the divine self-communication is again qualified by the openness of the sinner towards God. The latter is expressed in his obedience to the Church, in which he performs those works of penance that are prescribed for the indulgence.

These ideas offer us an approach to the understanding of the Church's treasury of merit. It must not be conceived in a material way, as a fixed store of spiritual goods—goods of satisfaction or expiation—or as a spiritual capital from which the Church can decide to dispense a certain amount. That would be to import a strange and distorting element into the Christian faith. It was the misconception which was in no small measure responsible for the Reformation. When the Church refers to its so-called treasury of merit in granting indulgences, this is a reference to Christ himself, to the crucified and risen Lord (and to the community of those brothers and sisters who have reached their fulfillment in and through Christ). The prayer to God that is included in the jurisdictional act of the Church is, like every prayer of the Church, performed in community with Christ the head. It takes place through Christ in the Holy Spirit, and its aim is that God should move the man who is already liberated from his sin as a guilty action, but not yet from his sinful involvement, through the impulse of grace to give himself more fully to the crucified Christ.

The Nature of Indulgences

Indulgences, then, must be understood as a sharing in the cross of Jesus Christ, a sharing both by the Church, which grants the indulgence, and by the person, who is seeking to gain it; for the cross of Christ is the source of satisfaction for the sin. This explanation shows that even in indulgences, the initiative is with God. What the Church does is an expression—and, here again, the *conditio sine qua non*—of the divine saving will.

We may see the connection between the jurisdictional and the subjective elements in the Church's practice of granting indulgences more clearly if we say that the Church's jurisdictional action fulfills primarily the function of prayer to God. Because of the help of God's grace which it confidently expects the sinner to receive, it remits its own punishment of him; moreover, because owing to the Church's authoritative action, God, in giving himself to the sinner, intensifies love in him, so that he is freed from those sinful involvements which remain (*reatus poenae*), it is no longer necessary for him to perform the full earthly penance, and hence it can be remitted. This last point emerges if we look at the history of indulgences. Although this explanation differs from other theological interpretations, it does not go counter to any part of the Church's teaching on the subject of indulgences. At any rate, it avoids the danger of a mechanization and legalization of Christianity which can lie in an excessively superficial interpretation of indulgences.

The Authority of the Church

The Church derives its authority to grant indulgences from the power of binding and loosing imparted to it by Christ. This authority cannot be directly deduced from this power, but in that the Church received from Christ the commission to bring into subjection the whole complex of sin (both the *reatus culpae* and the *reatus poenae*—the falling into guilt and the incurring of punishment), thus removing every obstacle to entrance into the kingdom of God, we can regard indulgences as part of the Church's power to bind and loose.

Indulgences for the Dead

Since the middle of the fifteenth century indulgences have also been applied to the dead. It has been the teaching of theologians that through indulgences the Church has the power to assist those among the deceased who are undergoing a process of purification. The indulgences do not mean, of course, that those to whom they are applied are absolved from their punishment: they are exclusively requests addressed to God. In giving an account of them, greater care must be exercised in avoiding the danger of dealing with salvation in a material and mechanical way than in the case of indulgences for the living. When a person on earth, moved by grace, gives himself more totally to Christ crucified in gaining an indulgence, he can unite with his intention a prayer that God will give himself to someone who has died, and with such intensity that the soul of the deceased will open itself more and more to him, with the effect that it will be increasingly purified and liberated from the whole complex of sin. (Cf. our account of purgatory, Volume VI.)[2]

[2]In preparation.

◄13

The Anointing of the Sick

SICKNESS AND DEATH AS BOUNDARY SITUATIONS

Sickness and death are special human situations. They are boundary situations: in sickness the limited condition—that is, the createdness—of every human life is revealed, and the end is foreshadowed which must ultimately come to pass. In mortal illness man experiences his inescapable dependence: he can refuse to accept it, but he cannot escape it. Thus he is confronted with the necessity of integrating his dependence, in obedience, with the whole of his existence. At the same time, in sickness and death, what a man has become over the course of his life appears. Nevertheless the biological end points beyond itself: sickness and death are eschatologically orientated—or, more precisely, in terminal illness man experiences his eschatological orientation. The hopes and desires, the dreams and ambitions of man far transcend his biological end. This gives rise to a contradiction between man's psychic-intellectual dynamism, in which he transcends himself, and the inexorable necessity of his death, a contradiction which must be resolved. The question is how can this be done?

In the light of one's association with Christ, sickness and death appear in a special way as participations in the cross of Christ, a participation which is grounded in faith and baptism. It shows itself in all the hardships and afflictions of life, but especially in death. Sharing in the cross of Christ, however, implies sharing in his resurrection. During the course of one's earthly life, to be sure, the saving efficacy of the resurrection is experienced more as a future hope than as a present possession; but because participation in the resurrection of Christ is inseparable from participation in his death, our death is made to appear in an eschatological light. Seen in this way, participation in the death of Christ becomes meaningful to us for the first time.

SPECIAL SACRAMENTALITY OF THE ANOINTING

Owing to the sacramentality of the Church as a whole, every act of a Christian has a sacramental, saving dimension: every participation in the death of Jesus is incorporated into the sacramental sphere. The great significance of sickness and death, however, make it understandable that the participation in the cross of Golgotha which they achieve is not determined by the sacramentality common to all human activity but acquires a special, concentrated sacramentality of its own. The sacrament for this is the anointing of the sick. In view of its significance for salvation, this sacrament is totally and essentially eschatological—even more so than the other sacraments, since it prepares a man for full participation in the resurrection of Jesus Christ.

This does not mean, of course, that it hastens the act of death. But even if the recipient of anointing regains his physical health, he is prepared through the sacrament for an existence filled with saving grace, a participation in the risen life of Jesus Christ. The sacrament accomplishes this by joining the individual's salvation history unreservedly to the general salvation history; or, conversely, general salvation history—Jesus Christ—comes to prevail unconditionally in the life of the concrete individual man. In the sacrament of the anointing of the sick, God communicates himself to man in order to make him capable of final and intimate dialogue with himself and summons him to it. Sickness or the danger of death is the occasion for this invitation: and should a man, recovering his health, delay in heeding the divine invitation, it will still not be silenced. The invitation remains ordered to its fulfillment.

THE SCRIPTURAL BASIS

Christ concerned himself with the sick and the dead in various ways, seeing in sickness and death not merely biological events but signs of man's disastrous situation. In the new world epoch he inaugurated, sickness and death no longer have a legitimate place. Even though, despite their radical defeat in the Lord's resurrection, they will remain until his return, they have no permanent future. Jesus saw a close connection between sickness and death, on the one hand, and sin and insubordination to God, on the other. It would, of course, be a misconception of the miraculous to attribute to Jesus the view that except for sin there would be no sickness and death in the world. Sickness and death would have occurred even in a world free from sin, but their meaning would have been quite different. Man, united with God and obedient to his will, would have been able to integrate the experiences of death into the whole of his life. Jesus' healing of the sick and raising of the dead are eschatological signs, heralding a limitless future free from sickness and death.

When Jesus commissions the apostles to proclaim the message of salvation and to heal the sick, it is part of the meaning of his own mission (Mk. 6,7-13; 16,15f.; Lk. 9,1f.; cf. Acts 3,1-16; 9,32f.; 14,8ff.; 28,8f.). The disciples heal the sick by means of an anointing with oil (Mark 6,13).

The Epistle of James (5,14ff.) provides the clearest reference to a sacrament of the sick:

Is one of you ill? He should send for the elders of the congregation to pray over him and anoint him with oil in the name of the Lord. The prayer offered in faith will save the sick man, the Lord will raise him from his bed, and any sins he may have committed will be forgiven. Therefore confess your sins to one another, and pray for one another, and then you will be healed. A good man's prayer is powerful and effective.

The community then is required to take care of the sick by calling in the elders, who are to perform the anointing with oil in the name of the Lord. This means that the saving power of Jesus is present and effective in the prayer and anointing. The expected result, according to this passage, is first of all bodily health. But if the passage in James is interpreted against the background of the entire New Testament, it must be admitted that for Jesus, who was always concerned with the whole person, the question is never one of physical health alone. The prayer of faith and the anointing are meant to bring complete health: they embrace body and soul at the same time. Viewed in this way, the anointing of the sick reveals its saving power even when it cannot prevent death, because through death the whole life of a man issues in victory. This is the function of the forgiveness of sin.

In evaluating the testimony of Scripture, it is to be noted that it develops in three stages. The sacramentality of the anointing of the sick rests on the sacramentality of the Church as a whole. Recognition of it as a sacrament develops out of faith's understanding of Jesus' acts of healing the sick and raising the dead. The Epistle of James provides a special reference to its sacramentality. A full recognition of the sacrament was attained only over the course of a long development.

THEOLOGICAL DEVELOPMENT IN ANTIQUITY AND IN THE MIDDLE AGES

Anointing the sick with oil was widespread in antiquity. Texts in which there is mention of the practice cannot without closer examination be used as evidence for the sacrament of the sick (cf. *The Teaching of the Twelve Apostles*, 10,7), but indications of it may be present in the prayer of consecration over the oil for the sick in the *Traditio Apostolica* of Hippolytus (c. 215) and in the consecratory prayer of Serapion of Thmuis from the fourth century.

A letter of Pope Innocent I (402-417) provides the first clear evidence for a sacrament of the anointing of the sick. Referring in his letter to an old Roman custom, he clearly considers the anointing with oil primarily as a sacrament of the sick and not of the dying. With regard to the fruit of the sacrament, he limits himself to citing the passage in James. Much the same can be said of the texts of Caesarius of Arles (c. 540), Cassiodorus (c. 550) and the Venerable Bede (the end of the seventh century). In Carolingian theology, anointing of the sick became a supplement to penance and was administered as a preparation for death.

In the Eastern Church the discussion is more concerned with an anointing which is to be administered to the dying and which was prefigured in the anointing of the Lord with oil before his death (John 12,3-8). In the period after Chrysostom, the under-standing of the anointing of the sick in connection with the sacra-ment of penance changed considerably. It was administered to those of the faithful who were suffering from spiritual or mental weakness. Finally, all sinners were anointed. Thus the anointing of the sick developed into a penintential anointing.

In the Western Church since the eleventh century, the anointing of the sick has generally been defined as a sacrament. Thus the view that it is not a remedy for sickness but a preparation for death has increasingly gained ground. The growing conviction that a man's ultimate decision—his final option with regard to his eternal destiny—concentrated itself in the moment of death, and there-fore the act of dying should be supported by its own sacrament, may have contributed to this development. By the end of the Mid-dle Ages, Christian understanding of the sacrament had developed from the more temporal concept of Christian antiquity—em-bracing both the earthly life and the hereafter, both body and soul—to an outlook which was almost exclusively spititualistic and eschatological. The Council of Trent prepared the ground for a synthesis. This synthesis, however, managed to penetrate the everyday faith of the people of God only with difficulty, or not at all.

THE TEACHING OF THE CHURCH

The Council of Trent, citing Mark 6,13 and James 5,14f., taught that the anointing of the sick was a sacrament. It pointed out further that according to the Church's apostolic tradition, the wording of James states the matter, the form, and the competent minister as well as the effect of the sacrament. According to the council, the Church understands as the matter the oil blessed by the bishop; as the form, the words: "Through this anointing," etc. . . . (DS 1694f., 1716; cf. DS 216, 860, 1259f., 2048).

The Second Vatican Council declared, in the Constitution on the Sacred Liturgy (No. 73): " 'Extreme unction,' which may also and more fittingly be called 'anointing of the sick,' is not a sacrament for those only who are at the point of death. Hence, as soon as any one of the faithful begins to be in danger of death from sickness or old age, the appropriate time for him to receive this sacrament has certainly already arrived."

THE SIGN

The sign of the sacrament of the anointing of the sick consists in the anointing with olive oil and the accompanying prayer. The oil must be consecrated by the bishop (DS 1718, 1324). The manner of anointing has undergone many changes in the course of time. The Second Vatican Council, in the Constitution on the Sacred Liturgy (No. 75), declared that the number of anointings should be adapted to the circumstances. As for the prayer, James's epistle only speaks in general of prayer over the sick person. The Church, however, has established a definite formula for the prayer; and the Second Vatican Council, in the constitution cited above (No. 75), says that the prayers accompanying the anointing are to be revised so as to correspond to the varying conditions of the sick who receive the sacrament.

THE SALVIFIC NATURE OF THE ANOINTING OF THE SICK

Although, as we have seen, the way in which the healing effect of the sacrament of the anointing of the sick is understood has undergone considerable change in the course of time, it can be established that the conviction that the sacrament had power to heal was consistently held from New Testament times right up to the Council of Trent. Whereas in Christian antiquity the idea of the healing of the body stood in the foreground, owing to the influence of Thomas Aquinas, the anointing of the sick came to be understood primarily as an aid for coming to grips with death. The Council of Trent (session 14, chapter 2, DS 1696) provided a synthesis of the interpretations which had emerged in the course of this development and at the same time stressed the eschatological orientation of the individual elements constituting the fruit of the sacrament. According to Scripture, all evil has its ultimate root in sin, in the isolation of man from God and from the community. The healing power of the sacrament attacks evil at its root. Because the anointing of the sick establishes a special bond with Christ, and through him with the Father in heaven, it blots out sin—our daily sins and if necessary even mortal sin in the case of a sick person who is not in a condition to receive the sacrament of penance but the tenor of whose life has manifested the desire to die a Christian. If it is in accordance with God's plan of salvation, the healing process of the anointing initiated at the root of evil leads to bodily health, and the person so cured must live in the future as one who has been healed—that is, in communion with Christ and the Church of the Living. If, on the other hand, it is according to God's plan that he should finish his earthly course, then the anointing of the sick equips him to make of his death the highest act of communion with the crucified Christ.

The individual moments in the sacrament's efficacy are traditionally termed the *res et sacramentum* and the *res*.

Individual Elements

The saving effect symbolized and caused by the external sign of the sacrament produces a special form of resemblance to Christ —not the indelible character deriving from baptism, confirmation, and orders but a real resemblance nonetheless. Through the anointing with the oil of the sick a man is incorporated by the Holy Spirit into the crucified and risen Christ in a special way, so that he becomes an image of the Christ who was crucified but, having undergone death, raised to the life of the resurrection. Thus he is able, in his death agony, to enter into the sphere of judgment and grace belonging to Christ's death, thereby making his own sickness and death a participation in the death and resurrection of Christ.

This particular imitation of Christ also means a special form of membership in the Church. Baptism and confirmation are the foundation of one's membership in the Church; in the anointing of the sick it undergoes a concrete transformation owing to the situation of the sick person. The Church bestows a special concern on him, taking him under the protection of her love and her prayer. Her prayers for him are directed to his total recovery, but the anointing of the sick person can either restore his bodily health or equip him for the consummation of his life.

The power to restore bodily health attributed to the anointing of the sick is not to be understood as a supplement to or substitute for medical efforts. Rather, it means that through his encounter with Christ the sick person is enabled to submit, in union with Christ, to the restrictions sickness imposes on his life, finding in this suffering a special opportunity for dedicating himself to the will of God. Thus he is able to take an active stand with respect to his illness. In sickness and its completion in death, man experiences his createdness: the last anointing gives him the power to affirm his creaturehood and acknowledge God as the Creator. Moreover, it gives him the opportunity of realizing his union with Christ in the most concrete and concentrated way. He is strengthened against the temptations of dejection, despair, impatience, and self-centeredness. In the midst of the afflictions of body and soul, God himself, who is active in the sacrament of the anointing of the sick as in every sacramental sign and who bestows himself on the recipient of the sacrament, inspires an unshaken confidence in his mercy and a triumphant staying power. If even Christ in his agony needed heavenly comfort (Lk. 22,43), how much more urgent is the need of man wounded by sin of divine assistance in this decisive hour? God gives this assistance according to the measure of the believer's readiness to proceed along the way which alone leads to fulfillment—letting go of this earthly life, to entrust himself without reserve to God.[1]

[1]See H. Schell, *Katholische Dogmatik*, III, 2d ed. (Paderborn, 1893), pp. 628f.

The *res* of the sacrament consists in an encounter with Christ, and through him with God, based on community with Christ and membership in the Church. This encounter takes place in the Holy Spirit. In the sacrament God bestows himself through Christ in the Holy Spirit on the sick person as one whom he summons to final fulfillment: he gives himself as the God of the future. God's giving of himself as one who summons a man into the perfect future implies the removal of everything in the man which is inimical to God. The proper sacrament for the overcoming of enmity with God, mortal sin, is penance; but if the reception of the sacrament of penance is no longer possible, the anointing of the sick takes its place, removing from the recipient everything which stands in the way of entering into beatifying dialogue with God and those of his brothers who have already reached this goal.

Whereas medieval theology seems to have held that the anointing of the sick wiped out all the sins, and the punishments due to sin, of one who received it with a simplicity devoid of self-will, so that no further purgation was necessary after death, theology since the Council of Trent has attributed rather less to the potentialities of the last anointing. It may be that Jansenism, with its harsh moral outlook, and the denial by the Reformers of any process of purgation after death have both contributed to this change. Nevertheless the view may be held that the anointing of the sick grants to one who opens himself completely to God, and on whom God can therefore confer himself without reserve, that intensity of love in which everything that is called sin and is related to sin is wiped out. This thesis has far-ranging significance if the contention that God gives to a man in the process of dying the final option of choosing love and community or rejection and isolation is valid. (See the doctrine of death in the treatise on the Last Things, Volume VI.)

MINISTER AND RECIPIENT

According to the Church's tradition and the Council of Trent (DS 1706), the anointing of the sick can be administered to any baptized person who is seriously ill. Thus it is not reserved to the dying (the opinion to the contrary developed in the Middle Ages has no foundation in the Church's tradition). On the other hand, the last anointing cannot be administered to someone risking death from causes other than sickness.

The indication in the Epistle of James that the anointing was performed by the elders—the presbyters—of the community is the origin of the theological judgment that the sacrament can be administered only by a priest. The medieval custom of a number of priests administering the sacrament was forbidden in the Western Church because it has given rise to inconveniences and abuses, but the practice survives in the Eastern Church even today. The idea it expresses is that the whole Christian community keeps a loving and prayerful watch over one of its sick or dying members.

As in the case of the sacrament of penance, the designation of the Father as the principal minister and the crucified Christ as the prototype of the recipient of the anointing conforms to the structure of this sacrament. Just as the Father embraced his suffering and dying Son as the representative of men with that love which is a judgment of grace, so he takes the sick person in whom he sees the image of his beloved Son into his healing care.

◄ 14

Marriage

HUMAN BEINGS AS MEN AND WOMEN

Paul asserts that the distinctions between persons based on the natural conditions of human society and the individual (man and wife, master and servant) should yield in face of the transcendent community of Christ. Nonetheless the question still arises of how individuals in their natural historical situations are to give concrete, daily expression to their union with Christ and all the other members of the Church which baptism has established. Ultimately, all Paul's epistles are exhortations to that conduct on the part of Christians which will be the right expression of their unity with Christ and with one another.

The specific condition of man and woman—their human sexuality—is part of the concrete situation in which every baptized Christian must fulfill his vocation. Thus the question arises: how are man and wife to encounter each other within the Church in such a way that justice will be done to their incorporation with Christ and the relationship it establishes between them? The first answer is: Act according to the nature of man and woman. But what is in accordance with the nature of man and woman? Ultimately, the definitive answer to this question, as to the more encompassing question, what is man? is given only by revelation as it is found in Scripture. Revelation gives us an insight into the essence of man and woman inasmuch as, beyond any definition, it shows us a decisive moment in the history of man and woman in which their reciprocal distinctiveness and relatedness appear.

First, we must try to situate the human phenomenon of man and woman in the context of the whole of created reality. The whole of creation is one progressively developing totality in which individual things and groups of things different from one another or opposed to one another are assembled. One articulation of this totality is the interdependence and diversity which constitutes the polarity of male and female in the realm of animals and plants. The distinction and mutual orientation of man and woman represent the highest development of the structural law of polarity governing the whole universe. Of man and woman Scripture says explicitly that God conceived and willed their union and distinction. According to the report of Genesis (the Priestly tradition: Gen. 1,27) God created mankind as man and woman. Since God willed to create man after his own image, he created him in this twofold form. Obviously, this does not mean that man is the image of God only in the union of husband and wife. Every individual is the image of God. However, the likeness to God is also realized in the unity of husband and wife. The Yahwist text of Genesis gives us more detailed information on the interdependence of man and woman. The author wants to show that woman is not on a level with the beasts and therefore is not a chattel which man can use as he pleases, but that she stands on the same personal plane as man himself. As we saw earlier, this text has a clearly polemical note which is aimed against the oppression and abuse of women.

According to the Priestly text, man and woman have been commissioned to rule over the earth jointly. Thus the image of God consists in their common endeavor to be the masters of subhuman reality; that commission of lordship, which the writer places in the mouth of God, is directed equally to the man and his wife. In this way, without reflecting on it, expression is given to the equality of man and woman.

The Yahwist text has God himself express the mutual relationship of man and woman. This interrelationship is so intense that, according to God's own words, man would have had to endure a loneliness gnawing at his very being had God not given him a helpmate as his companion. The woman is able to free man from his loneliness. And because he needs her he experiences his desire for her with a force that impels him to leave father and mother for his wife (Gen. 2,23). The encounter of man and woman presupposes their diversity. This diversity is not merely external but permeates and determines the whole essence of man as husband and woman as wife. Precisely what this diversity consists in Scripture does not clearly say. It obviously presupposes that the reader has some notion of it.

Many attempts have been made to analyse the essence of man and that of woman. These analyses have produced a number of valuable insights, but they still remain on the level of probability. This is understandable, since man and woman for all their diversity are one in their humanity: a man is a human being and a woman is a human being. However one may conceive the distinction between the two, the fullness of being-human, according to the testimony of Genesis, is achieved only in the encounter of man and woman. Furthermore, not only is this encounter the concrete embodiment of integral humanity; it is only in the encounter with the partner that each man and woman achieves the fullness of his or her own selfhood. The loneliness of man, which God himself has emphasized, thus turns out to be the loneliness of someone incomplete, a deficiency in the very realization of selfhood. Scripture does not depict the intimate encounter of man and woman in a spiritual manner; rather, in opposition to all spiritualistic tendencies, it portrays it as an encounter in the flesh (Gen. 2,24). It is communion on every level of their being, embracing both body and soul. (The life of virginity advocated in the New Testament must be viewed in the light of the eschatological nature of the Christian dispensation.)

In spite of the heavy emphasis on the equality of man and woman, and in spite of the polemic against the suppression of women, one cannot fail to perceive, especially in the case of the Yahwist text, that the presentation of Scripture reflects the thinking of a patriarchal society.

The transcending of self from I to Thou and from Thou to I is not, according to the description of Genesis, simply an act of the present moment, but a step into the future. In the encounter which leads to the unity of the flesh, man and wife are commanded to multiply and to fill the earth. Through their children they have an effect which extends into the future. Indeed, they create the future through the bearing of children. According to the wording of the Priestly text, the union of man and wife extends beyond the partners themselves into human history, initiating it and carrying it forward. Furthermore, as a result of the lordship over creation with which they have been charged, their union even has an impact on the infrahuman world. The two movements of transcendence—in history and in space—unify themselves, for the cultivation of the earth provides for the foundation of further settlements.

Genesis testifies that sin has had a destructive influence on the relationship of man and wife: woman has become more and more an object of man's lust. Nevertheless, a look at human history shows that among primitive peoples the equality of man and woman held sway. Indeed, early agrarian society was matriarchal. The woman was the determinant factor. However, with changes in the organization of society and economic relationships (the transition to stock breeding) matriarchy was replaced by patriarchy. What is of greater importance is that all the cultures in which Christianity has taken concrete form—the Hebraic as well as the Greek, the Roman, and the Germanic—have been characterized by a harsh patriarchalism which made man the unequivocal master in religious, moral, social, and economic matters. In the course of historical developments, even the unity and indissolubility of marriage were called into question and impaired.

THE NATURAL STATUS OF MARRIAGE

The beginnings of marriage as a sacral institution reach back to the very beginning of mankind in the Old Testament. The man and his wife were brought together by God himself. In the Fathers of the Church we occasionally encounter the notion that God served as the "giver of the bride" for the first couple. Marriage was described as a covenant before God (Prov. 2,17; Mal. 2,14). When, in the course of history, God concluded a covenant with men (the covenant with Moses and the Israelite tribes), the bond of intimacy created by the covenant was represented by the image of marriage. Conversely, marriage was an expression of God's relation to his people.

In the Old Testament marriage was basically understood not as a private affair but as a familial and patriarchal institution. The conditions for the conclusion of the marriage contract were often handled by the head of the family in such a way that the whole procedure looked like a sale (Ex. 22,15f.; Gen. 24,2-61; 34,1-24; 28,6; 22,8; Judges 14,2f.). Nevertheless the bridegroom could make his own decision (Gen. 26,34f.; 29,14-30; 38,1-5; Sir. 16,19f.). In Genesis 24,5.8.58 there is mention of consent on the part of the young girl. Though the bride became the property of her husband through a payment or the performance of some service, he could not simply do with her whatever he liked. Taking the bride home, the carrying out of the marriage proper, was distinct from the "betrothal." The primary consideration was the bearing of children (Gen. 1,28; 24,16; Sir. 16,19ff.). Progeny meant an increase in the influence of the family and an expansion of the people of God. Behind it all lay the hope that every generation would contribute a link in the chain at whose end the Messiah would stand. But despite this emphasis on progeny, the fact that marriage is a community of persons was not lost sight of (cf. Gen. 2,18-25; 24,67; 1 Sam. 1,5-8; Prov. 5,15-20; 31,10-31; Sir. 25; 36,21-26; Ex. 20,14.17). The man, however, clearly takes precedence: though a husband's sexual lapses are disapproved of, they are condemned less sharply than any fault on the part of the wife. There was a constant threat to the unity and indissolubility of marriage, and certain institutional arrangements must be understood as concessions to human weakness. In particular, the regulations affecting divorce (Deut. 24,1-4) are aimed at stemming a growing abuse (Deut. 22,13-19; Lev. 21,14; Jer. 3,1). By Jesus' day, monogamy more or less prevailed in Israel; and thus for the most part Jesus himself had no need to concern himself with stressing the unity of marriage but had to come to grips with the question of divorce. In this whole area the Old Testament distinguishes itself from the New primarily through its undervaluing and neglect of virginity.

THE SACRAMENTALITY OF MARRIAGE

Scripture

Jesus remained unmarried. Marriage, if we are to judge by Jesus, is a provisional form of existence: celibacy is adapted to the task of preaching and inaugurating the kingdom of God. Even though marriage is a basic form of human history, its place is within human history: with the passing of this aeon it too will pass away (Mk. 12,25). Nevertheless Jesus paid special attention to marriage, not only restoring marriage which had been weakened by sin to its original form but even making it a step on the way of salvation he had opened up to men. The simple fact that he gave the world an instruction on marriage (Mt. 19,6) indicates its sacramental nature. Jesus Christ was conscious of being sent to build up the kingdom of God, and he did not consider it his immediate task to arrange the things of this world. If he gave an instruction on marriage, it is an indication that he did not want marriage to be understood simply as a thing of this world, but rather as an element in the kingdom of God, an event within the province of the divine law which he proclaimed. Thus his instruction on marriage is related to the preaching of the gospel and is in fact a part of that preaching.

The most explicit reference to the sacramentality of marriage is in the Epistle to the Ephesians (5,21-33):

Be subject to one another out of reverence for Christ. Wives, be subject to your husbands as to the Lord; for the man is the head of the woman, just as Christ also is the head of the church. Christ is, indeed, the Saviour of the body; but just as the church is subject to Christ, so must women be to their husbands in everything. Husbands, love your wives, as Christ also loved the church and gave himself up for it, to consecrate it, cleansing it by water and word, so that he might present the church to himself all glorious, with no stain or wrinkle or anything of the sort, but holy and without blemish. In the same way men also are bound to love their wives, as they love their own bodies. In loving his wife a man loves himself. For no one ever hated his own flesh; on the contrary, he provides and cares for it; and that is how Christ treats the church, because it is his body, of which we are living parts (flesh of his flesh and bone of his bone). Thus it is that (in the words of Scripture) "a man shall leave his father and mother and shall be joined to his wife, and the two shall become one flesh." This is a great mystery. I for my part refer it to Christ and to the church, but it applies also individually: each of you must love his wife as his very self; and the woman must see to it that she pays her husband all respect.

This passage occurs in a context in which Paul is setting up the rules for living together within the Christian community. One of the things he is trying to determine is the proper conduct of man and wife. The conduct that is to be characteristic of the wife is obedience, that of the husband love. The reason Paul offers for this is important for our question. As the foundation for his own demands he cites the fact that marriage is a re-enactment of the mutual relationship of Christ and the church. The conduct of husband and wife towards each other must correspond to Christ's conduct towards the church, and vice versa. The relationship of Christ to the church was established by the devotion of Jesus, that is, by his self-surrender for the sake of the church. The initiative of Jesus establishes his position as head of the church and at the same time implies his function as Saviour. When Paul says of Christ that he is both the head and the Saviour of the church and in so doing calls the church the body of Christ, the question arises: what is meant by the church saved by Christ, the body saved by him? The Church founded on Pentecost—which did not yet, at the moment of Genesis, exist—cannot be meant, nor can the Old Testament people of God. We must, with H. Schlier,[1] understand "church" here as the church pre-existing in Christ himself in virtue of God's predestining election, the church which in its members was in need of Christ's self-sacrifice and saving work because it had relinquished its election. Christ has "consecrated" the church; that is, he has transferred it to the sphere of God's holiness and has presented it to himself as an immaculate

---

[1]*Der Brief an die Epheser*, 2d ed. (Dusseldorf, 1958), p. 255.

bride purified by baptism. The demand to exercise this love of Christ's is placed before man.

The apostle adds yet another idea: Christ provides for and is concerned for the church which is his body—that is, for the members constituting that body. Similarly, the husband in imitation of Christ should provide for his wife and care for her: she occupies a position parallel to the church as the body of Christ. Here Paul changes the word "body" to "flesh" and employs a proverb widely known in his time: No one ever hated his own flesh. When the husband loves his wife, he loves himself, for he loves his own flesh. To elucidate this last thesis Paul recalls the text of Genesis 2,14. Of the text and the practice indicated in it Paul says that it is a great mystery, namely a type of Christ and the church. Marriage, then, is both concealing and revealing. The text of Genesis presents a prophecy in action of the union between Christ and the Church. Marriage as instituted by God is a symbolic anticipation of the relation of Christ to the Church, for he is the head of the Church, the Church is his body and the individual members of the Church are the parts of his body. Thus Paul interprets the Genesis passage as a promise.

The Epistle to the Ephesians explains the connection between the love implanted in creation by God and the love of Christ. According to Paul, Adam is a type of Christ (cf. Rom. 5,13; 1 Cor. 15,44ff.). Adam already contains in himself the future Savior. In Christ, on the other hand, the original man reappears. The salvation in Christ foreseen by God is already concealed in creation. Correspondingly, in Christ there is a rediscovery of creation. Thus, the love of Adam points to the love of Christ. The latter is the meaning of the former. The love of one creature for another has as its object the saving love of Christ and is ultimately revealed therein. When Jesus came and won for himself the Church as his bride, then it was finally revealed who the man is who abandons everything in order to cling to his wife. Since Christ and in Christ, marriage shares in the mystery of the marriage of Christ and the Church and thus is itself a mystery. Of course, it must be emphasized that the word *mysterium,* or its Latin translation *sacramentum,* is not the basis for the Catholic understanding of marriage as a sacrament. Rather, the whole passage, verses 21-33, opens the possibility for understanding marriage as a sacrament in the later sense of the term.[2] If originally marriage was a prototype of the relation of Christ to the Church, then in the era introduced by Christ it becomes among the baptized a re-presentation of that relationship. However, the marriage of men who have yet to be reached by the preaching of Christ retains the character of a symbolic anticipation.

It is striking that Paul emphasizes that it is he himself who refers the practice attested in Genesis 2,24 to the relationship of Christ and the Church. He obviously is aware of another interpretation. It is more than likely that in the background of his own explanation there stands the widespread gnostic conception found in Hellenistic Judaism of a heavenly marriage and its human imitation. If this is correct, then the text of the apostle Paul is a rejection of gnosticism: both of the sort which expresses itself in promiscuous sexual intercourse and that which repudiates marriage, principally for spiritualistic and ascetic reasons.[3]

Viewed against the background of the typological interpretation of marriage, the union of Christ and the Church becomes the union in which every marriage finds its fulfillment. Conversely, in the era introduced by Christ marriage is an image of the union of Christ and the Church. This conception of marriage motivates the instructions which Paul gives to husband and wife. We must go a step further: Marriage is not a mere image of the communion between Christ and the Church. Rather, the original itself is active in its image. The original becomes visible in its image. The relationship of Christ to the Church can only be understood if one understands marriage. Conversely, marriage can only be understood if one reflects on the union of Christ and the Church.

Baptism is, of course, required if the marriage partners are to represent the relationship of Christ to the Church. For baptism gives men the mark necessary if they are to represent Christ. In the marriage ceremony the baptized couple re-present the event in which Christ through his death gave himself up to the Church, and the Church in turn surrendered itself to him in order to

[2]Schlier, *op. cit.*, p. 263.
[3]*Ibid.*, pp. 264-276; cf. 1 Tim. 4,1-5.

protect and foster through his help the life it has received from him.

As a result of its relationship to the union of Christ and the Church, marriage is a sign of salvation under the new covenant. Husband and wife play the roles of Christ and the Church. Since the unbaptized lack the capacity for such roles, their marriage is not a sacrament. In vigorously setting forth his eschatological hope, Paul could not entirely avoid a certain onesided undervaluing of marriage (1 Cor. 7,1.8). Furthermore, he repeatedly emphasizes the subordination of the wife to her husband (Eph. 5,21-24; 1 Cor. 14,34f.; 11,1-15; 1 Tim. 2,11-15). Contemporary exegesis, however, goes to great pains to examine the historical and cultural conditions of the apostle's statements. In this way, too much is not demanded of the text, and the principle of the distinction between the form of an expression and its content is preserved. For the rest, one must bear in mind that the passage on marriage in the Epistle to the Ephesians can only be understood in the framework of the sacramentality of the Church as a whole. The encounter of two members of the Church in marriage is a major event in the sacramental life of the Church. The fact that during his historical life Jesus bestowed a special concern on marriage demonstrates the importance of the marital relationship within the Church as a whole. It is correct to conclude that Christ, ever present and active in the Church as his mystical body, has not let marriage slip from his saving concern, but that he is always salvifically active and present in the marriage partners in a manner corresponding to their special encounter.

The Post-Apostolic Development

In the post-apostolic period, in opposition to Manichaean and Gnostic contempt for married life, marriage was always considered a part of life in the Church. It is worthy of note that the Church Fathers and Doctors, although they witnessed the depravity of pagan marriage, did not let this discredit marriage itself in their eyes. The tendency to undervalue the woman which infiltrated theological thought for a time owing to the acceptance of the Aristotelian biology of reproduction could not last. In the twelfth century marriage was included in the seven sacramental signs which in a special way were designated by the technical term "sacrament."

First of all, the settlement of the marriage in the process by which a man and woman bind themselves to one another for ever is sacramental. The sacrament of marriage takes place in this settlement. Nevertheless, the whole of married life following upon this act is incorporated into the realm of the sacramental *(sacramentum in fieri, sacramentum in esse)*. Finally, the fact that marriage is a sacrament means that the baptized cannot contract a marriage without receiving a sacrament.

The Teaching of the Church

Following theological developments in the twelfth century, the Second Lateran Council (1193) included marriage in the seven sacraments (DS 718; see further DS 761, 769; 793f. against the Waldensians; the Council of Lyons; DS 1327, the Council of Florence). The belief that marriage is truly and properly one of the seven sacraments of the New Law, that is, of the New Covenant, and that it has been instituted by Christ the Lord, is most clearly expressed by the Council of Trent (DS 1801). Trent presents a salvation-history view of the origin of the sacrament of marriage when it declares:

The first parent of the human race, under the inspiration of the Divine Spirit, proclaimed the perpetual and indissoluble bond of matrimony when he said: "This at last is bone of my bones, flesh of my flesh. . . . Therefore a man leaves his father and his mother and cleaves to his wife, and they become one flesh" (Gen. 2,23f.).

Christ our Lord taught more clearly that only two persons are joined and united by this marriage bond. He referred to the final words of the quotation above as words spoken by God and said: "It follows that they are no longer two individuals: they are one flesh" (Matt. 19,6); and immediately after this with the words, "What God has joined together, man must not separate" (Matt. 19,6), he confirmed the stability of that same bond which had been declared by Adam so long before.

Moreover, Christ himself, who instituted the holy sacraments and brought them to perfection, merited for us by his passion the grace that brings natural love to perfection, and strengthens the indissoluble unity, and sanctifies the spouses. The Apostle Paul intimates this when he says: "Husbands, love your wives, as Christ also loved the church and gave himself up for it" (Eph. 5,25); and he immediately adds: "This is a great mystery. I for my part refer it to Christ and to the church" (Eph. 5,32).

Therefore, since matrimony under the law of the gospel is, because of the grace given through Christ, superior to the marriage unions of earlier times, our Holy Fathers, the councils, and the tradition of the universal Church have always rightly taught that matrimony should be included among the sacraments of the new Law.[4]

Since Trent the popes have taken up and authoritatively commented on questions not clarified by the Tridentine declaration, even though they themselves have not pronounced any infallible decisions; thus, see Pius IX (1848-1878; DS 2965-2974), Leo XIII (1878-1903; DS 3142-3146), Pius X (1903-1914; DS 3451), Pius XI (1922-1939, DS 3700-3724), Pius XII (1939-1958, in many statements), John XXIII (encyclical *Mater et Magistra,* 1961), the Second Vatican Council *(Lumen Gentium, Gaudium et Spes,* and *Sacrosanctum Concilium),* and Paul VI (the encyclical *Humanae Vitae,* 1968). The sacramentality of marriage contracted by two Christians has therefore been confirmed anew and the proper mutual behavior of the spouses in accordance with the sacramentality of their marriage has been proclaimed.

The Protestant Teaching on Marriage

Primarily, the Reformers attacked the role of canon law in marriage. Marriage, they held, is not a sacrament, for Scripture says nothing about its sacramentality. Marriage does not belong to the dispensation of grace, but to the original order of creation in which it was instituted. Since it is an external and secular matter, it should be regulated not by the church but by the state. The state has to protect its indissolubility. As the consequence of this theological position, the established churches in Germany dependent

[4]*The Church Teaches,* p. 336.

upon the state have accepted obligatory civil marriage as corresponding to the supposed secularity of marriage.

A radically new consciousness emerged after the Second World War. Karl Barth interpreted marriage in the created order as an analogue of the covenant of grace in Jesus Christ. In general the Lutherans remained faithful to the traditional line. Nevertheless, they did emphasize that marriage in Jesus Christ can only be realized in conformity with the marriage instructions in the fifth chapter of the Epistle to the Ephesians. There is no distinction between the marriage of the baptized and that of the unbaptized. However, there is a distinction between the secular and the church marriage ceremony. The blessing of the church must always follow the civil ceremony, even in a mixed marriage. What Scripture offers us are instructions on the behavior of husband and wife in the Lord.

THE SIGN

The view that the exchange of the mutual desire to marry on the part of the persons contracting a marriage—thus, the marriage contract—is the external sign of the sacrament is the product of a long development. The Church has made no binding statement on this, however. In order to understand the theological thesis one must start from the fact that Christian marriage is the salvific representation of the relationship of Christ as the head to the Church as his body. This relationship represents the bond which Christ has established between himself and the Church, and the bond to Jesus Christ which the Church has accepted. It represents the New Covenant. It is a covenant within the Covenant (a covenant in miniature, a household church). Marriage accordingly is characterized by a bond, namely, two sexually diverse persons mutually bind themselves into a sexual community. Through this mutual bond rights and duties are exchanged. The marriage bond is of a juridical nature. The juridical or legal nature of marriage means that in marriage husband and wife belong irrevocably and exclusively to one another, and the independence otherwise proper to man as a personal being is mutually limited (1 Cor. 7,4). The mutual right of each spouse to have the other at his or her disposal is not power over a thing, however. The right which one spouse has over the other in marriage justifies one in demanding that the other grant him or her bodily communion. To the claim of the one there corresponds the obligation of the other. Nonetheless, the property of the marriage settlement that makes it a contract does not prevent it from being a union of love. In fact, it is precisely love which impels the spouses to no longer wish to belong to themselves, but to belong forever and exclusively to each other. This willingness is sealed by the contract. For in the contract the earnestness and power of love manifest themselves. Indeed, the connection between the contract and love reveals that the marriage bond is a unique kind of contract. Thus, even though the word "contract" is used, it must be understood in an analogous sense.

The chief distinction of the marriage contract from other contracts is in the fact that it grants a claim not to a thing but to a person, and the juridical state it establishes remains forever independent of the will of either party concluding the contract. Just as on the one hand the contract is an expression of the intensity of love, it is at the same time a protection against the dangers and threats to which love, like every human relationship, is exposed.

The view once advocated by theologians (e.g., Hinkmar of Reims [d. 882] or by the school of Bologna) that it is not the contract but the consummation of the marriage that constitutes a sacramental marriage, lives on in the Church's conviction that, though every contractually concluded marriage is indeed a sacrament, it only becomes absolutely indissoluble through its consummation. Thus marriages which have not yet been consummated can under certain conditions be dissolved. The reason for this thesis is that only the consummated marriage represents the relationship between Christ and the Church perfectly. In analysing the sign of the sacrament of marriage, it might be better not to introduce the concepts of matter and form, which are frequently employed in theology for interpreting a sacramental sign. With respect to the form of the contract, the Church has enacted specific regulations for safeguarding the contract.

MINISTER AND RECIPIENT OF THE SACRAMENT

The ministers of the sacrament are those who effect the sign—that is, those who conclude the contract—the marriage partners. Thus, in the strict sense of the term, they are mediators of grace for one another. It is of course important to remember that the human minister of the sacrament is only an instrument of God, who is himself always the primary minister. This is clear if one reflects that grace is primarily the self-communication of God: he is present in the sacramental action of the marriage contract as in an efficacious sign. Insofar as marriage does not consist simply in the act by which the contract is concluded, but establishes the married state of life, the contracting partners continue throughout life to be mediators of grace for one another. In marriage the sacramental effectiveness of the laity (in the Western Church, the priest is at present barred from marriage by the Church's law of celibacy) reaches its peak intensity, although this is by no means the only way the laity can mediate grace. Whatever married people accomplish in their mutual encounter, whether in the ordinary activity of everyday life or in the communion of their bodies, that encounter is a grace-mediating event. When one person gives himself to the other, God also gives himself to the two of them under the sign of this human gift of self. The love of one for the other is an efficacious sign of God's gift of himself to the two marriage partners. In their mutual love they have the guarantee that God bestows himself upon both of them.

In view of what has been said above, the question arises: what does the Church do, what is the function at a marriage of the priest commissioned by the Church? According to a view widely held today, the priest's role is that of an official witness to the marriage contract. This view is based on the ecclesial requirement of form, according to which a marriage in which at least one of the partners is Catholic must be contracted before a priest and two witnesses.[5]

The following must be said in any critical analysis of the problem at issue here: from the beginning there has existed in the Church the conviction that marriage is an event which concerns not only the marriage partners themselves but the entire Church, insofar as the marriage partners are members of the Church and through their marriage take up a new position in it. Through the procreation of children they are instrumental in the spread of the Church on earth. They contribute to the future of the Church and, insofar as the Church is the beginning of the kingdom of God, to the kingdom itself.

Ignatius of Antioch declared that marriage should only be contracted with the consent of the bishop and should only take place in his presence (*Letter to Polycarp,* 5). According to Tertullian, marriage should be contracted in the presence of the Christian community gathered for eucharistic worship. Tertullian, of course, recognized a marriage without the knowledge or participation of the ecclesial community (clandestine marriage). Before the Council of Trent the Church recognized every marriage as valid, even though clandestine marriages were prohibited. The council established a definite form for marriage. After many wide-ranging

---

[5]Following Vatican II, especially the Decree on Ecumenism, the Church has relaxed its requirements of matrimonial form. The two significant documents on this subject are Pope Paul's *Apostolic Letter on Mixed Marriages,* March 31, 1970, and the *Statement of the National Conference of Catholic Bishops on the Implementation of the Apostolic Letter on Mixed Marriages,* January 1, 1971. Recognizing that in a pluralistic society mixed marriages between Catholics and non-Catholics were increasing, these documents, stressing mercy and unity, said that "where there are serious difficulties in observing canonical form in a mixed marriage, the local Ordinary of the Catholic party or of the place where the marriage is to occur, may dispense the Catholic from the observance of the form for a just pastoral cause." So, for a good reason, such as achieving family harmony and avoiding family alienation, the marriage may take place outside a Catholic church and before someone who is not a Catholic priest. A dispensation from *place* (rather than from *form*) is all that is required when the marriage takes place in a non-Catholic church before a Catholic priest.

changes the aforementioned form for the performance of a marriage was prescribed by the Code of Canon Law. Thus, the priest must take the initiative, in that he questions the spouses on their intention to marry and accepts their declarations of intent. The regulations at present in force mean that baptized Catholics cannot contract a sacramental and therefore indissoluble marriage with one another if they announce their intention to marry in any other way.

Since Pope Paul's *Apostolic Letter on Mixed Marriages* (March 31, 1971) there is no longer any question that the marriage of a Catholic to a non-Catholic Christian is valid, sacred, and lawful, provided that the necessary dispensations have been obtained. The *Apostolic Letter* makes it quite clear that a "communion of spiritual benefits" exists between the couple thus united. The recognition of the validity of a mixed marriage which is concluded in the presence of a Protestant minister alone implies the recognition of the Protestant community, that is, of the existence of ecclesial elements in it. Thus the problem of the mixed marriage is but a part of the whole ecumenical problematic. Today this problematic is essentially determined by the fact that at the Second Vatican Council the major non-Catholic Christian communities were, on the basis of the ecclesial elements contained in them, recognized as Churches. The problem can be reduced to the question: How is this recognition to be related to the conscious faith of Catholics that the one Church founded by Jesus Christ has its concrete existence in the Roman Catholic Church?

The changes which have been made by the Church in the course of its history in the form prescribed for marriage lead us once again to the question whether, and to what extent, the Church has authority over the external sign. As on previous occasions it is necessary to emphasize at this point that the core symbol of marriage consists in the contract. This central symbol cannot be reformed or abrogated by the Church. Nonetheless the Church can specify how the contract should be concluded. Its authority to do so is based on the fact that marriage is a sacrament and therefore has been entrusted to the administration of the Church (1 Cor. 4,1). As a result of the sacramentality of marriage, both the marriage contract and the conduct of one living in the state of marriage are expressions of the life of the Church, the Christian sacrament in its entirety. Out of regard for the local temporal, cultural or even political situation, the Church can make different regulations suited to the practice of Christian living. It is not necessary that these regulations be uniform throughout the Church as a whole. Thus it is, for example, that one marriage form is pre-scribed for the Western Church, another for the Eastern Churches united to the Catholic Church. On February 22, 1949, the *Motu proprio "Crebrae Allatae"* of Pius XII on marriage law for the Eastern Church decreed: "Only those marriages are valid which are contracted according to the sacred rite and in the presence of the pastor or local ordinary or an authorized priest and at least two witnesses. A sacred rite is one at which a priest is present and gives a blessing." According to this decree, it is impossible to contract a marriage in the absence of an authorized priest. In particular, in the Eastern Church the priestly benediction is part of the sacramental sign. This decree, of course, only holds for the Eastern Church. Nonetheless, it raises the question whether in the Western Church also a greater role than that of a qualified witness should not be ascribed to the priest.

One will have to admit that in the Western Church the activity of the priest in asking for and accepting the declaration of consent is incorporated into the sacramental sign. The structure of the sign is complex. It consists of the declaration of intent on the part of the spouses and the activity of the priest. The cooperation of the priest in the contract is the cooperation of the Church of which he is the representative. The following difficulty should not be overlooked: if one simply declares that the marriage partners confer the sacrament of marriage on each other, then the execution of the sign is too sharply divided into two parts. In reality the execution of the sign forms an indivisible whole carried out by both spouses.

One will best do justice to these facts by not treating the ques-tion of the minister of the sacrament of marriage in the same way as in the case of the other sacraments. It must be admitted that the marriage partners and the assisting priest in one unified symbolic action execute that sign in virtue of which the sacrament of marriage takes place. Nevertheless each of the spouses remains the mediator of grace for the other. Each is a minister of the sacrament of marriage (cf. Pius XII in an address to engaged couples, April 29, 1942).

In this explanation the married couple still administer the sacrament to themselves. However, the mutual administration of the sacrament is more accurately explained in that the sacramental sign is seen in its structural unity and the place for the activity of the laity is exhibited within the whole sign. At the same time it is proper that in an event which has such an impact on the whole life of the Church as marriage, the Church itself should be officially represented, for the marriage partners are members of the Church. The activity of the lay people, who actually contract the marriage, would be incapable of bringing about their marriage without the saving activity of the whole Church. The saving activity of the Church, on the other hand, would be unable to get under way without the ministering activity of the marriage partners. The connection between the two also makes it clear why in special cases a marriage can be contracted without a priest being present. In such a case the Church as a transindividual subject is active without being concretely represented.

·15

Marriage and Salvation

Our understanding of the sanctifying character of marriage is derived from the fact that it is a salvific representation of the union between Christ and the Church. This explanation of the saving efficacy of the sacrament has its focus in the interhuman relationship specific to marriage. Moreover, since the individual person must always be the bearer of the grace which is uniquely his or her own, the consequence, when marriage achieves its true meaning, is that the two partners each come to resemble Christ in a new way.

IMAGE OF CHRIST AND THE CHURCH

When, in the Epistle to the Ephesians, Paul sees the relationship of husband to wife as modelled on the relationship of Christ to the Church, his conclusion is that the man enjoys a special relationship to Christ—and indeed his instructions to the wife are based on the relationship of the Church to Christ. However, it should be made quite clear that both husband and wife in marriage become like Christ in a new way. In marriage the Christian's resemblance to Christ based on his encounter with Christ in baptism and confirmation undergoes a special change. Even though marriage does not imprint an indelible mark, the resemblance to Christ which it brings about is a close approach to such a sacramental character.

282

For marriage confers on the contracting parties, the husband and wife, a special and eternal relationship to Christ and correspondingly a special position within the Church. In virtue of the "character" of Christ imprinted by marriage the spouses resemble Christ, for throughout his entire life and above all in his death he devoted himself to the Father in boundless love. Marriage means consecration to a life of love similar to that of Christ. The love which determines the relationship of Christ to the Church is the inner law of marriage (Eph. 5,25).

The designation of the sacramental fruit of marriage as its resemblance, expressed in the marriage bond itself, to the covenant of Christ with the Church does justice to the essence of marriage as well as to the essence of grace. Marriage is a special interhuman relationship. Grace, on the other hand, signifies a relation of God to man. It has the character of a covenant in which God is the initiator and it continues to depend upon that covenant. Grace is of its nature a dialogue. Thus it is fitting that grace be both symbolized and effected by an interhuman relationship.

MARRIAGE AS THE CHURCH IN MINIATURE

As a result of their resemblance to Christ the spouses as spouses live their lives in Christ, that is, in the sphere of his grace. Jesus Christ himself is present in marriage through the Holy Spirit. His saying holds: "For where two or three have met together in my name, I am there among them." Insofar as the presence of Christ through the Holy Spirit is constitutive for the Church itself, marriage represents a church in miniature, a "household church." Today, of course, marriage as a social institution is not as highly esteemed as previously. It is not understood as an economic or a sovereign unit. Within the Church, however, its significance has remained fundamentally the same. There the ecclesial view of marriage is linked to its christological meaning. The new status of married people in the Church is expressed in the fact that they are called upon to provide the body of Christ with new members. They present these to the Church. The Church on its part accepts them and through baptism incorporates them into Christ and grafts them onto her own community. The parents have both the qualifications and the obligation to assist the new members of the Church whom they have begotten, their children, towards responsible participation in the life of the people of God. In this way the parents make a contribution to the growth of the body of Christ. By their marriage they receive both the capacity and the mission to exercise in a concrete way the priesthood they received in baptism—their participation in the ruling, teaching, and priestly activity of Christ—in the service of their children. The spouses are sanctified and consecrated for this service.

THE SELF-COMMUNICATION OF GOD IN MARRIAGE

The new relation to Christ implies a new relation to God the Father. Indeed, since God always takes the initiative, it is more accurate to say that under the sign of the matrimonial community God communicates himself to the two persons united in marriage in a new way. This communication possesses the structure of every divine self-communication. It takes place through Christ by the working of the Holy Spirit. It is stamped by the specific essence of marriage. Its efficacious sign is the contract of marriage with the resulting marriage bond.

MARITAL BEHAVIOR

To say that marriage is a salvific representation of the relationship "Christ-Church" means that the spouses have both the power and the obligation to behave towards one another in the manner revealed in that relationship. It is a relationship sustained by love. In Scripture man is enjoined to practice the form of love which bears the name *agape* (not *eros*). Agape is the type of love which proves itself in sacrifice (1 Cor. 13). Nevertheless, the love of eros is obviously not excluded. This is most emphatically clear in Paul and in the Old Testament writings. One-sided spiritualization is alien to the apostle. However, the love of eros, a love that is by nature impetuous and inclined to violence, must allow itself to be governed by the love of agape, a love which gives of itself and serves the beloved. This need not mean that the intimacy or passionateness of married love suffers. According to Paul, the transformation of eros into agape, or better the interfusion of eros with agape, is a lifelong task (see Col. 3,18; also 1 Pet. 3,1-7). Since in the love of the husband the love of Christ for the Church —indeed, the love of God himself—is both represented and operative, a profound mystery lies behind Paul's admonition. At the same time, the scope of agape's activity is clear. It includes mutual responsibility, concern, respect, and patience (1 Cor. 7,14; Mt. 20,26f.; Lk. 22,24-27). The responsibility of the spouses embraces both the earthly and the future heavenly life of the respective marriage partners. It is therefore total.

Such reflections place in their proper light the demands for the conduct of married life imposed with decisiveness by Paul and the First Epistle of Peter (probably influenced by Paul). Accordingly, the wife ought to be subject to her husband. There is the question of how far the historically and culturally conditioned notions employed in expressing revelation are at work here. Nevertheless we cannot disregard the fact that the hierarchical order in marriage corresponds to the conviction of Christian faith. But how this hierarchical order is to be realized is a question. One would lapse into empty formalism were he simply to emphasize the hierarchical element without taking into consideration the content, the meaning respectively of obeying and commanding. This can only be derived from the relationship of Christ to the Church. Christ has given himself up unconditionally and without reserve for the Church. This act of surrender entails an obligation on the Church's part. It is not free to accept or reject the gift of salvation of Jesus, its head. In this respect the Church is called upon to obey. Its obedience nonetheless is the obedience of love. Its obedience is its answer to the love of Jesus Christ.

With respect to the question of the equal rights of the spouses which is today the subject of such lively dispute, the following must be said: in the area of sexual intercourse there is complete equality. This is absolutely necessary because the conjugal act is an encounter of the partners affecting the very inner core of the person and therefore can only be performed meaningfully if both enter into it of their own free will. Marriage, however, extends beyond bodily communion to a whole life in common. It possesses a domestic and a social dimension. This becomes especially clear in the case of the family. In the realm of the spouses' common life, authority is indispensable, lest the marital unity of two-in-one should fall apart, resulting in two parallel but separate units. Mutual consent is, of course, the ideal; but when this is not attainable, the decision must fall to one of the spouses. This legitimate authority belongs primarily to the husband and secondarily (should the husband abdicate it) to the wife. The juridical element in marriage should be understood as a framework within which the self-binding love of husband and wife can live. (For the primacy of the husband, see the statements in the marriage encyclical of Leo XIII, Feb. 10, 1880, and those of Pius XI in *Casti Connubii*, Jan. 31, 1930, as well as the statements of Pius XII.) So understood, to command as well as to obey emerges as a form of love. Thus the existence of hierarchy within marriage can be insisted upon without thereby discrediting or minimizing the position of the wife.

COMMUNITY AND FRUITFULNESS

Part of the saving efficacy of the sacrament of marriage is that it makes it possible to harmonize the "objective" meaning of marriage with the personal desire for physical and psychological companionship which brings the spouses together and binds them to one another. The course of history manifests considerable discrepancy in this regard, and it required a lengthy unfolding of divine revelation concerning marriage until the full scope of marriage was recognized and the individual elements in its structure were correctly understood. As we saw, in the Old Testament hope for progeny stood in the foreground, although the element of personal encounter was not forgotten. The Middle Ages also was dominated by an objectivistic approach to marriage. Marriage was intended to serve the expansion of the Church through the procreation and education of children and to check unchastity through love. However, even in that period the concept of marriage as a form of lifetime companionship was by no means pushed to the periphery (cf. *The Roman Catechism*). With the evolution of personalism in modern times, the element of personal encounter has more and more taken the first place, while the procreation of children has moved to second place.

Actually no one of the factors ingredient in marriage can dislodge or supplant the other. No one of them thrives by neglecting the other; indeed, the one is related to the other. If the personalist element were separated from the objective, a purely subjective and individualistic concept of marriage would result. If the objective element were separated from the personal, then marriage would sink to a subhuman level.

First of all it should be noted that the emphasis on personal encounter is not in itself to be identified with subjectivism. According to the Yahwist text, God himself is only stating the facts when he says that it is not good for man to be alone. In this instance man's longing for a feminine complement is accounted for in terms of his God-given essence. Conversely, the same holds for the woman. Were the personal encounter lacking—that is, the gift of I to Thou born of love—and only the procreation of children taken into consideration, then an extreme instance of a personal objectivism could arise in which man was employed simply as an instrument, a functionary in the service of the future. Fecundity without love would not attain the dimension of the truly human. Conversely, a love which did not wish to bear fruit would be a form of self-defeating make-believe. Love objectifies itself in the child. The child is the fruit, the manifestation, and in its innermost sense, the guarantee of love. Fruitfulness is an essential ingredient in the signification of marriage by which it is an image of the encounter "Christ-Church." The conjugal act in which the encounter and union of I and Thou is realized in its greatest intensity is not closed in upon itself. It necessarily presses beyond itself. This transcendence is not a new or alien addition. Rather it gives to the conjugal act its ultimate meaning. In the face of the population explosion, and the economic and cultural possibilities and limits of the human situation, the question arises how the principle just set forth is actually and concretely to be realized. With this in mind moral theologians must take into account the numerous economic, medical, and cultural factors in arriving at the theological answer—or perhaps the lack of an answer.

MARRIAGE AND THE WORLD

The marriage partners, in spite of the intimacy of their relationship to one another, cannot isolate themselves from the Church and the world. Over and above their particular married existence they have a social and an ecclesial existence. Indeed, it is only as members of the Church and of mankind as a whole, as creatures within the universe, that they can realize a marital community. Thus it is that the realities of church and society extend even into the realm of marriage. Conversely, the mutual dedication characteristic of marriage is a step into the world. Marriage is a school for all genuine fraternal and social conduct. The man who in marriage grows in selfless love and responsible concern is preserved from the egoistic misuse of men and things as well as from selfish indifference. Thus marriage has an incalculable, far-ranging effect.

MARRIAGE AND ESCHATOLOGY

The marriage partners also experience the limits of their union. Even in marriage, desire for the other, which over and over again impels the human I towards the Thou and to complete union with him, can find no ultimate fulfillment, for within the world there is no such fulfillment. This experience directs married couples beyond this passing world to that future moment in which God will bestow himself on his creatures in order to fulfill them. Although according to the words of Jesus there is no marriage in the kingdom of God, nonetheless the unity achieved in marriage blossoms into its greatest fullness and intensity in the kingdom of God. Thus marriage is not only eschatologically orientated in the sense that through the procreation of children every marriage extends into the distant future, or in the sense that it belongs to this world which is passing; but also, and above all, in the sense that leaving behind what is transitory, it approaches the ultimate future, where in a new and transformed manner, freed from the limits of historical existence, it will become fully what it has always desired to be.

◄16

The Unity and Indissolubility of Marriage

Unity and indissolubility are elements of every marriage. In sacramental marriage they receive a deeper foundation and source of support: the sacrament provides at once the capacity and the obligation for the partners to accept and preserve the unity and indissolubility of the marriage. If the contracting parties exclude unity and indissolubility, then there is no genuine intention to marry, for something other than a sacramental marriage is intended. Unity and indissolubility are not extrinsic requirements which can be made stricter or liberalized at will: they are essential properties of the sacrament of marriage.

UNITY

As the history of marriage shows, not only has it been difficult for man, in the course of his development, to preserve the unity and indissolubility of marriage; it has been difficult for him even to recognize it. The Old Testament manifests no awareness of a universal obligation to monogamy. The admonitions of the later wisdom books presuppose that monogamy is the predominant form of marriage (Prov. 5,15-23; 31,10-31; Sir. 26,9ff.; Wis. 3,13-4,6); and, as we have already pointed out, by Jesus' time monogamy had in fact come to prevail. In the New Testament it is a matter of course.

If one seeks the reason for the unity of sacramental marriage, the fundamental answer is that it is an image of the relationship of Christ to the Church. Christ founded not two churches but only one. The Church has not two heads or more, but only one. Christ remains forever bound to the Church, and the Church remains forever the community of Christ in the Holy Spirit. The Fathers of the Church were so convinced of the unity of marriage by this reasoning alone that many of them even condemned remarriage after the death of a spouse or would allow it only as a respectable form of adultery (Athenagoras, Justin Martyr); or at least they counseled against it (the Shepherd of Hermas, Ambrose, Rufinus of Verona). Even today the Greek Orthodox Church follows a procedure deriving from an ancient synod in imposing a penance on those who have entered a second or third marriage (withholding the eucharist at specific times).

At the Council of Trent the Church enunciated the dogma that to have more than one wife at a time was forbidden to Christians by divine law (DS 1802). The fact of the matter is that it is only in the sacramental sphere of marriage that reasons derived from its essence have achieved their full force. Marriage is a personal encounter, not the mere use of an object. A person is a human being who possesses himself in his uniqueness and diversity, and in this self-possession he gives himself to the other in the conjugal act without reserve. Genuine love consists in this I-Thou relationship. A multiplicity of sexual relationships does not testify to an abundant capacity for love but to the opposite. Infidelity is the offspring of incapacity and weakness in the commitment of the I for the Thou. Fidelity is the vital strength of love.

INDISSOLUBILITY

Scripture

As far as the indissolubility of marriage is concerned, the Old Testament did provide for divorce. Even at the time of Jesus, it was not only possible but common. According to Mark and Luke (Mk. 10,9; Lk. 16,18; cf. 1 Cor. 7,10f.), Jesus proclaimed the indissolubility of marriage in opposition to that practice.

The Gospel of Luke gives us what is most probably the oldest tradition of the words of Jesus about the indissolubility of marriage (Lk. 16,18): "A man who divorces his wife and marries another commits adultery; and anyone who marries a woman divorced from her husband commits adultery." This statement probably derives from the collection of Jesus' words which Luke and Matthew used as a common source *(Q)*. The context in which Luke uses the statement makes plain that it is a question of the validity and the interpretation of the Old Testament law. The passage is preceded by the statement that heaven and earth will pass away before even a jot of the law is abrogated. It is clear from this that Jesus demanded in an absolute way that marriage should not be dissolved.

This is confirmed by a second source, namely, the relevant passage in Mark (10,1-12) and, with a serious difference, in Matthew (19,1-12). The structure of the two passages is different, but the same event forms their subject matter and both represent the same piece of tradition. The difference between them consists chiefly in this: that in Mark, Jesus asks first about the Mosaic law and emphasizes the order of creation in contrast to the Pharisees' reference to the Law of Moses; in Matthew, however, the relevant passages of Genesis (Gen. 1,27; 2,4) are quoted and then the Pharisees raise the objection that Moses commanded them to make out a letter of divorce and thereby to let the woman go.

The text of the Marcan passage is as follows (Mk. 10,2-12):

The question was put to him: "Is it lawful for a man to divorce his wife?" This was to test him. He asked in return, "What did Moses command you?" They answered, "Moses permitted a man to divorce his wife by note of dismissal." Jesus said to them, "It is because your minds were closed that he made this rule for you; but in the beginning, at the creation, God made them male and female. For this reason a man shall leave his father and mother, and be made one with his wife; and the two shall become one flesh. It follows that they are no longer two individuals: they are one flesh. What God has joined together, man must not separate."

When they were indoors again the disciples questioned him about this matter; he said to them, "Whoever divorces his wife and marries

another commits adultery against her: so too, if she divorces her
husband and marries another, she commits adultery."

The passage in Matthew is as follows (Mt. 19,3-12):

Some Pharisees came and tested him by asking, "Is it lawful for a man
to divorce his wife on any and every ground?" He asked in return,
"Have you never read that the Creator made them from the beginning
male and female?"; and he added, "For this reason a man shall
leave his father and mother, and be made one with his wife; and the
two shall become one flesh. It follows that they are no longer two
individuals: they are one flesh. What God has joined together, man
must not separate." "Why then," they objected, "did Moses lay it
down that a man might divorce his wife by note of dismissal?" He
answered, "It was because your minds were closed that Moses gave
you permission to divorce your wives; but it was not like that when
all began. I tell you, if a man divorces his wife, for any cause other
than unchastity, and marries another, he commits adultery."
        The disciples said to him, "If that is the position with husband
and wife, it is better not to marry." To this he replied, "That is
something which not everyone can accept, but only those for whom
God has appointed it. For while some are incapable of marriage
because they were born so, or were made so by men, there are others
who have themselves renounced marriage for the sake of the kingdom
of Heaven. Let those accept it who can."

Another similar and significant statement of Jesus occurs in
Matthew in the context of the Sermon on the Mount (Mt. 5,31f.):

They were told, "A man who divorces his wife must give her a note
of dismissal. But what I tell you is this: If a man divorces his wife
for any cause other than unchastity he involves her in adultery; and
anyone who marries a woman so divorced commits adultery."

With these words Jesus contrasts his own new conception of
marriage clearly and specifically with that of Moses. According
to Mosaic law, a man had the right to divorce his wife. This
right was recognized before the time of Moses; he simply regulated
it by prescribing a bill of divorce. Grounds for divorce were
given in Deut. 24,1 as "something contrary" that a man dis-

covered in his wife. This "contrary" was interpreted in widely differing ways. While the school of Shammai understood by it something morally disgraceful (not only adultery), the school of Hillel accepted anything that displeased the man as grounds for divorce. It is in contrast to these rulings that Jesus sets up his new command which rejects divorce absolutely.

In view of the clarity and absoluteness of Jesus' words and the contrast which he emphasizes with the ordinance of the Old Testament, and given the shock felt by his hearers, there can be no question but that Jesus rejected any remarriage after divorce. But this only makes the question more difficult as to what is meant by the additions in Matthew referring to unchastity. In both passages an exception is made to the rule. There can also be no doubt about this. Exegetes and theologians have gone to endless trouble to interpret the passages, but a satisfactory interpretation has still not yet been achieved. Any explanation must assume that the words in question belong to the original text of the gospels and are not later interpolations, but this is not necessarily to say that they come from Jesus himself.

In any event it would be a direct contradiction to the words of Jesus reported by Mark and Luke, and it would run contrary to the meaning of his ordinance, if he had allowed an exception. In that case he would simply be repeating the doctrine of the school of Shammai: he would be giving only a new, somewhat stricter interpretation of the law of Moses. But the whole point of his statement is that he reverses the Mosaic law in order to restore the original will of God. God's law allows for no exception. It is not possible to take the passages as relating to a separation of bed and board which would not, nevertheless, allow for remarriage: this kind of separation was unknown to the Hebrews of Jesus' time.[1]

There have been two principal attempts at a solution of this problem. One is this: that the Matthean passage was added, in the course of time, to the statements reported in Mark and Luke in response to a need of the community to make the conditions

[1] J. Schmid, *Das Evangelium nach Matthäus*, 4th ed. (Regensburg, 1965), pp. 10ff.

of marriage less rigorous. It must be remembered that to both the Christians coming out of Judaism and those converted from paganism (but to the latter more especially), following Jesus' words literally would constitute an almost unbearable burden. The communities for which Matthew's gospel was meant considered themselves justified in making Jesus' statement less stringent. In this case the passage in Matthew does not represent a statement of Jesus but an addition made either by the evangelist himself or by the Matthean community; it does not interpret Jesus' statement but changes it for the milder. In support of this explanation it is pointed out that Paul likewise introduces a relaxation of Jesus' command to his proclamation (1 Cor. 7,12-15). But whereas in Matthew the only exception allowed is on the grounds of unchastity, in Paul the refusal of the marriage partner to accept the Christian faith makes divorce and remarriage possible. Despite the law of God, which he does not doubt, Paul clearly considers it his prerogative to make this exception to it. Although the Church maintained and further developed Paul's teaching (cf. the "Pauline privilege" in canon law), it did not preserve the position adopted in Matthew.

According to another interpretation of the Matthean passage, the addition has reference not to a proper marriage but to an illegitimate one. The sense would be: remarriage after separation is forbidden so long as it is a case of a genuine marriage, but if there was not a genuine marriage, then naturally after separation there would be no hindrance to remarriage. This explanation of the word *porneia* is just as possible as the translation of it by the word unchastity. The context would seem to favor it over the first interpretation given above.

In the Eastern Church the Matthean passage had the effect that the remarriage of divorced persons was permitted under certain conditions. The divine command of indissolubility was and is maintained, but in certain situations a remarriage is permitted through confidence in God's mercy towards human weakness. A similar understanding of the indissolubility of marriage was accepted by the Churches of the Reformation. In the view of the Eastern Church the meaning of Christian marriage is that it is a witness to the kingdom of God. At the same time, however, marriage is caught up in the chaos of sin. Because of its reference to Christ it is indissoluble. But yet at the same time it is always being dissolved by sin and ignorance, passion and selfishness, lack of faith and love. The Church does not dissolve the marriage but recognizes that here and now a marriage is actually broken by human weakness and sinfulness.

The Tradition of the Church

The general orientation of the Church's tradition has been clearly towards the unconditional indissolubility of marriage. In the ancient Church this was maintained chiefly by Ambrose and Augustine. However, a number of notable Church Fathers, theologians, and bishops express a milder view. The Eastern Churches often base themselves on a statement of Origen in his commentary on Mt. 19,3-12:

Besides this it has happened that even some bishops, despite what is said in Scripture, have permitted a woman to marry again while her former husband was still alive. They have done this even though it is written that the woman is bound so long as her husband lives and that she should be treated as an adulteress if she marries another while her husband still lives. And yet they have by no means acted without good reason. Clearly they have tolerated this weakness in order to avoid greater evils, despite what was commanded from the beginning and is written in Scripture.

About 150 years later we find similar views in Epiphanius of Salamis and in Basil of Cappadocia. Epiphanius says:

If a man has one wife, he is duly praised and honored among the members of the Church. But even he who is not content with having had one, after she is dead, or has separated himself from her because of fornication, adultery, or some other grounds, is not condemned by the word of God, and he is not excluded from the Church or from life but his behavior is tolerated because of his weakness. Not so that he can have two wives at the same time, that is, while the first is still alive, but so that if he is separated from the first he can live legally in a given case with another. For the sacred word and holy Church have pity on him, especially when this man is otherwise devout and lives according to the law of God. *(Haereses, 59, 4)*

Basil states:

I do not know whether one should consider as an adulteress a woman who lives with a man who was abandoned by his first wife. Such an accusation is raised only against a woman who has betrayed her husband. *(Letters to Amphilochius,* canon 9, No. 188)

In the West even Augustine, who otherwise maintains the indissolubility of marriage emphatically, says in his work *De Fide et Operibus,* written in 413:

The man who divorces his wife when he has caught her in adultery and marries another should obviously not be put on the same level as those who divorce their wives for other grounds than adultery and marry again. In the divine Scriptures it is by no means clear whether the man, who without doubt is permitted to divorce his wife when she commits adultery, is himself to be considered an adulterer if he then goes on to marry another. It is my opinion, anyway, that in this case he commits a pardonable error.

It should be noted from these statements that marriage partners who separate and marry again because of special circumstances were not excluded from the Church, that is, not excommunicated.

The Teaching of the Church

At the Council of Trent (DS 1805) the Catholic Church enunciated against the Reformers the proposition that the marriage bond cannot be dissolved on account of heterodoxy or incompatibility or willful desertion. It went on to insist further (DS 1807):

If anyone says that the Church is in error when it has taught and does teach according to the doctrine of the Gospels and apostles that the marriage bond cannot be dissolved because of adultery on the part of either the husband or the wife; and that neither party, not even the innocent one who gave no cause for the adultery, can contract another marriage while the other party is still living; and that adultery is committed both by the husband who dismisses his adulterous wife and marries again and by the wife who dismisses her adulterous husband and marries again: let him be anathema.[2]

According to the formulations of Trent, a marriage cannot be dissolved on the basis of the grounds mentioned (heterodoxy, incompatibility, desertion, adultery). It would be hair-splitting to suggest that the Church might accept other grounds for dissolution. The council Fathers, at the request of the representative of the Republic of Venice, adopted the milder version of the anathema cited above in order to avoid portraying the Greeks as heretics (they held that divorce was permissible in case of adultery). The grounds for divorce cited and rejected by the Church point out the chief situations which might mislead the marriage partners into believing that their marriage could be dissolved. In these motives for divorce all the other possible human situations are implicit. Thus it is the teaching of the Church (even though it is not a formal dogma: *sententia fidei proxima*) that under no conditions can a marriage be dissolved. Of course, only a validly contracted and consummated marriage is meant: no doubt must exist as to the existence of the marriage itself. It is likewise necessary to distinguish between the dissolution of a marriage and the permission given to the spouses to live apart.

The Church's teaching has to come to grips with the crucial passages in Matthew. Probably it must be admitted outright that a satisfactory interpretation of the meaning of the two passages is not possible.

Theological Reflection

The indissolubility of marriage as well as its unity can be derived by theological reflection from its sacramentality: sacramental marriage is wholly structured according to the Christ-Church relationship. Nothing can ever disrupt this relationship: the love of Christ for the Church and the Church for Christ will never end. The human relationship structured according to this same pattern—

[2] *The Church Teaches*, pp. 337f.

the dedication of Christ to the Church and the Church's loving response—shares the same permanence. To the degree that sacramental marriage participates in this indestructible relationship, it is permeated and determined by it. If marriage were allowed to come to an end with the loss of love on the part of the spouses, it would become detached from its sacramental moorings only to drift in the sea of subjectivism and individualism. The door would be opened to arbitrariness, human frailty, and restless desire. Hence, fundamental as mutual love is to contracting a marriage worthy of the human person—and, indeed, to married life itself—the partners are nonetheless deprived of the power to dispose of the marriage itself. The solidarity of marriage is distinct from that of every other human encounter based on love; for other encounters bring into existence a kind of community which actually comes to an end if love dies; but when two people contract a marriage they enter into a community whose essence they have not created but which has been predetermined by God through Jesus Christ.

The marriage partners are bound together not only by psychological understanding and love but also by the love of Christ and the Church. An exclusively existential interpretation of marriage would contradict its objective content. The visible manifestation of the objective—prior to any human decision—and ontological character of marriage is the child resulting from the conjugal community. Against the background of the reasons for the indissolubility of marriage derived from its sacramentality, the principles deduced from the natural law achieve their force. They are the same as those for the unity of marriage. If a person in full possession of himself places himself completely at the disposal of another, insofar as this is possible without the loss of personal integrity, and is accepted by the other, then the two partners remain forever influenced by that event. Their knowledge of one another reaches a depth which only a complete bodily and mental union can plumb. The impression made on the marriage partners by the very nature of conjugal community can never be sloughed off. Reflection on this point, of course, reaches the level of abolute certitude only when the mutual dedication of marriage is seen as supported by the love of Christ.

Index

299